PRIMARY READING SIMPLIFIED

PRIMARY READING SIMPLIFIED

A PRACTICAL GUIDE TO CLASSROOM TEACHING & WHOLE-SCHOOL IMPLEMENTATION

CHRISTOPHER SUCH

CORWIN

A SAGE Publishing Company

1 Oliver's Yard
55 City Road
London EC1Y 1SP

CORWIN
A Sage company
2455 Teller Road
Thousand Oaks
California 91320
(800)233-9936
www.corwin.com

Unit No 323-333, Third Floor, F-Block
International Trade Tower
Nehru Place, New Delhi – 110 019

8 Marina View Suite 43-053
Asia Square Tower 1
Singapore 018960

Editor: James Clark
Assistant editor: Esosa Otabor
Production editor: Sarah Sewell
Marketing manager: Dilhara Attygalle
Cover design: Wendy Scott
Typeset by: C&M Digitals (P), Ltd, Chennai, India
Printed in the UK

British Library Cataloguing in Publication data

A catalogue record for this book is available from the
British Library

ISBN 978-1-03-620142-5
ISBN 978-1-03-620141-8 (pbk)

For Silvia

CONTENTS

ABOUT THE AUTHOR

Christopher Such is a primary school teacher, school leader, teacher educator and consultant who has worked in schools since 2006. As part of Ambition Institute's learning design team, he co-designed their National Professional Qualification in Leading Literacy (NPQLL). He has contributed to the initial teacher training programmes for Teach East, Torch SCITT and Ambition Institute, focusing on reading and mathematics pedagogy. In his work as an education consultant, he has worked with schools, multi-academy trusts, English hubs and wider organisations to develop teachers' understanding of reading and implement approaches to evidence-informed classroom teaching that prioritise meaningful experiences with texts. His first book, *The Art and Science of Teaching Primary Reading*, is required reading on many initial teacher training programmes and higher education courses. He is the author of the education blog *Primary Colour*, and he can be found on social media platforms via the username @Suchmo83.

ACKNOWLEDGEMENTS

First, I'd like to thank everyone at Sage who helped bring this book to fruition.

Second, I'd like to thank the learning design team at Ambition Institute, especially Chloe Wardle and Ryan Yung, who provided the flexibility that allowed me to complete the first draft.

Third, I'd like to thank those who over the years have challenged my thinking, provided encouragement and offered feedback on my writing, especially Kieran Mackle, Neil Almond, Elliot Morgan, Lloyd Williams-Jones, Shannen Doherty, Matt Swain, Adam Smith, Sarah Cottingham, Philip Salisbury, Kathy Rastle, Sarah Bagshaw-McCormick, Katie McHugh, Lucy Newman, Jon Biddle and Andrew Currie.

Fourth, I'd like to thank everyone at Fulbridge Academy who implemented the first version of the approach to reading shared in this book.

Finally, I'd like to thank my family, especially my wife and best friend, Silvia. L'úbim t'a.

INTRODUCTION

This book is my attempt to address one of the most daunting problems in education: how do we maximise the chances that all pupils in our schools will become capable, confident readers? My first book, *The Art and Science of Teaching Primary Reading*, was designed to help teachers and school leaders understand key principles derived from the wealth of research on reading development and instruction. The idea was that these principles could be used to devise a multitude of sensible approaches to teaching reading. I was determined not to advocate one specific approach, but instead to empower schools to find their own way.

However, I have become increasingly convinced that there is an appetite for much more than a set of evidence-informed principles. The aim of this book is to detail how I approach classroom teaching and whole-school coordination of reading, and to do justice to every practicality, including those to which research provides scant guidance.

In other words, my last book offered a bird's eye view of the terrain of reading instruction so that teachers and school leaders could safely plot their own paths. In contrast, this book describes *my* preferred route through that terrain, addressing every potential problem faced along the way. It is certainly not the only effective approach, but it is one that has been refined over several years to allow all teachers to thrive. To be exact, a single guiding belief underpins this book:

Any approach to teaching reading should be judged both on the scope it provides for expert teachers to excel and on the support it provides for novice teachers to achieve adequacy.

Much of this book's contents has already been put into practice by many schools I have supported. The feedback on this has been overwhelmingly positive, and I wouldn't have written this book if I didn't think this approach had the potential to be effective. However, it would be wrong to suggest that this book describes a foolproof method of achieving stunning results in every possible context. No such thing exists, nor is it ever likely to. Ultimately, all significant change in a school relies on conscientious implementation by teachers and school leaders. This book offers an approach that makes this implementation as simple as possible without compromising every pupil's right to meaningful reading experiences. I hope you find it useful.

HOW TO READ
THIS BOOK

One of the joys of working with young people is that they provide challenges you could never have imagined. This means it is impossible to create a truly comprehensive list of problems that teachers and school leaders might face when teaching reading. However, there are several common questions faced in every school by those seeking to improve reading. Regardless of whether you follow the exact advice offered in this book, if you have a good answer to the questions listed below, then you're almost certainly doing justice to your pupils and ensuring they have every opportunity to become capable, confident readers.

There are two ways to use this book. First, and most obviously, this book has been designed so that you can read it from start to finish. But it has also been designed so you can skip to the parts of the book that are most relevant to the questions you are looking to address in your classroom or across your school.

FOR CLASSROOM TEACHERS

What do I need to know about reading and how it develops? **Turn to Chapter 1 – What Every Teacher Needs to Know about Reading**

How do I teach pupils to begin to decode words? **Turn to Chapter 3 – Teaching Phonics**

How do I lay the foundations of language comprehension while pupils are still learning the basics of decoding? **Turn to Chapter 4 – Supporting Spoken Language Development**

How do I introduce pupils to whole-class reading in year 1? **Turn to Chapter 7 – Scaffolded Reading**

How do I help pupils become fluent when they are just beginning to read? **Turn to Chapter 8 – Fluency Reading**

How do I ensure pupils get the vast amount of text experience required to become capable, confident readers? **Turn to Chapter 9 – Extended Reading**

How do I support pupils to develop strategic, critical, appreciative dispositions towards reading? **Turn to Chapter 10 – Close Reading**

How do I foster independent reading in my classroom? **Turn to Chapter 17 – Nurturing a Reading Culture**

How do I develop pupils' vocabulary and knowledge of the world? **Turn to Chapter 18 – Developing Vocabulary**

How do I teach spelling in a way that will support reading development? **Turn to Chapter 19 – Supporting Reading through Writing**

How do I ensure pupils feel prepared for statutory reading assessments? **Turn to Chapter 20 – Preparing Pupils for External Assessments**

How do I identify pupils who need extra support and provide interventions that target their individual barriers to reading development? **Turn to Chapter 21 – Identifying and Addressing Barriers to Reading Development**

How do I make the most of opportunities for one-to-one reading? **Turn to Chapter 22 – Maximising the Impact of One-to-One Reading**

FOR THOSE RESPONSIBLE FOR READING ACROSS A SCHOOL

How do I support colleagues to have a shared understanding of reading development? **Turn to Chapter 1 – What Every Teacher Needs to Know about Reading**

How do I ensure that phonics provision is effective? **Turn to Chapter 3 – Teaching Phonics**

How do I ensure that pupils' language comprehension develops while they are learning the basics of decoding? **Turn to Chapter 4 – Supporting Spoken Language Development**

How do I structure a timetable to ensure a balance between fluency development, breadth of text experience and meaningful discussion of texts? **Turn to Part III – Organising Classroom Teaching**

How do I implement changes to how reading is taught across the school in a sustainable way that encourages buy-in from colleagues? **Turn to Part IV – Implementing Change across a School**

How do I build a diverse, challenging reading curriculum that balances narrative fiction and other forms of texts? **Turn to Chapter 16 – Building a Reading Curriculum**

How do I foster independent reading across the school? **Turn to Chapter 17 – Nurturing a Reading Culture**

How do I support other leaders across the school to develop a curriculum that builds pupils' vocabulary and knowledge of the world? **Turn to Chapter 18 – Developing Vocabulary**

How do I organise spelling instruction across the school in a way that supports reading development? **Turn to Chapter 19 – Supporting Reading through Writing**

How do I ensure pupils feel prepared for statutory reading assessments? **Turn to Chapter 20 – Preparing Pupils for External Assessments**

How do I employ a systematic approach to assessment and intervention that tackles pupils' specific barriers to reading? **Turn to Chapter 21 – Identifying and Addressing Barriers to Reading Development**

How do I support my colleagues to make the most of opportunities for one-to-one reading? **Turn to Chapter 22 – Maximising the Impact of One-to-One Reading**

This book is written in reference to English schools. Table 0.1 is presented to support readers from other countries to access this book.

Table 0.1 Ages of year groups in English schools

	Year group	Age in years
	Reception	4–5
Key stage 1	Year 1	5–6
	Year 2	6–7
Key stage 2	Year 3	7–8
	Year 4	8–9
	Year 5	9–10
	Year 6	10–11

PART I
UNDERSTANDING READING

1

WHAT EVERY TEACHER NEEDS TO KNOW ABOUT READING

WHY IS IT ESSENTIAL FOR TEACHERS TO HAVE AN EVIDENCE-INFORMED UNDERSTANDING OF READING DEVELOPMENT?

All teachers need to have an evidence-informed understanding of what reading is, how it develops and how this development can be facilitated in the classroom. There are several reasons for this:

Understanding reading development helps us to avoid ineffective strategies and allows us to adapt effective ones to our own contexts without accidentally removing 'active ingredients' (i.e. the parts of a strategy that render it ineffective if removed – see Sharples et al., (2024) for more on 'active ingredients').

Well-informed teachers recognise the priorities of reading development and how these sometimes conflict with each other, allowing them to find a reasonable balance. For example, teachers need to give pupils opportunities to explore a lot of unfamiliar texts so that they can build up their knowledge of the English writing system and language more generally. However, we also need to cultivate pupils' understanding of their active role in comprehension by engaging them in text discussions. Focusing on one of these priorities inevitably reduces the time available to focus on the other. By having an evidence-informed understanding of reading development, teachers can reach sensible conclusions about how much time to dedicate to each of these priorities and how this balance might change as pupils become stronger readers.

By understanding reading development, teachers are better able to communicate about their teaching with each other. As a result, we can more effectively accumulate professional wisdom about reading within schools and across the profession. And this communication is especially vital when we are identifying and supporting those pupils who experience the greatest difficulty in learning to read.

Figure 1.1 A concept map detailing key ideas about reading

Crucially, a shared understanding of reading development allows those in charge of reading across a school to explain the rationale behind suggested changes to reading instruction. Teachers are more likely to buy into new ideas if they know the reasons behind them (Mccrea, 2023). And this knowledge means they are better placed to give constructive feedback on what is working and what might be adapted so that changes have a higher likelihood of success.

In short, it's essential that teachers understand reading development, and a key responsibility of school leaders is to ensure their colleagues build this understanding.

WHAT DO TEACHERS NEED TO KNOW ABOUT READING DEVELOPMENT?

Ideally, every teacher should be an expert in the evidence related to reading. However, it requires hundreds of hours of study to even scratch the surface of the research into reading, and teachers are busy people with countless other demands placed upon the limited time they have available for professional development. And in terms of class-room utility, there are diminishing returns available to those who devote a lot of time to investigating the research into reading. While all teachers should continue to build their knowledge of reading development throughout their career, thankfully the most valuable theoretical understanding can be grasped in just a few hours of learning.

As a starting point, on the facing page you will see a concept map that attempts to summarise the key understanding of reading development that every teacher needs (see Figure 1.1).

Let's explore this concept map together, starting at the top (see Figure 1.2).

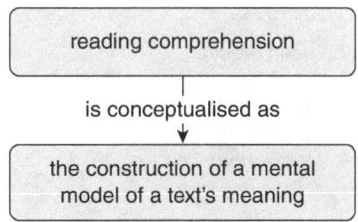

Figure 1.2 Extract from the reading concept map – reading comprehension

The ultimate goal of reading is comprehension. We can think of reading comprehension as the building of a mental model that represents the meaning we have derived from a text (Kintsch, 1988; Zwaan & Radvansky, 1998). We rarely memorise the words as they are displayed in the text unless we intentionally seek to do so. Instead, as we read, we are engaged in a constructive process in which we create our own version of the text's meaning. This process depends on our unique knowledge of the language in the text and the world this language describes (Oakhill et al., 2014).

So, how do we do this? There are two underlying capabilities upon which reading comprehension depends: word recognition and language comprehension (Hoover & Tunmer, 2022; see Figure 1.3).

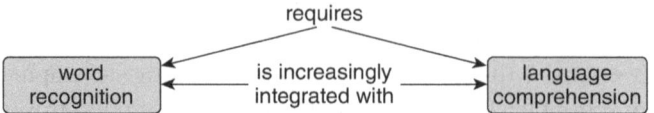

Figure 1.3 Extract from the reading map – word recognition and language comprehension

Word recognition is our ability to identify the words on a page. Language comprehension is our ability to build meaning from those words. If either of these capabilities is lacking, then reading development will stall. The knowledge and skills that support these two capabilities are not entirely separate, and as expertise develops, these capabilities become more and more intertwined (Scarborough, 2001).

Let's explore the integrated bodies of knowledge and skills behind these two capabilities, starting with word recognition (see Figure 1.4).

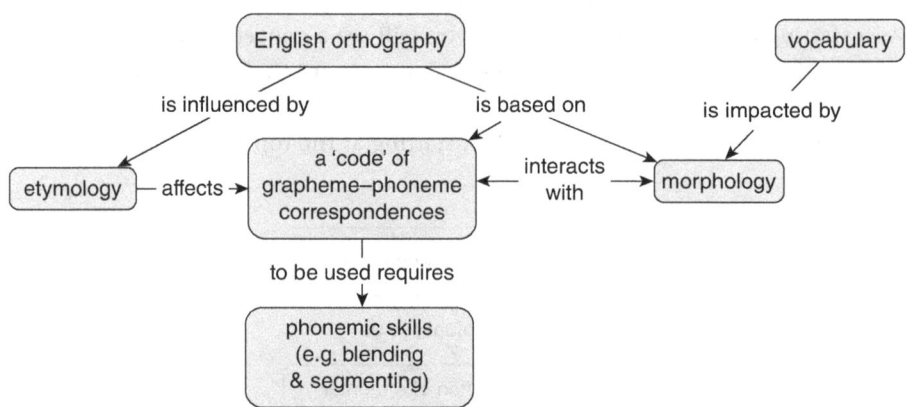

Figure 1.4 Extract from the reading map – understanding related to word recognition

Our ability to recognise words is primarily the result of our expertise with the English writing system (also called English **orthography**). At the heart of this system are relationships between visual symbols and spoken sounds.

The sounds represented in the English writing system are **phonemes,** the smallest chunks of spoken sound that can distinguish one word from another (e.g. the difference between 'cat' and 'bat' is a single phoneme at the start of each word). Put simply, phonemes can be thought of as basic chunks of spoken sound that we can break a word into for the purposes of reading. For example, the spoken word 'shop' can be deconstructed into three phonemes: /sh/, /o/ and /p/. (Henceforth, forward slashes will be used to show phonemes.) The visual symbols representing these phonemes are letters of the alphabet operating individually or in groups, called **graphemes**. For example, the written word 'shop' represents the three phonemes in the spoken word using the graphemes 'sh', 'o' and 'p'.

Across the English writing system, the various relationships between graphemes and phonemes (known as **grapheme–phoneme correspondences** or GPCs) can be thought of as a code that must be learned by a pupil if they are to become able to recognise words. Pupils need to become experts in this code of GPCs, and they need to become experts in using this code. Part of this means learning how to **blend** phonemes together to reconstitute a word (e.g. /sh/ /o/ /p/ → shop) and how to do the reverse, called **segmenting**. The ability to identify and manipulate phonemes in this way is called **phonemic awareness**. When a pupil uses their knowledge of GPCs and blending to identify a word, this is called **decoding**.

The code of GPCs in the English writing system is complex. A given phoneme is often represented by different graphemes in different words (e.g. /sh/ can be represented by 'sh' in 'shop', by 'ch' in 'chef', etc). And a given grapheme can represent different phonemes (e.g. 'a' represents different phonemes in 'apple', 'acorn', 'wash', etc).

However, the English writing system is more than just a code of GPCs. Letters do not always represent sounds (e.g. consider the word 'Wednesday') and the correspondences between graphemes and phonemes in a word can be ambiguous. Thus, determining correspondences between graphemes and phonemes often requires a 'best fit' approach or an acceptance that part of a word is not profitably, or accurately, described through identification of GPCs.

We can begin to make sense of this complexity by considering the representation of meaning visible in the English writing system. In every language, words are made up of **morphemes**, which for the purposes of teaching can be understood as basic elements that have relatively consistent meanings across words. For example, the word 'unhelpful' contains three morphemes: un-help-ful. In this word, 'help' is a **root**, which means it provides the core of the word's meaning. In contrast, 'un' and 'ful' are **affixes** which attach to a root to change the word's meaning. To be more precise, 'un-' is a type of affix called a **prefix** as it comes before the root. And '-ful' is a type of affix called a **suffix** because it comes after the root. In the English writing system, morphemes are often spelled consistently, even when this involves inconsistencies in the relationships between letters and sounds (e.g. notice the consistent spelling of the past tense morpheme in 'walked' and 'hinted', despite the represented sounds being different at the end of the two words). The convoluted history of how words are spelled in

English (i.e. their **etymology**) also adds to the complexity of the English writing system (Crystal, 2013).

How do pupils develop the necessary expertise in this writing system that allows them to recognise words? It requires a mixture of explicit teaching and meaningful text experience (see Figure 1.5).

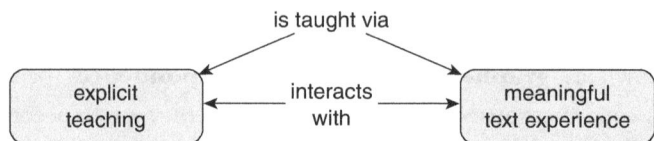

Figure 1.5 Extract from the reading map – explicit teaching and meaningful text experience

The teaching of the correspondences between letters and sounds is called **phonics**. There is a robust evidence base suggesting that systematic phonics – the teaching of phonics using an organised curriculum – is an effective way to teach pupils to begin to recognise words (Brooks, 2023; Ehri et al., 2001; Torgerson et al., 2019). And pupils should also be taught how to spell words through further understanding of phonics, **morphology** (i.e. the study of morphemes) and other patterns seen in English spellings.

Critically, however, learning phonics is just the start of a pupil's journey to word recognition expertise. Phonics introduces pupils to the most common GPCs but not all of them. Pupils learn how to navigate the wider complexities of the English writing system through vast amounts of decoding experience (Seidenberg, 2017; Share, 1995). An important process pupils use to build up this knowledge of the English writing system is **mispronunciation correction**, also known as set for variability (Colenbrander et al., 2022). This involves pupils decoding words that contain at least one unfamiliar GPC by using the GPCs they already know and then self-correcting their initial attempt, something that relies on the pupil having the word in their spoken vocabulary. For example, a pupil might initially decode 'wasp' in a way that rhymes with 'clasp', before correcting this mispronunciation using their vocabulary knowledge. (See Chapter 3 for more on this.)

As a pupil's word recognition improves, their reading develops a sense of flow, which is called **reading fluency** (see Figure 1.6).

This flow can be observed most easily when pupils read aloud. The **accuracy**, **automaticity** and **prosody** of oral reading are proxies that can be used to assess the reading fluency of most pupils (Kuhn et al., 2010):

- *Accuracy*: the correct identification of words
- *Automaticity*: the rate and effortlessness of word recognition
- *Prosody*: the patterns of stress and intonation in spoken language.

Increased reading fluency frees up cognitive resources that can be dedicated to making meaning from the identified words (Pikulski & Chard, 2005). Put another way, reading fluency supports language comprehension. This relationship is reciprocal: greater fluency makes comprehension easier, *and* greater comprehension helps reading to flow.

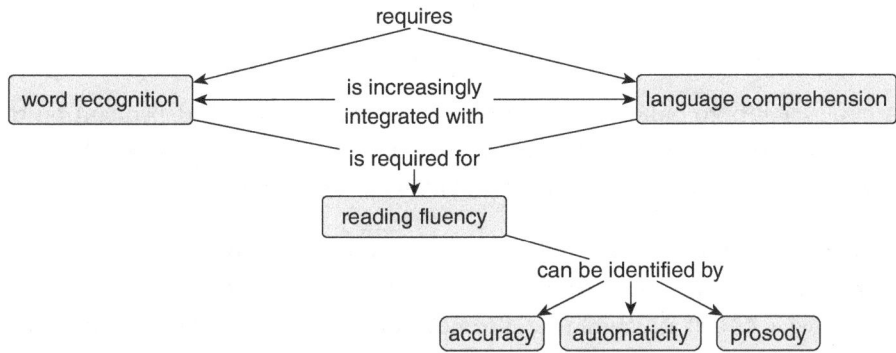

Figure 1.6 Extract from the reading map – reading fluency

Given its importance, how do teachers support fluency development? As with word recognition, the answer is a mixture of explicit teaching and meaningful text experience (see Figure 1.7).

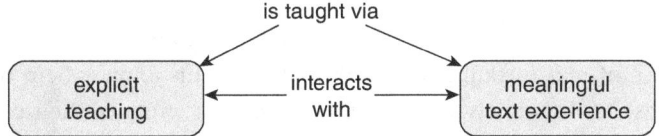

Figure 1.7 Extract from the reading map – explicit teaching and meaningful text experience

In the context of reading fluency, explicit teaching consists of expert modelling of reading and opportunities for pupils to reach fluency with a text through accurate decoding experience offered by activities like repeated reading. And extensive, meaningful text experience provides pupils with knowledge of written language that helps reading to flow.

We've discussed word recognition, so let's now consider the other underlying capability required for reading: language comprehension (see Figure 1.8).

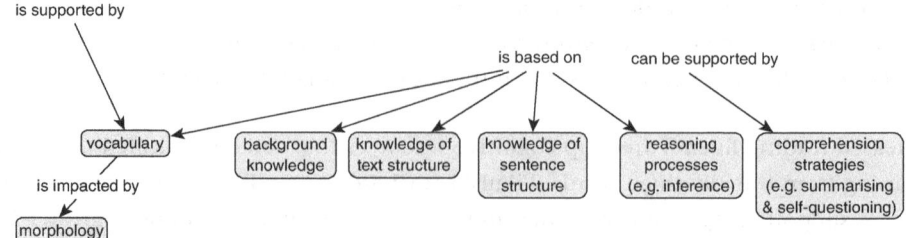

Figure 1.8 Extract from the reading map – understanding related to language comprehension

A pupil's ability to build meaning from the words they read is dependent on their understanding of written language and the world it describes (Castles et al., 2018). This can be divided into interconnected bodies of knowledge and processes:

- Vocabulary is the knowledge of the words and phrases in the text.
- Background knowledge is knowledge of the wider world relevant to the text.
- Knowledge of text structure relates to how texts are organised beyond the sentence level, often in ways that align with the text type, genre, purpose and audience.
- Knowledge of sentence structure relates to how words are organised within sentences.
- Reasoning processes are the application of the above types of knowledge to allow the reader to make meaning that goes beyond what is literally stated in the text.

Pupils are more able to understand what they read if they are tuned in to their own role in making sense of text (Oakhill et al., 2005, 2014). This allows them to adjust their focus in response to their goals and to actively repair or enhance their comprehension through strategies such as re-reading, summarising and self-questioning.

How might teachers develop their pupils' reading comprehension? Once again, effective teaching comprises a mixture of explicit teaching and meaningful text experience (see Figure 1.9).

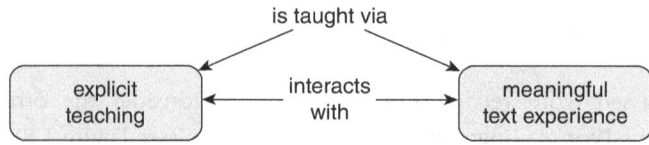

Figure 1.9 Extract from the reading map – explicit teaching and meaningful text experience

While spoken language and written language are not identical (Rastle, 2019), there *is* a shared pool of linguistic knowledge that supports both (Aitchison, 2012). This means that pupils' speaking and listening capabilities should be supported through productive classroom talk (Knight, 2020). Teachers should also read aloud to pupils and explore a wealth of texts chosen for the variety of their content and structure. And the knowledge of the world that pupils acquire from the wider curriculum will also play a key role in their ability to comprehend the texts they read.

HOW SHOULD WE SUPPORT OUR COLLEAGUES TO UNDERSTAND MORE ABOUT READING DEVELOPMENT?

It can be difficult to know where to begin when we want to support colleagues to know more about reading development. As a general rule, the most useful time to introduce an aspect of this understanding to teachers is shortly before they need to use it in practice. Theoretical concepts that are used by teachers to understand practical changes in their classroom are much more likely to be remembered.

We will explore the relationship between theory and practice, and the ingredients of effective professional development, in subsequent chapters. For now, it's enough to recognise the value of acquiring an evidence-informed understanding of reading development and the value of supporting our colleagues to do the same.

--- This Chapter in a Nutshell ---

- It is essential that all teachers have an evidence-informed understanding of reading development so that they can discuss their classroom practice, offer constructive feedback on whole-school initiatives and support struggling readers.
- School leaders should understand reading development so that they can balance different priorities and promote effective approaches to teaching reading.
- Reading comprehension is a constructive process that requires the ability to recognise words and the ability to build meaning from words.
- Word recognition relies on knowledge of the English writing system and how to use it. At the heart of this writing system is a complex code of relationships between letters and sounds.
- Language comprehension relies on knowledge of written language and the world this language describes alongside an appreciation of a reader's role in actively constructing meaning.

───────────────────────── Further Reading ─────────────────────────

- *The Art and Science of Teaching Primary Reading* (Such, 2021)
- Ending the reading wars: Reading acquisition from novice to expert (Castles et al., 2018)
- *Understanding and Teaching Primary English* (Clements & Tobin, 2021)
- *Reading for Life* (Stone, 2018)

───────────────────────── Retrieval Quiz ─────────────────────────

- What is the cause of the complexity of the English writing system?
- What is reading fluency? And how is it commonly assessed?
- Describe the integrated bodies of knowledge and processes that underpin language comprehension.

───────────────────────── Questions for Professional Discussions ─────────────────────────

- To what extent are your colleagues familiar with the evidence relating to reading development?
- Which of these words are commonly used in your context – grapheme, phoneme, morpheme, fluency, prosody?
- Which words in the list above do you think are most useful to support productive discussion in a school?

REFERENCES

Aitchison, J. (2012). *Words in the Mind: An Introduction to the Mental Lexicon*. John Wiley & Sons.

Brooks, G. (2023). Disputing recent attempts to reject the evidence in favour of systematic phonics instruction. *Review of Education, 11*(2), e3408.

Castles, A., Rastle, K. & Nation, K. (2018). Ending the reading wars: Reading acquisition from novice to expert. *Psychological Science in the Public Interest, 19*(1), 5–51.

Clements, J. & Tobin, M. (2021). *Understanding and Teaching Primary English: Theory Into Practice*. Sage.

Colenbrander, D., Kohnen, S., Beyersmann, E., Robidoux, S., Wegener, S., Arrow, T., Nation, K. & Castles, A. (2022). Teaching children to read irregular words: A comparison of three instructional methods. *Scientific Studies of Reading, 26*(6), 545–564.

Crystal, D. (2013). *Spell It Out: The Singular Story of English Spelling*. Profile Books.

Ehri, L. C., Nunes, S. R., Stahl, S. A. & Willows, D. M. (2001). Systematic phonics instruction helps students learn to read: Evidence from the National Reading Panel's meta-analysis. *Review of Educational Research*, *71*(3), 393–447.

Hoover, W. A. & Tunmer, W. E. (2022). The primacy of science in communicating advances in the science of reading. *Reading Research Quarterly*, *57*(2), 399–408.

Kintsch, W. (1988). The role of knowledge in discourse comprehension: A construction–integration model. *Psychological Review*, *95*(2), 163.

Knight, R. (2020). *Classroom Talk*. Critical Publishing.

Kuhn, M. R., Schwanenflugel, P. J. & Meisinger, E. B. (2010). Aligning theory and assessment of reading fluency: Automaticity, prosody, and definitions of fluency. *Reading Research Quarterly*, *45*(2), 230–251.

Mccrea, P. (2023). *Developing Expert Teaching*. Self published.

Oakhill, J., Cain, K. & Elbro, C. (2014). *Understanding and Teaching Reading Comprehension: A Handbook*. Routledge.

Oakhill, J. V., Hartt, J. & Samols, D. (2005). Levels of comprehension monitoring and working memory in good and poor comprehenders. *Reading and Writing*, *18*, 657–686.

Pikulski, J. J. & Chard, D. J. (2005). Fluency: Bridge between decoding and reading comprehension. *The Reading Teacher*, *58*(6), 510–519.

Rastle, K. (2019). EPS mid-career prize lecture 2017: Writing systems, reading, and language. *Quarterly Journal of Experimental Psychology*, *72*(4), 677–692.

Scarborough, H. (2001). Connecting early language and literacy to later reading (dis)abilities: Evidence, theory, and practice. In S. B. Neuman & D. K. Dickinson (Eds.), *Handbook of Early Literacy Research* (pp. 97–110). Guilford Press.

Seidenberg, M. (2017). *Language at the Speed of Sight: How We Read, Why So Many Can't, and What Can Be Done about It*. Basic Books.

Share, D. L. (1995). Phonological recoding and self-teaching: Sine qua non of reading acquisition. *Cognition*, *55*(2), 151–218.

Sharples, J., Eaton, J. & Boughelaf, J. (2024). *A School's Guide to Implementation: Guidance Report*. Education Endowment Foundation.

Stone, L. (2018). *Reading for Life: High Quality Literacy Instruction for All*. Routledge.

Such, C. (2021). *The Art and Science of Teaching Primary Reading*. Sage Corwin.

Torgerson, C., Brooks, G., Gascoine, L. & Higgins, S. (2019). Phonics: Reading policy and the evidence of effectiveness from a systematic 'tertiary' review. *Research Papers in Education*, *34*(2), 208–238.

Zwaan, R. A. & Radvansky, G. A. (1998). Situation models in language comprehension and memory. *Psychological Bulletin*, *123*(2), 162.

2

COMPREHENSION CONCEPTUALISED

WHY IS IT IMPORTANT FOR TEACHERS TO HAVE A PRODUCTIVE CONCEPTION OF READING COMPREHENSION?

Teachers' ideas about the nature of reading comprehension have a profound impact on their classroom practice. Common misconceptions frequently lead to teaching that is inefficient and stultifying.

For example, in pursuit of improved assessment outcomes, many teachers in English schools spend countless hours trying to teach pupils how to answer specific types of comprehension questions that align with the content domains of the end-of-key stage 2 reading assessments. This is fuelled by a belief that pupils who succeed on comprehension assessments must possess a narrow set of discrete, transferable comprehension skills that align with the way assessment questions are categorised: *pupils who can retrieve information from texts have well-developed 'retrieval skills'; pupils who answer questions that require prediction have well-developed 'prediction skills';* and so on.

But this conception of reading comprehension is bogus. Such comprehension skills 'lack any kind of psychological reality' (Shanahan, 2018). The truth is that pupils who can retrieve, predict, etc. are those who have understood the text because of their fluent word recognition and their understanding of the specific language used in that text.

Many teachers who might otherwise spend precious classroom time developing pupils' understanding and appreciation of written language – something that genuinely would support improved outcomes – instead target illusory skills. They inadvertently replace meaningful instruction with years of unnecessary test preparation (though a small, timely amount of this preparation is justifiable – see Chapter 20 for more on this). And all of this comes about because of misconceptions about the nature of reading comprehension.

WHY ARE MISCONCEPTIONS ABOUT READING COMPREHENSION SO COMMON?

Misconceptions about reading comprehension come about for various reasons.

First, teachers and school leaders scarcely have the time to reflect on the nature of the subjects they teach. It is understandable that when presented with a high-stakes assessment that purports to measure reading comprehension, educators would think it sensible to align their teaching with the structure of that assessment.

Second, countless resources have been created and sold to schools that reinforce misconceptions. Revision guides and off-the-shelf teaching materials often purport to teach pupils 'inference skills', 'prediction skills', etc., encouraging superficial teaching.

Third, while those responsible for school accountability have belatedly tried to address misconceptions about reading comprehension (Ofsted, 2022), these messages have clearly still not reached all those whose day-to-day job it is to assess the quality of education in schools.

Finally, it can be tricky to pin down what reading comprehension is, even for those who dedicate their lives to studying it. After all, to comprehend requires the application of knowledge, and the nature of knowledge is hardly the most accessible of subjects. Putting aside the endless labyrinths of epistemology, there are various plausible definitions of what reading comprehension entails. Cain (2010, p. 3) defines comprehension as 'Retrieving the sense of individual words, combining clauses to make sentences, and making meaning from successive sentences and paragraphs.' Snow (2002, p. 11) defines it as 'the process of simultaneously extracting and constructing meaning through interaction and involvement with written language'. Castles et al. (2018, p. 28) define it as 'the orchestrated product of a set of linguistic and cognitive processes operating on text and interacting with background knowledge, features of the text, and the purpose and goals of the reading situation'. And Tennent (2014, p. 23) argues that there is 'no conclusive definition of reading comprehension'. It's a lot for teachers to wrap their heads around.

Essentially, though, reading comprehension is difficult to define because the knowledge required to construct meaning is specific to the contents of the text being read. And the contents of a text could be literally anything. Imagine you are handed a piece of writing in a sealed envelope. The hidden text could be about the Cold War, the art of Hokusai, the role of enzymes in the nitrogen cycle… anything at all. What would you need to know to be certain you could comprehend the hidden text once you had opened the envelope? The answer is 'everything'. To guarantee you could construct meaning from the hidden text, you would need to have the capability to fluently recognise the words on the page, *and* you would need to know everything there is to know about the English language and the world it describes.

All of this means that reading comprehension is a bit of a nightmare for anyone trying to construct a neat list of things we want pupils to learn. In mathematics, we might list the knowledge and skills relating to place value, arithmetic, fractions, geometry, etc. that we want pupils to learn by the end of primary school. We can do something similar for science, geography, history, etc. But reading comprehension? In theory, we could take on the impossible job of listing the tens of thousands of words we want pupils to understand; we could attempt to add what we believed to be the most useful phrases, idioms, metaphors, rhetorical devices, structural text features, genres and sentence formations; and we could list everything we want pupils to know about the world they live in, including – but not limited to – the concepts of every other academic subject in the primary curriculum. However, even if a list like this could be written, what practical purpose could it ever serve? Such a list would always either be too short to be meaningful or too long to be useful. Knowledge of the English language and the world it describes is not a constrained skill (Dougherty Stahl, 2011; Paris, 2005; Snow & Matthews, 2016). It is an unconstrained body of interconnected knowledge that simply refuses to be itemised.

WHAT IS A BETTER WAY TO THINK ABOUT READING COMPREHENSION?

When it comes to conceptualising reading comprehension, we are left with two options: we can either pretend that a pupil's capability can be divided into a small set of transferable 'skills', giving us something to *try* to teach and a related assessment checklist. Or we can accept that reading comprehension is based in part on our grasp of the vast construct that is the entirety of written English and the world to which it relates. The first option allows us to create a superficial artefact to point towards when someone in authority demands we show them how we are defining and measuring progress. But the latter option guides us towards effective teaching and better outcomes for pupils.

In short, we can either participate in a shared delusion for the benefit of those who think everything in education can be boiled down to a basic tick list of criteria, or we can recognise the complexity of reading comprehension and teach accordingly. I advocate the latter, and the rest of this book is written on the assumption that you do too.

Let's sum up the argument so far:

1   *Reading comprehension relies on fluent word recognition.*
2   *Reading comprehension also relies on our understanding of written English and the world to which it relates.*

However, there is more to know about comprehension that can help us, so let's build on the two points above:

3   *Reading comprehension exists on a continuum.*

Imagine a story describing 'a forest, high in the mountains'. If a reader doesn't know what a forest is, then we can safely say that they will not comprehend this part of the story. But what about the reader who knows that forests high in the mountains are likely to be evergreen? Have they comprehended the text to a higher level than someone who instead imagines a forest of deciduous trees? What about someone who has trekked through alpine forests and can vividly remember the sight and scent of pine trees? Is it only their more detailed perspective that allows for adequate comprehension? These are not questions with clear answers. Comprehension exists on a continuum, so it can be difficult to ascertain the extent to which a person has made sense of a text.

It can be equally difficult to know where comprehension ends and prior knowledge begins. If we were to probe a reader's understanding of a text, the sorts of questions we could ask range from those that relate entirely to the literal contents of the text alone to those that only tangentially address the text's contents and require various bits of knowledge not within the text. It is hard to define exactly what counts as comprehension and what counts merely as prior knowledge when reading a text.

4   *Reading comprehension involves subjective elements.*

Readers bring unique experiences and knowledge to texts. Two readers can have adequately grasped a text and yet each be emphasising or ignoring different aspects of it. For example, every person possesses a different network of associations for every word in the language they know. If asked to visualise a car in their mind's eye, every person would likely bring to mind something slightly different (or nothing at all in the case of those with aphantasia). This individuality plays out in every text we read, both in the meanings we construct and in our subjective interpretations of those meanings. Engaging with the subjectivity of interpretation, and developing pupils' understanding of themselves as readers, is a key part of teaching reading comprehension.

5   *Comprehension of challenging texts requires conscious effort, which can be*
     supported by particular strategies.

If reading comprehension were always a wholly automatic process based on our knowledge of the relevant written language alone, then there would be no need to consciously grapple with text. However, sometimes texts provide us with challenges. Perhaps a few too many concepts are unfamiliar to us, or our understanding of a few too many words is limited. Under such circumstances, we might simply accept that the text is currently beyond our reach, but it is also possible that with further effort we might be able to construct meaning to an adequate degree. To achieve this, we might re-read the text, summarise passages or ask ourselves questions as we progress. Capable readers are conscious of their own comprehension levels and adapt their focus and use of strategies based on their reading goals (Oakhill et al., 2005, 2014).

WHAT DOES THIS ALL MEAN FOR CLASSROOM TEACHING?

Let's consider the practical implications for teaching reading comprehension of points 1–5 below:

1   *Reading comprehension relies on fluent word recognition.* Word recognition and reading fluency can, and should, be taught. Both rely on a mixture of explicit teaching and meaningful text experience. The teaching of reading comprehension should be undertaken with the development of fluency firmly in mind.

2   *Reading comprehension also relies on our understanding of written English and the world to which it relates.* If you were asked to read a text on an entirely unfamiliar subject, you would probably struggle to understand it to a useful level. Certain critical concepts would be beyond your grasp, for the time being at least. But this doesn't mean you would lack *all* the knowledge required to understand the text. On the contrary, you would be likely to understand *most* of the words; you would probably be familiar with the syntax (i.e. the ordering of words and phrases); you might be familiar with the way the text is structured. The more we learn about written language, the more we increase our chances of understanding other texts we might encounter, even ones with some totally unfamiliar components. Consequently, a central aim of teaching reading comprehension must be the development of pupils' understanding of written language and the wider world. Increasing pupils' breadth of experience with written English is paramount.

3   *Reading comprehension exists on a continuum.* While sometimes we might describe a pupil's comprehension of a text as successful or unsuccessful, we need to recognise that this dichotomy is often misleading. A struggling pupil rarely comprehends absolutely nothing even when they struggle to build meaning as they read a text, and there is almost always scope to deepen the understanding of even the strongest readers. We need to bear in mind that the complexity of the questions we ask pupils will influence our judgements of their comprehension.

4   *Reading comprehension involves subjective elements.* Because the meaning a reader builds from a text inevitably differs from that built by others, it can be tempting to think that the teacher's role is solely to stimulate pupils' own understanding and to equip them with the strategies and dispositions to achieve this more effectively. In this view, as stated by Tennent et al. (2016, p. 35), 'guiding readers is not about the teacher telling pupils what they *should* understand from the text'. There is much to value in this perspective. Part of teaching reading must always be to nurture and value pupils' subjective responses to texts. But teaching reading comprehension also involves supporting pupils' understanding of written English and the world to which it relates. The teacher in the classroom knows *a lot* about this, and they should share this knowledge with their pupils.

Winograd and Johnston (1987) drew a distinction between 'sense' – the individual's experience of a text – and 'meaning' – the socially shared knowledge of that same text. This is a useful way to frame a teacher's priorities. If we focus only on guiding pupils' subjective sense-making with a text, then we reduce the teaching of comprehension to the mere facilitation of independent reading. Equally, if we focus only on ensuring pupils acquire more of the socially shared knowledge of written English, then we fail to teach them about their personal relationship to written language and the world it describes. Often it is valuable to guide pupils to learn new things about written language for themselves, to reach new meanings and to recognise the inherent individuality of their ideas. But just as often, pupils' understanding of a text is best facilitated by a teacher explaining concepts, considering the relative merit of different positions and choosing in advance the aspects of a text they want pupils to better understand. Effective instruction requires us to bring into harmony these different aspects of teaching reading comprehension.

5 *Comprehension of challenging texts requires conscious effort, which can be supported by particular strategies.* Through our teaching, we want pupils to develop their awareness of when texts are challenging and how to use strategies in response. We can model this for pupils before guiding their initial use of these strategies and giving them opportunities to put them into practice independently. And all of this can be achieved as an integrated part of meaningful experiences with texts chosen for their content and variety.

This Chapter in a Nutshell

- It is counterproductive to conceptualise reading comprehension as a set of discrete, transferable skills used to answer specific types of assessment questions. The ability to answer such questions is a *consequence* of comprehension.
- Reading comprehension relies on fluent word recognition.
- A reader's comprehension of a text is dependent on their understanding of the written language used in that text. Thus, a reader's ability to comprehend texts in general is dependent on their wider understanding of written language.
- A teacher's judgement of a pupil's understanding of a text is influenced by what they ask the pupil to do to demonstrate their understanding.
- The meaning that a reader constructs from a text is inevitably personal, but this shouldn't prevent teachers from sharing their own knowledge as part of classroom practice.

---------------------------- Further Reading ----------------------------

- *Understanding and Teaching Reading Comprehension: A Handbook* (Oakhill et al., 2014)
- *Understanding Reading Comprehension: Processes and Practices* (Tennent, 2014)
- The role of background knowledge in reading comprehension: A critical review (Smith et al., 2021)
- How does understanding work? A look at the construction–integration model of comprehension (Young, 2022)

---------------------------- Retrieval Quiz ----------------------------

- What does it mean to suggest that a reader's comprehension of a text exists on a continuum?
- Why is it paramount to develop pupils' breadth of experience with written English?
- In what way can reading comprehension be considered subjective?

---------------------------- Questions for Professional Discussions ----------------------------

- To what extent do text discussions in your context reflect the aim of building pupils' knowledge of written English through meaningful experiences with a variety of texts chosen for this purpose?
- How are pupils in your context supported to recognise their active role in setting reading goals and matching their focus to those goals?
- To what extent is reading comprehension conceptualised as a set of transferable skills in your context?

REFERENCES

Cain, K. (2010). *Reading Development and Difficulties* (Vol. 8). John Wiley & Sons.

Castles, A., Rastle, K. & Nation, K. (2018). Ending the reading wars: Reading acquisition from novice to expert. *Psychological Science in the Public Interest, 19*(1), 5–51.

Dougherty Stahl, K. A. (2011). Applying new visions of reading development in today's classrooms. *The Reading Teacher, 65*(1), 52–56.

Oakhill, J., Cain, K. & Elbro, C. (2014). *Understanding and Teaching Reading Comprehension: A Handbook*. Routledge.

Oakhill, J. V., Hartt, J. & Samols, D. (2005). Levels of comprehension monitoring and working memory in good and poor comprehenders. *Reading and Writing, 18*, 657–686.

Ofsted (2022). *Research Review Series: English.* www.gov.uk/government/publications/ curriculum-research-review-series-english/curriculum-research-review-series-english

Paris, S. G. (2005). Reinterpreting the development of reading skills. *Reading Research Quarterly, 40*(2), 184–202.

Shanahan, T. (2018). Comprehension skills or strategies: Is there a difference and does it matter? Blog. www.shanahanonliteracy.com/blog/comprehension-skills-or-strategies-is-there-a-difference-and-does-it-matter

Smith, R., Snow, P., Serry, T. & Hammond, L. (2021) The role of background knowledge in reading comprehension: A critical review. *Reading Psychology, 3,* 214–240.

Snow, C. (2002). *Reading for Understanding: Toward an R&D Program in Reading Comprehension.* Rand Corporation.

Snow, C. E. & Matthews, T. J. (2016). Reading and language in the early grades. *The Future of Children, 26*(2), 57–74.

Tennent, W. (2014). *Understanding Reading Comprehension: Processes and Practices.* Sage.

Tennent, W., Reedy, D., Hobsbaum, A. & Gamble, N. (2016). *Guiding Readers – Layers of Meaning: A Handbook for Teaching Reading Comprehension to 7–11-Year-Olds.* Trentham Books.

Winograd, P. & Johnston, P. (1987). Some considerations for advancing the teaching of reading comprehension. *Educational Psychologist, 22*(3–4), 213–230.

Young, S. H. (2022). How does understanding work? A look at the construction–integration model of comprehension. Blog. www.scotthyoung.com/blog/2022/02/22/

PART II
LAYING FOUNDATIONS FOR READING DEVELOPMENT

3
TEACHING PHONICS

WHAT IS PHONICS?

Few aspects of primary education are the focus of as much debate, and as many misconceptions, as the teaching of phonics. It is worth pinning down exactly what is meant by phonics and its associated terminology before we proceed any further:

As we saw in Chapter 1, at the heart of the English writing system are relationships between the sounds of spoken language and the letters used to represent them. Specifically, these are correspondences between basic chunks of spoken sound we can break words into for the purposes of reading, called phonemes, and the individual letters or small groups of letters that represent them, called graphemes. These are commonly called grapheme–phoneme correspondences or GPCs. Phonics is any attempt to teach the correspondences between letters and sounds and how to use them. Using these correspondences involves blending identified phonemes together to reconstitute words (e.g. /c/ /a/ /t/ → 'cat') and segmenting phonemes within words (e.g. 'dog' → /d/ /o/ /g/). This identification and manipulation of phonemes, called phonemic awareness, is sometimes discussed as something separate from phonics (National Reading Panel, 2000). However, evidence suggests that phonemic awareness is best taught in the presence of letters, and consequently it is an integral part of teaching phonics (Moats, 2019).

The word 'phonics' is also sometimes used to describe the knowledge and skills relating to the relationships between letters and sounds, in the same way that 'science' might be used to describe the processes of systematic observation undertaken by scientists *and* the things we know about the world from these observations.

Systematic phonics is the attempt to teach phonics with a defined scope and sequence (i.e. an organised curriculum of what will be taught and in what order). In most cases, this means starting with the simplest and most common GPCs and incrementally introducing greater complexity.

Synthetic phonics is the teaching of phonics in which pupils are introduced to GPCs individually and shown how to blend these into words. This contrasts with approaches that initially introduce pupils to words before deriving GPCs from analysis of these words. A key advantage of synthetic phonics is that it makes it easier to ensure targeted GPCs are taught explicitly and in a predetermined sequence (Castles et al., 2018).

WHY SHOULD WE TEACH PHONICS?

The argument for teaching phonics is simple: to use the English writing system, all readers must acquire an understanding of GPCs and how to use them. Thus, it makes sense to teach pupils the most common GPCs and the related skills, using a specified curriculum to gradually build pupils' understanding. Of course, learning to read requires much more than expertise with GPCs, but developing this expertise is a necessary condition of becoming a fluent reader.

When some argue 'phonics doesn't work for everyone' or 'not all pupils learn the same way', they are misunderstanding what phonics actually is. One way or another, if a pupil is to become a fluent reader, then they must acquire knowledge of the code of GPCs that is central to the English writing system. We can teach them this (i.e. phonics), or we can hope pupils will work it out for themselves. Some pupils do seem to have the ability to derive GPCs for themselves with minimal teaching, but these pupils are categorically *not* those who struggle to recognise words. The more difficult a pupil finds it to learn GPCs and how to use them (i.e. how to decode), the more they need patient, persistent teaching of phonics that takes account of this difficulty and the impact it can have on motivation and self-efficacy (Wagner et al., 2022).

WHAT ARE THE LIMITS OF PHONICS?

We've seen that phonics is most accurately and productively defined as the attempt to teach pupils to begin to recognise words for themselves using common relationships between letters and sounds. However, phonics is also sometimes described simply as a method of teaching reading. While understandable, this latter framing of phonics is unfortunate for two reasons:

1 It downplays the importance of various other aspects of teaching reading that constitute an effective curriculum.
2 It implies that *all* those who are struggling with reading need to be supported through phonics.

To counter these issues, it is helpful to understand the limits of phonics.

The goal of phonics is to teach pupils enough about GPCs so that they can begin to recognise words for themselves. No phonics programme aims to teach all the GPCs that might be identified in written English; nor would it be sensible to do so. Instead, the goal of phonics is to teach pupils an initial knowledge of the most common GPCs, enough to allow them to begin adding to this knowledge through their own text experience.

It is also worth reiterating that the English writing system is more than just a code of correspondences between letters and sounds. In some words in English, it is of no use to try to attribute phonemes to every letter (e.g. 'cupboard', 'one', 'Gloucester').

Knowledge of GPCs and their application is essential, but expert word recognition is more than just application of this knowledge (Wagner et al., 2022).

Learning to recognise words can be compared to learning to play chess. It is beneficial for those new to chess to be explicitly taught the basics of how the different pieces move. But further expertise then requires the application of this basic knowledge to new situations, learning the complexities of the game through vast experience of actually playing chess. Subsequent explicit teaching of more complex aspects of chess continues to be useful, but there is no substitute for plenty of experience playing the game.

Similarly, it is beneficial for those new to recognising words to be explicitly taught the basics about GPCs and how to use them. But further expertise then requires the application of this basic knowledge to new situations, learning the complexities of the English writing system through vast experience actually recognising unfamiliar words. Subsequent explicit teaching of more complex aspects of the English writing system continues to be useful, but there is no substitute for plenty of experience recognising words.

HOW DO PUPILS BECOME MORE EXPERT AT RECOGNISING WORDS?

What does this word recognition development look like in practice? Some words that are unfamiliar to a novice reader are simple to decode. Even if a pupil has never seen the word 'stuck' written down before, their first attempt at decoding it will easily provide them with new knowledge of how this word is spelled. After decoding this word a few times, the pupil will become able to recognise this word without conscious effort (Dehaene, 2009; Ehri, 2014).

However, what about unfamiliar words that aren't so easy to decode? Imagine a pupil encounters the word 'cafe' in text for the first time. If they were to read the word aloud, their initial attempts at decoding the word might sound like 'caif' or 'caffee'. After a moment, though, they might realise there is a word already in their vocabulary that sounds quite like 'caffee'... cafe! And from this they have learned something new about the English writing system. They have made a useful connection between the spelling and pronunciation of this word, and they have also learned that the letter 'e' sometimes represents an /ay/ sound. We saw in Chapter 1 that this process is called mispronunciation correction (Colenbrander et al., 2022). Again, with repeated exposure to this word, the pupil becomes able to recognise it without conscious decoding.

It is the accumulation of these moments of learning that builds pupils' word recognition expertise. This is the reason why pupils must be encouraged to use their knowledge of GPCs throughout the entirety of each word they encounter, paying attention to every letter. Where pupils don't do this – often decoding just part of the word and then guessing from context – they miss an opportunity to increase their understanding of the English writing system. Over time, these missed opportunities add up, leading to diminished word recognition expertise, the consequences of which often only reveal themselves after several years of impeded development.

HOW SHOULD PHONICS BE TAUGHT?

The short answer to this question is that it makes sense to teach phonics in the way that aligns with your school's chosen systematic phonics programme. However, there are some principles that teachers should bear in mind, regardless of the specific phonics programme they are using:

- Ensure phonics is taught for the allotted time each day.
- Embed the use of GPCs throughout the entire word as the go-to approach to recognising unfamiliar words. Put another way, you should make sure every pupil decodes unfamiliar words through reference to every letter in the word. Many pupils who develop a 'partial-decode-then-guess' strategy find their development hampered by this over the long term. This can be identified when pupils guess words in ways that suggest they are not paying attention to all the letters in that word, e.g. incorrectly identifying 'jumping' as 'jumped' or 'junking' or 'leaping'.
- Use consistent routines that allow pupils to focus their attention on the learning at hand.
- Ensure teaching is focused and pacy to allow pupils to get plenty of practice decoding and spelling words.
- Enunciate the individual phonemes within words in ways that support pupils to develop phonemic awareness. This means minimising the 'uh' sound (also known as schwa) that can follow consonant phonemes (e.g. 'm' should be pronounced as 'mmm' not 'muh'). Sometimes, it is only possible to minimise this sound; it can't always be removed entirely. While evidence on this aspect of phonics instruction is currently lacking, the experience of countless teachers of early reading suggests that enunciating phonemes in this way is helpful. It is also worth noting that phonemes are abstract entities that are identified within words for the purposes of reading, so – strictly speaking – there isn't a 'pure' or 'correct' way to pronounce any given phoneme.
- Be consistent with any terminology that is part of your school's phonics programme.
- Ensure the teaching of GPCs within words takes account of the accents used by pupils in the classroom (e.g. the vowel sound in the middle of the word 'pass' will differ based on the pupils' accents, and teaching should reflect this).
- Align decodable books that pupils read with the learning they have undertaken through the school's phonics programme. This means the words that pupils encounter in decodable books should either include GPCs they have learned or be whole words to which they have already been introduced.

- Use **responsive teaching**. In other words, assess pupils' learning regularly so that extra support can be provided where required. In some cases, this might entail support that allows pupils to 'keep up' with the pace of learning of their peers. In other cases, it might entail more frequent support that allows pupils to 'catch up' with the pace of learning of their peers.

As well as ensuring the above is taking place, there are further considerations for those who lead phonics across a school:

- Give relevant training to every person who teaches phonics or decoding interventions in your school, including teachers in key stage 2, teaching assistants and colleagues new to the school.
- Offer pupils' parents/carers opportunities to understand how phonics is taught in your school and how they can support their child at home. (See Chapters 17 and 22 for more on this.)
- Help teachers to organise and monitor the in-class provision and interventions provided for pupils who need extra support learning to decode. This support can be adapted through changes to teacher–pupil ratio, changes to frequency/length of interventions, changes to frequency of modelling or targeting of specific barriers to decoding, such as specific gaps in GPC knowledge, difficulties with blending or difficulties decoding polysyllabic words (i.e. words with more than one syllable).

It is worth taking a moment to consider in more detail the support offered to pupils through interventions. Obviously, what constitutes an appropriate pace of learning in any area of the curriculum is set arbitrarily. It can thus seem odd to suggest that a pupil is somehow 'behind' the pace of learning of their peers. However, primary education requires large groups of pupils to be taught by individual teachers, so pragmatism dictates that, where possible, pupils should be given extra support to allow them to be taught alongside the rest of their peers. (For more on assessment and interventions, see Chapter 21.)

Alternatively, phonics can be taught with pupils placed into different groups based on their current attainment. This allows teaching to move at different paces and focus on the immediate needs of pupils. However, this can be challenging to organise, especially in small schools. Regardless of how phonics teaching is organised, pupils who require extra support should receive it.

SHOULD THE TEACHING OF MORPHOLOGY BE EMBEDDED INTO PHONICS INSTRUCTION?

In Chapter 1, we learned that words are composed of morphemes, which we can think of as basic chunks of meaning from which words are built. The study of these morphemes is called morphology. Some argue that because of the impact of these morphemes on spelling, GPCs should be taught primarily in the context of word families that make a word's morphology clearer (Bowers, 2022). However, organising the teaching of GPCs in this way makes it close to impossible to organise phonics instruction systematically (i.e. to incrementally introduce pupils to increasingly more complex and less common GPCs). And evidence suggests that systematic phonics is an essential component of decoding instruction (Castles et al., 2018).

This does not mean we should avoid sensitising pupils to the morphological patterns in the English writing system during the teaching of phonics. For example, the relatively consistent way words are pluralised (i.e. by adding the letter 's') can be pointed out to pupils (Department for Education, 2013). As pupils encounter other common morphemes, especially affixes (prefixes and suffixes) like 'un-' and '-ing', their meaning can be introduced and their existence in other familiar words can be discussed. This supports pupils in understanding the meaning of the words they decode, a key part of phonics instruction. And this understanding can be subsequently developed as pupils learn about morphemes in the context of vocabulary and spelling (see Chapters 18 and 19).

WHY IS DECODABLE TEXT VALUABLE?

Decodable text is any text that primarily uses GPCs that are already familiar to pupils. In other words, these texts are phonically controlled to ensure they do not exceed pupils' nascent GPC knowledge, in line with the phonics programme they are learning from. Such text may also include words containing unfamiliar GPCs if the words in their entirety are already familiar to pupils. As such, whether or not a text is decodable depends on the knowledge of the pupil relative to the text.

There is scant research that focuses specifically on the use of decodable text in early reading instruction. We are left to our experience, intuition and understanding of learning more broadly to help us determine how to make use of such text. Anyone who has sat alongside a novice reader and watched them fail to decode many of the words in a 'normal' text will know the value of decodable text. Pupils' motivation to engage in any activity is linked to the extent to which they can feel successful while practising. Decodable text offers pupils the opportunity to practise what they have learned and, crucially, to embed the key strategy of attending to every letter in a word, all while experiencing a motivating sense of success.

Texts that align with pupils' limited knowledge from the first few weeks of phonics will be unavoidably narrow in the range of words they require pupils to recognise. Such texts are often derided as artificial, but such protestations miss the point: pupils who do not learn to recognise words for themselves will never want to read independently, whatever the quality of the books in front of them. Regardless, all pupils will experience a wide array of 'normal' texts across the curriculum throughout their time in school. Decoding practice with texts that are controlled so that pupils can experience much-needed success is an essential part of any reading curriculum.

WHAT ARE THE LIMITS OF DECODABLE TEXT?

At the very beginning of pupils' journey to reading proficiency, it is essential they prac-tise accurate decoding, and decodable text is designed for this purpose. However, pupils should engage with 'normal' texts as well, especially in partnership with an adult. Ideally, in the first two years of learning to read, pupils should have access to decodable texts that are aligned with their developing understanding of GPCs *in addition to* free choice from a selection of children's books. Decodable texts provide necessary decoding practice while 'normal' books selected by pupils can be shared with parents/carers to build motivation for reading and develop pupils' understanding of written English more generally. Beyond this, pupils can experience the variety of written English beyond decodable books when teachers read aloud and point at the words under a document camera (i.e. a visualiser) or when they read aloud using oversized books (sometimes called 'big books'). One way or another, at no point should pupils' experiences of writ-ten language be limited to decodable text only.

At the early stages of learning to decode, it would be counterproductive to require pupils to persistently decode unfamiliar words that weren't based on their newly devel-oped understanding of GPCs. To do so would be to encourage them to identify words without reference to all the letters within them. If pupils are successful in identifying words without paying attention to all the letters, they might embed a 'partial-decode-then-guess' strategy that is likely to impede their reading development. And if they are not successful in doing this, then they are likely to find these reading experiences demotivating. One way or another, at the very early stages of decoding proficiency, it is a bad idea to expect pupils to persistently identify unfamiliar words containing unknown GPCs.

However, this early stage of decoding proficiency doesn't last forever. At the core of criticisms about the artificiality of decodable text is an issue worth consideration. As described earlier in this chapter, a crucial part of a pupil's journey to reading pro-ficiency is the countless experiences with unfamiliar words containing unfamiliar GPCs. And decodable text is designed to *minimise* such experiences. This means we need to have a clear idea of how to manage pupils' transition from decodable text to 'normal' text.

WHEN AND HOW SHOULD PUPILS TRANSITION TO READING 'NORMAL' TEXTS?

As stated above, it is not problematic for pupils to engage with 'normal' books at any stage of their reading development. Shared experiences of good books are always ben-eficial. However, at the early stages of learning to decode, it is a bad idea to require pupils to persistently decode unfamiliar words containing unknown GPCs. This means we need to think carefully about when we begin asking pupils to do this. In other words, the transition from decodable books to 'normal' books requires consideration.

When pupils start reading 'normal' books (i.e. texts that are not phonically controlled), they will need to use the set of GPCs they have already learned. This knowledge bootstraps their learning of the rest of the complexities of the English writing system through mispronunciation correction. To achieve this, pupils need to:

- Know enough of the most common GPCs so that they can deal with most of the unfamiliar words they face
- Have developed as an embedded habit the strategy of decoding through the entire word (i.e. paying attention to all the letters) when dealing with unfamiliar words
- Know that unfamiliar GPCs exist and that they can figure these out by identifying unfamiliar words
- Have the requisite vocabulary that will allow them to use the meaning of words to correct near-miss decoding attempts with many of the unfamiliar words they encounter.

It is difficult to know when the best moment is to ask a pupil to begin regularly dealing with words that contain unfamiliar GPCs (i.e. practising reading with 'normal' texts). Some pupils will be ready to independently read such texts inside their first year of reading instruction. Others will benefit from much more time practising with decodable text. As a general rule, the vast majority of pupils are ready for 'normal' texts by the end of their second year of formal reading instruction (i.e. the end of year 1 in English schools). However, there is no need for all pupils to wait this long. As already stated, pupils should be engaging with 'normal' texts at *every* stage, assuming they are not expected to regularly decode words with unfamiliar GPCs. But we can judge when a pupil is ready to profitably move their reading practice to 'normal' texts by hearing them read aloud. As soon as a pupil can successfully decode most words in an age-appropriate 'normal' text – decoding through the entirety of each word – then they are ready for independent reading of 'normal' texts. This doesn't mean every word needs to be decoded accurately although 90% of words is a sensible minimum. But it does mean that pupils should *not* be resorting to a 'partial-decode-then-guess' strategy for unfamiliar words. The use of a 'partial-decode-then-guess' strategy for word identification is a clear warning sign that the habit of decoding using all the letters in a word has not fully developed and further practice with decodable text is likely to be beneficial. (For further discussion of productive one-to-one reading, see Chapter 22.)

When making the transition from decodable text to 'normal' text, the choice of book matters. No initial reader is going to successfully recognise more than 90% of the words in *Pride and Prejudice* or even *Charlotte's Web*. Pupils' first experiences with 'normal' text should provide a gentle introduction to the complexities of the English writing system.

When pupils make this transition at a young age, this is not a problem as they can simply begin reading the age-appropriate texts from their classroom or school library. (As we will discuss in Chapter 17, there is no need for elaborate book-banding systems beyond the support they offer teachers in recommending books to children.) However, where pupils make this transition at a later age – perhaps even at secondary school or in adulthood – it is vital that texts provide pupils with the same gentle introduction to the complexities of written English but in the context of age-appropriate content and presentation. Many providers of decodable books have designed texts for this purpose, sometimes called 'Hi-Lo' books.

This Chapter in a Nutshell

- Phonics is the attempt to teach correspondences between letters and sounds and phonemic skills. Systematic phonics includes a defined scope and sequence (i.e. which correspondences are learned and in what order). Synthetic phonics is the teaching of phonics in which pupils are introduced to GPCs individually and shown how to blend these into words.
- All fluent readers are experts in the code of GPCs at the heart of the English writing system. The central goal of teaching phonics is for every pupil to acquire enough knowledge of the most common GPCs so that they can begin recognising words for themselves. Where pupils lack this knowledge, there is no reason not to teach it to them.
- Once pupils *can* begin recognising words for themselves in 'normal' texts, they can then learn the true complexity of the English writing system through vast amounts of text experience. This is a vital, though often underappreciated, component of a pupil's journey to reading proficiency.
- Phonics lessons should embed the strategy of using GPCs throughout the entirety of each word as the go-to approach to recognising unfamiliar words. Phonics lessons also benefit from routines that allow for plenty of focused practice of decoding and spelling words.
- Phonics teachers should take care to enunciate phonemes in ways that support the development of pupils' phonemic awareness, minimising the 'uh' sound (schwa) after consonant sounds.
- Regular assessment should be used to identify pupils who require further support. This support can be adapted through changes to teacher–pupil ratio, changes to frequency/length of interventions, changes to frequency of modelling and targeting of specific barriers to decoding.
- Decodable text is designed to provide initial readers with accurate decoding practice using GPCs they have already learned. The transition to practising decoding with 'normal' texts should be monitored to ensure pupils do not begin to employ a counterproductive 'partial-decode-then-guess' strategy.

—————————— Further Reading ——————————

- Ending the reading wars: Reading acquisition from novice to expert (Castles et al., 2018)
- *Early Reading Instruction: What Science Really Tells Us about How to Teach Reading* (McGuinness, 2006)
- Teaching children to read irregular words: A comparison of three instructional methods (Colenbrander et al., 2022)
- Connected phonation is more effective than segmented phonation for teaching beginning readers to decode unfamiliar words (Gonzalez-Frey & Ehri, 2021)

—————————— Retrieval Quiz ——————————

- What is meant by 'systematic phonics'?
- What are the limits of phonics?
- How might elements of morphology be included in early reading instruction?

—————————— Questions for Professional Discussions ——————————

- To what extent do all teachers and teaching assistants in your school have an adequate grasp of the underlying purpose of phonics?
- When, if ever, are pupils in your school introduced to the role of morphemes within words? How is this achieved?
- How does your school support pupils to make the transition from decodable texts to 'normal' texts at a time that matches their individual reading capabilities?

REFERENCES

Bowers, P. (2022). Structured word inquiry (SWI): Literacy instruction that makes sense of English spelling for students of all ages and abilities. *Patoss Summer 2022 Bulletin*, 35(1).

Castles, A., Rastle, K. & Nation, K. (2018). Ending the reading wars: Reading acquisition from novice to expert. *Psychological Science in the Public Interest*, 19(1), 5–51.

Colenbrander, D., Kohnen, S., Beyersmann, E., Robidoux, S., Wegener, S., Arrow, T., Nation, K. & Castles, A. (2022). Teaching children to read irregular words: A comparison of three instructional methods. *Scientific Studies of Reading*, 26(6), 545–564.

Dehaene, S. (2009). *Reading in the Brain*. Penguin.

Department for Education (2013). English Programmes of Study: Key Stages 1 and 2. National Curriculum in England https://assets.publishing.service.gov.uk/media/5a7de93840f0b62305b7f8ee/PRIMARY_national_curriculum_-_English_220714.pdf

Ehri, L. C. (2014). Orthographic mapping in the acquisition of sight word reading, spelling memory, and vocabulary learning. *Scientific Studies of Reading, 18*(1), 5–21.

Gonzalez-Frey, S. M. & Ehri, L. C. (2021). Connected phonation is more effective than segmented phonation for teaching beginning readers to decode unfamiliar words. *Scientific Studies of Reading, 25*(3), 272–285.

McGuinness, D. (2006). *Early Reading Instruction: What Science Really Tells Us about How to Teach Reading.* MIT Press.

Moats, L. (2019). Phonics and spelling: Learning the structure of language at the word level. In D. A. Kilpatrick., R. M. Joshi & R. K. Wagner (Eds), *Reading Development and Difficulties* (pp. 39–62). Springer International Publishing.

National Reading Panel (2000). *Teaching Children to Read: An Evidence-Based Assessment of the Scientific Research Literature on Reading and Its Implications for Reading Instruction: Reports of the Subgroups.* National Institute of Child Health and Human Development, National Institutes of Health [in the US Department of Health and Human Services].

Wagner, R. K., Zirps, F. A. & Wood, S. G. (2022). Developmental dyslexia. In M. J. Snowling, C. Hulme & K. Nation, K. (Eds), *The Science of Reading: A Handbook* (pp. 533–555). John Wiley & Sons.

4

SUPPORTING SPOKEN LANGUAGE DEVELOPMENT

WHY IS SPOKEN LANGUAGE DEVELOPMENT IMPORTANT TO READING?

There are undoubted differences between spoken language and written language (Oakhill et al., 2014; Rastle, 2019). Beyond the different media of transmission (i.e. spoken sound vs visual symbols), each mode of communication has distinct constraints and affordances. Written language lacks the rhythm, intonation and facial expressions of spoken language that can contribute to meaning although typographical features such as punctuation and italics go some way to compensating for this. Written language tends to be more formal and syntactically complex. A reader cannot ask for an author to clarify their message, but written language offers a reader greater control over the pace of comprehension. And certain chunks of meaningful information are more apparent in spelling than in sound (e.g. the suffixes in 'walked', 'hinted' and 'scored' all indicate the past tense in a way that is easier to discern from the spelling than from the sounds of these words).

However, there is considerable overlap between the knowledge that allows us to comprehend spoken language and that which allows us to comprehend written language (Huettig & Pickering, 2019; Seidenberg, 2017). Reading and listening rely on a shared well of understanding about the meaning of words individually and in concert (Aitchison, 2012). A central role of any school is to support the development of pupils' spoken language capabilities, not least because of the impact on their reading development.

HOW CAN PUPILS' SPOKEN LANGUAGE DEVELOPMENT BE NURTURED IN THEIR FIRST YEARS AT SCHOOL?

In contrast to other aspects of literacy, young people's ability to speak develops relatively instinctively if they interact within a language community. Sensitivity to the sounds of their mother's language emerges before birth, and the development of spoken language over the first few years of life progresses at an astonishing rate (O'Grady, 2005). There is plenty that schools can do to enhance this area of pupils' learning, especially in the first years of their education. Singing songs, sharing rhymes, engaging in role play and sharing storybooks are all valuable in their own right, not least for the joy they bring, but they also contribute to a pupil's grasp of spoken language (Hamilton & Hayiou-Thomas, 2022).

Dockrell et al.'s (2012) 'Communication Supporting Classroom Observation Tool' suggests that in the first years at school, the support offered to pupils can be considered in reference to three dimensions:

1 *Language learning environment*: The learning environment for pupils needs to be set up to encourage spoken interactions. This means, for example, that there are clearly defined learning areas; background noise is managed to allow children and adults to hear one another; and resources are available that encourage imaginative play and discussion.

2 *Language learning opportunities*: Structured opportunities are provided to pupils for discussion with adults and peers. This includes interactive reading and small-group activities.

3 *Language learning interactions*: The way in which adults talk with children supports spoken interaction. This means, for example, that adults physically get down to pupils' level and encourage conversations through careful use of pacing, pausing, responding and turn-taking in ways that signal the value of pupils' utterances and build on them.

Dockrell et al.'s (2012) 'Communication Supporting Classroom Observation Tool' is a useful way to consider spoken language provision in environments where pupils often move freely around. As such, in English schools this tool is most relevant in reception classrooms and in some key stage 1 classrooms in which continuous provision is part of teaching (i.e. where pupils freely access and explore areas and resources around the classroom as part of their learning).

There is some evidence that early spoken language interventions can be valuable for pupils who might benefit from extra support in this area (Sibieta et al., 2016). These tend to involve frequent small-group discussions with pupils, alongside one-to-one discussions that focus on vocabulary and listening. Targeting pupils for extra informal support (i.e. further opportunities for discussion with adults and peers) is also likely to be worthwhile.

HOW CAN COLLABORATIVE LEARNING STRUCTURES BE USED TO SUPPORT PUPILS' SPOKEN LANGUAGE DEVELOPMENT?

In the formal classroom settings that are more common as pupils progress, the role of whole-class structures for collaborative talk becomes increasingly important. Collaborative learning activities that are designed carefully can ensure pupils work together through productive talk (Bilton & Duff, 2021; Knight, 2020). These benefit from well-understood routines. It is often more effective for a teacher to use a small set of collaborative structures rather than trying to use a wide array of practices their pupils are consequently less familiar with. Two collaborative structures that are particularly useful are 'think-pair-share' (Lyman, 1981) and 'rally coach' (Kagan, 1994):

1   *Think-pair-share*: Pupils are given time to individually consider a question before discussing their ideas with a partner to refine their thinking. Finally, pupils are selected to present their answers to the class.
2   *Rally coach*: In pairs, one pupil answers a question while being coached on how to complete the answer by their partner. The pupils then switch roles, alternating as they progress through different questions.

WHAT KIND OF CLASSROOM TALK BETWEEN TEACHERS AND PUPILS IS MOST LIKELY TO SUPPORT PUPILS' SPOKEN LANGUAGE DEVELOPMENT?

In many classrooms, the most common form of classroom talk between teachers and pupils takes the form of 'initiation-response-feedback', also known as 'initiation-response-evaluation' (Clements & Tobin, 2021; Mercer & Dawes, 2014). This involves a teacher asking a question, receiving a short response from a pupil and then giving evaluative feedback on that response. While this sort of talk has its uses, such as assessing the understanding of an individual pupil, it is likely to contribute little to pupils' spoken language development. Alexander (2008) argues that talk based around dialogue is most likely to develop pupils' reasoning and accelerate their facility with spoken language. In line with this aim, Bilton & Duff (2021) recommend the following ways to increase the quantity and quality of classroom talk:

* Ask open questions, such as questions that require pupils to explain, reason or argue.
* Probe with follow-up questions that require pupils to expand on their answers.
* Build on pupils' responses to move the dialogue forward.
* Encourage pupils to ask their own questions.
* Ensure every pupil has opportunities to articulate their ideas and be listened to.
* Create a classroom culture that encourages dialogue (e.g. by teaching pupils to listen when others are speaking).
* Incorporate opportunities for dialogue into lesson plans and classroom activities.

The discussion of texts, sometimes known as 'book talk', is an essential part of any school's curriculum. It is particularly valuable because it develops pupils' knowledge of written language and their understanding of themselves as readers. This form of discussion will be discussed in depth in Chapters 5 and 10.

HOW CAN PICTURE BOOKS, VIDEOS AND OTHER FORMS OF MEDIA PROVIDE OPPORTUNITIES FOR CLASSROOM TALK?

Picture books, those containing solely pictures or those containing words and pictures together, provide powerful opportunities for classroom discussion. Pictures provide an immediate way to connect pupils to the setting or characters within a story or the content of a non-fiction book. This provides impetus for vibrant classroom talk for pupils of all ages although it is especially useful for young pupils for whom it provides a scaffold to ensure as many as possible can participate in the discussion.

An entire picture book can be shared at pace so that pupils can reflect on it. Alternatively, single pages or even sections of single pages can be lingered on, and pupils can be invited to draw conclusions based on what they see and to make predictions. While there is no reason to assume that reasoning about pictures or videos is a skill that transfers meaningfully to reasoning about written language, supporting pupils' spoken language development is beneficial to all aspects of literacy, and picture books, videos and other forms of media can play a useful role in this.

HOW CAN WE SUPPORT THE SPOKEN LANGUAGE DEVELOPMENT OF BILINGUAL AND MULTILINGUAL PUPILS?

Bilingual pupils are those who speak two languages, and multilingual pupils are those who speak more than two languages. Pupils in English schools are identified as speaking English as an additional language (EAL) if they are exposed to a language other than English at home (Department for Education, 2020). It is important to recognise that pupils defined as EAL are a heterogenous group (Sharples, 2021; The Bell Foundation, 2024). Teachers should make no assumptions about a pupil's spoken language abilities in English based on a pupil's designation as speaking EAL. However, pupils who speak languages other than English can be supported in ways that are specific to their language capabilities:

- They should be encouraged to use *both* English and any other languages they know. This is beneficial for their spoken language development and their broader learning outcomes because it allows them to make sense of new concepts using all their language knowledge.
- Pupils at different levels of proficiency in English are likely to need different levels of support. Where pupils are relatively new to English, teachers will need

to use clear examples and offer concrete language support (including translation where this is beneficial to the individual pupil).

- Assessment of pupils' wider capabilities will need to take account of their current proficiency in English as this will influence how the pupils engage with any form of assessment.
- Teachers should recognise that bilingualism/multilingualism is an asset to the pupil and the school community. The variety of language spoken in every classroom should be celebrated.

For more on how to support bilingual and multilingual pupils, see Chapter 21.

This Chapter in a Nutshell

- While there are important differences between spoken language and written language, there is considerable overlap between the knowledge that supports each of these capabilities. As such, supporting pupils' spoken language development is a key part of teaching reading.
- In the earliest stages of school, specifically reception and other year groups where continuous provision is used, provision relating to spoken language development can be considered in reference to three dimensions: the language learning environment, language learning opportunities (i.e. small-group discussion) and language learning interactions (i.e. the ways language is used by adults with pupils).
- Early spoken language interventions can be beneficial for pupils who require extra support.
- Collaborative learning structures, such as 'think-pair-share' and 'rally-coach', are pedagogical tools that can be used to build productive talk into everyday teaching.
- Classrooms in which dialogue is part of everyday teaching are likely to demonstrate a higher quality and quantity of productive talk.
- Picture books, videos and other forms of media can provide the impetus for productive classroom talk.
- Bilingual and multilingual pupils are a heterogenous group who should be encouraged to use and develop all their spoken languages in the classroom.

Further Reading

- *How Children Learn Language* (O'Grady, 2005)
- *Classroom Talk* (Knight, 2020)
- *Developing a Communication Supporting Classrooms Observation Tool* (Dockrell et al., 2012)
- *Towards Dialogic Teaching: Rethinking Classroom Talk* (Alexander, 2008)
- What is EAL in education? (The Bell Foundation, 2024)

──────────────────────── Retrieval Quiz ────────────────────────

- Name three ways in which written language and spoken language differ.
- Describe the collaborative learning structure 'think-pair-share'.
- Name three ways that the quantity and quality of classroom talk can be increased.

──────────── Questions for Professional Discussions ────────────

- To what extent is spoken language development seen as key to reading development in your school?
- Which subjects across the curriculum might be well-suited to the use of 'think-pair-share'?
- How are bilingual and multilingual pupils in your school encouraged to use and develop all their spoken language capabilities?

REFERENCES

Aitchison, J. (2012). *Words in the Mind: An Introduction to the Mental Lexicon.* John Wiley & Sons.

Alexander, R. J. (2008). *Towards Dialogic Teaching: Rethinking Classroom Talk.* Routledge

Bilton, C. & Duff, A. (2021). *Improving Literacy in Key Stage 2: Guidance Report.* Education Endowment Foundation.

Clements, J. & Tobin, M. (2021). *Understanding and Teaching Primary English: Theory Into Practice.* Sage.

Department for Education (2020). *English Proficiency of Pupils with English as an Additional Language.* www.gov.uk/government/publications/english-proficiency-pupils-with-english-as-additional-language

Dockrell, J. E., Bakopoulou, I., Law, J., Spencer, S. & Lindsay, G. (2012) *Developing a Communication Supporting Classrooms Observation Tool.* https://assets.publishing.service.gov.uk/media/5a7c50b7ed915d338141dfdf/DFE-RR247-BCRP8.pdf

Hamilton, L. G. & Hayiou-Thomas, M. E. (2022). The foundations of literacy. In M. J. Snowling, C. Hulme & K. Nation, K. (Eds), *The Science of Reading: A Handbook.* (pp. 533–555). John Wiley & Sons.

Huettig, F. & Pickering, M. J. (2019). Literacy advantages beyond reading: Prediction of spoken language. *Trends in Cognitive Sciences, 23*(6), 464–475.

Kagan, S. (1994). *Cooperative Learning.* Kagan Publishing.

Knight, R. (2020). *Classroom Talk.* Critical Publishing.

Lyman, F. (1981). The responsive classroom discussion: The inclusion of all students. In A. Anderson (Ed.), *Mainstreaming Digest* (pp. 109–113). University of Maryland College of Education.

Mercer, N. & Dawes, L. (2014). The study of talk between teachers and students, from the 1970s until the 2010s. *Oxford Review of Education, 40*(4), 430–445.

O'Grady, W. (2005). *How Children Learn Language.* Cambridge University Press.

Oakhill, J., Cain, K. & Elbro, C. (2014). *Understanding and Teaching Reading Comprehension: A Handbook.* Routledge.

Rastle, K. (2019). EPS mid-career prize lecture 2017: Writing systems, reading, and language. *Quarterly Journal of Experimental Psychology, 72*(4), 677–692.

Seidenberg, M. (2017). *Language at the Speed of Sight: How We Read, Why So Many Can't, and What Can Be Done about It.* Basic Books.

Sharples, R. (2021). *Teaching EAL: Evidence-Based Strategies for the Classroom and School.* Multilingual Matters.

Sibieta, L., Kotecha, M. & Skipp, A. (2016). *Nuffield Early Language Intervention: Evaluation Report and Executive Summary.* Education Endowment Foundation.

The Bell Foundation (2024). What is EAL in education? www.bell-foundation.org.uk/eal-programme/guidance/classroom-guidance/what-is-eal-in-education

PART III

ORGANISING CLASSROOM TEACHING

5

DISCUSSION OF TEXT: QUESTIONING, EXPLANATION AND DIALOGUE

WHY DO WE NEED TO DISCUSS TEXT?

In Chapter 1, we considered the idea that capable readers are those who can recognise words well enough to flow through text *and* who know enough about written language to build meaning from those words (Hoover & Tunmer, 2022). On this basis, it is not immediately clear why engaging pupils in discussions about texts would be a necessary part of teaching reading. One could argue that to build pupils' understanding of written English, teachers only need to read various texts aloud to pupils, explaining as they go. And assuming the pupils are fairly fluent already, a lot of independent reading time could be used to further develop their word recognition capabilities. So why *are* text discussions central to reading lessons?

> *First*, it's close to impossible to predict exactly which parts of a text pupils will comprehend. Pupils often surprise their teachers by their prior knowledge (or lack thereof) on a given subject. And even when it seems pupils should be able to grasp a writer's meaning, it is possible for them to be tripped up by an unfamiliar phrase or a complex sentence structure. Only through engaging pupils in discussion can teachers match their explanations to the needs of their class.

> *Second*, by using techniques that involve the whole class in discussion, teachers can ensure all pupils are thinking about the written language contained within texts. And by putting their knowledge of new words into practice, pupils increase the chances that this knowledge will be remembered (Beck et al., 2013; Zimmerman & Reed, 2017).

Third, effective readers are those that understand their role in the reading process, setting reading goals and responding strategically to parts of text that require greater attention (Oakhill et al., 2005). Through discussion, teachers can model the thought processes of expert readers and gradually encourage pupils to react more strategically to challenging text.

Fourth, text discussions can help pupils to understand the subjective nature of aspects of comprehension. These discussions can nurture and validate pupils' own ideas and opinions, building their identity as readers and emphasising the value of reading.

Fifth, while the central purpose of reading lessons is to support pupils' reading development, it is possible for the benefits to go beyond literacy. At their best, text discussions teach pupils how to interact with their peers in sophisticated ways. They encourage pupils to communicate their thoughts clearly, to build on the ideas of others and to disagree with sensitivity.

WHAT ASPECTS OF TEXTS SHOULD DISCUSSIONS FOCUS UPON?

No aspect of a text is off limits. We can, and should, direct pupils' attention to any aspect that is worth discussing and encourage them to identify such aspects themselves, asking questions of their own.

It can be helpful to think about the different levels we might explore within a text:

- Word/phrase level – for example:
  - o Meanings of the word/phrase in context
  - o Endophors, which are words/phrases that derive their meaning from the surrounding text (e.g. pronouns like 'it' or 'they', or phrases like 'the stranger' referring to a character previously introduced)
  - o Sensitivity analysis, which involves considering the way an alternative word/phrase choice would impact meaning (Lemov et al., 2016).
- Sentence/line level – for example:
  - o Meaning of a sentence/line in context
  - o Phrase and clause structure
  - o Punctuation
  - o Connectives (e.g. conjunctions, joining phrases).
- Paragraph/chapter level – for example:
  - o Meaning of a paragraph/chapter in context
  - o Paragraph/chapter coherence (e.g. how meaning builds across a paragraph/chapter)
  - o Use of organisational devices (e.g. subheadings).

- Text level
  - o Meaning of a text
  - o Relationship of a text to conventions of text type, genre, audience or purpose.

At each of these levels, language choices can be explored at face value or analysed by considering an author's purpose, style, etc. and by considering comparisons to other potential language choices and other texts.

WHAT IS REQUIRED FOR TEXT DISCUSSIONS TO BE EFFECTIVE?

There are three essential elements to text discussions: *explanation, questioning* and *dialogue*. These three elements rarely exist in isolation from each other, but it is worth considering them separately so that we can recognise the purpose of each and how they might be balanced. To do this, we first need to address the role teachers play in lessons, the implicit assumptions in much that has been written about the teaching of reading and the detachment of this from common classroom practice.

Many teachers have been told at some point in their career that they should minimise the amount of talking they do in the classroom. While teachers can often become more effective in their explanations and modelling by being more concise, this is different to simply aiming to talk as little as possible. Thankfully, most classroom teachers and school leaders recognise that explicit instruction does not conflict with the aim of cultivating pupils' autonomy, and they are increasingly confident in pushing back against those who suggest otherwise.

However, the teaching of reading appears to have bucked this positive trend. It is not difficult to find examples of teachers being advised to avoid sharing their knowledge of written English for fear this will impede the *real* task of helping pupils to learn the 'skill' of independently comprehending text. It is much better, or so it is claimed, for teachers to only ever nudge pupils towards their own discoveries and to avoid ever deciding in advance what it is pupils might learn from a text. Ironically, this advice has coincided with many teachers – as a result of accountability pressures – moving in the extreme opposite direction, towards a lifeless caricature of explicit instruction, in which they model question-answering procedures with disconnected bits of text before pupils practise these procedures independently.

I am not going to blandly state that a better way to discuss texts with pupils is to find a middle ground between these perspectives. Both viewpoints sideline the content being explored, with texts chosen less for the ideas and language they contain, and more for the discovery they might elicit or the test rehearsal they supposedly provide. Of course, it is not an inherently bad thing for pupils to learn without relying on the knowledge of their teacher, nor is it unwise to prepare pupils for the assessments that are an inevitable part of education. But neither of these should be the central aim of reading lessons, which instead should exist to introduce pupils to the breadth of written English through exploration of texts chosen for this purpose. In this light, the roles of *explanation, questioning* and *dialogue* become clear:

- *Explaining to pupils* what we know about a text isn't a pedagogical last resort. Instead, it is a tool to be used whenever we want pupils to have immediate access to something we know that will aid their understanding of a text.
- *Asking questions* is a means of getting pupils to think about written language in ways that wouldn't happen in our absence, one that awakens them to their responsibility in making meaning from words.
- *Engaging pupils* in dialogue is a strategy for probing pupils' understanding, deepening their learning and helping them to recognise how their ideas might differ from those of others.

The balance between these three elements of text discussion depends on what we want pupils to learn about written English and their relationship to it, something that is inseparable from the content of the texts we choose to explore. (Exactly how these three elements of text discussion can be balanced will be exemplified in Chapters 7, 8, 9 and 10.)

WHAT MIGHT EFFECTIVE EXPLANATION LOOK LIKE?

When sharing a text with a class, it is common to find ourselves unsure whether a word, phrase, sentence, paragraph or aspect of the whole text makes sense to all the pupils in the room. We are then left with a decision: do we probe pupils' understanding and encourage them to make connections for themselves by asking a question? Or do we simply give a clear explanation and move on. There are two circumstances in which an explanation is likely to be preferable:

1   We are keen to maintain the pace of reading, and we suspect asking a question will break the flow more than we want.
2   Understanding the word, phrase, sentence, paragraph, chapter or aspect of the whole text in question requires knowledge we think pupils are unlikely to have.

In most cases, it is best to keep our explanations brief. If this is the explanation of a word or phrase, then it might be a succinct, pupil-friendly definition with an example (e.g. 'The word "makeshift" describes a poor-quality solution to a problem, one that is only used until a better solution is found. If you weren't allowed to use the football goals on the school field, then two jumpers might be used as a *makeshift* solution to that problem.') We might not provide an example if we think the text itself provides an adequate example to help pupils learn the word (e.g. 'The word "makeshift" here means the shelter they have built is a solution that isn't ideal and isn't meant to last long.') Equally, where we think pupils' comprehension of a sentence, paragraph or chapter is likely to have broken down, we might paraphrase or summarise (e.g. 'We see here that Hugo wasn't sure whether to trust Isabelle at first, but he decided to share his secret with her.')

The brevity and quality of our explanations are supported by preparation. Sometimes we need to react in the moment to unexpected responses from pupils. But often when we read a text before a lesson, we can predict where pupils might need an explanation, and we can make a note of how we will explain something. This might even include the use of a picture if what we want to describe is easier to show than to explain in words. Where possible, it suffices in our planning to quickly search online for a representative image or a set of images that will build pupils' understanding.

In some cases, we might even provide pupils with explanations and images for unfamiliar vocabulary *before* we dive into reading a chunk of text. Generally, it is better to explain in the moment rather than in advance so that pupils have the text's context to support them in their understanding. However, where the required explanation is lengthy enough to interrupt the flow of text more than we would like, pre-teaching vocabulary before reading is a useful option.

HOW CAN EXPLANATIONS SUPPORT PUPILS TO BECOME MORE STRATEGIC READERS?

Explanations of words, phrases, sentences and paragraphs are not the only sort of explanation that is valuable. A key part of teaching reading is to nurture pupils' understanding of their role as strategic readers, which means we want them to recognise what they can do when faced with text that is challenging to comprehend. We can begin to achieve this by narrating our thinking, explaining our strategies for when the going gets tough. For example, we might explain that a sentence or paragraph we just read was quite complicated, so we think it's a good idea to re-read it (e.g. 'I'm not sure I understood all that. Let's re-read that paragraph.') We might explain that we're keen to keep track of what we have understood in an information text by summarising (e.g. 'There's a lot going on in that section. I think it is basically saying that our cardiovascular system benefits from a balanced diet and regular exercise.') Or we might model how to self-question in response to challenging text, in other words creating and answering questions that get to the heart of a section (e.g. 'If I wanted to know the most important thing from this chapter, I would ask "What strange things seem to have happened in Ade's world?"')

WHAT MIGHT EFFECTIVE QUESTIONING LOOK LIKE?

The aim of questioning in reading lessons is to provoke pupils to build meaning from written language for themselves, habituating them to the cognitive effort this can demand and demonstrating the value of their individual interpretations of texts.

However, to achieve this, we need all pupils to engage with the questions we ask. Too often, only a small selection of pupils actively think about the questions asked by their teacher. This lack of engagement is reinforced if we solely seek answers from pupils who volunteer a response by putting their hand up. The only way to ensure all pupils are thinking about the questions we ask is for everyone in the class to know they might be asked to share their thinking. This requires an environment in which pupils feel safe in the knowledge that their responses will be treated sensitively and respectfully (something that will be discussed later in this chapter), and it also requires strategies that are designed to elicit participation from the entire class:

- *Think-Pair-Share*: Give all pupils time to independently think about a question and discuss their thoughts with a partner. Then, ask some pupils to share their ideas (Lyman, 1981).
- *Pose-Pause-Pounce-Bounce*: Give pupils adequate thinking time before asking a pupil to share their ideas. Then, ask another pupil to share, ideally by building on the answer before. In some cases, a pupil might offer no answer, saying something like, 'I don't know.' Ask this first pupil to listen carefully as you elicit responses from other pupils, and then go back to the first pupil, asking them to share their interpretation of what they heard from their peers.
- *Mini whiteboards*: Ask all pupils to jot down a response to a question on their mini whiteboards. If the question allows responses of many pupils to be quickly gauged, systematically view the responses of the whole class, table by table or row by row, depending on the classroom seating arrangement. This makes most sense with questions that require short answers. In contrast, if the question does not allow responses to be systematically viewed, seek responses from a small selection of pupils. By moving around the room as pupils write on mini whiteboards, you can identify responses that are most worth further exploration, including misconceptions and interesting perspectives. Particularly thought-provoking responses might even be shared with the entire class by placing a pupil's mini whiteboard under a document camera.
- *Signals for questions or to build on peers' ideas*: By giving pupils a specific way of showing they want to ask a question or build on the answer of a classmate, you can bring their contributions to the fore at apposite moments, demonstrating that their thoughts are valued. Specific hand gestures can be used in a classroom – or, ideally, across an entire school – so that a pupil can signal to their teacher when they wish to ask a question, build on a classmate's answer or provide an opposing viewpoint. For example, pupils could place one fist on top of another to show they wish to build on an answer. The exact gestures are less important than pupils having a clear understanding of how and when to use them.
- *Written answers*: Ask pupils to independently write in response to a question. Reading lessons should be predominantly spent reading texts and discussing them, but a little time spent writing can reinforce pupils' thinking and ensure all pupils have an extra reason to pay attention to text discussions. (That said,

it might be valuable for pupils to do more writing in response to text in reading lessons if this is absent across the wider curriculum. This is discussed further in Chapter 19.)

HOW CAN THE QUESTIONS WE ASK COMPLEMENT THE WAY WE ARE READING A TEXT?

It can be helpful to think of the questions we ask in reading lessons as serving two distinct purposes: establishing meaning and analysing meaning (Lemov et al., 2016).

Questions that establish meaning provoke pupils to make basic sense of a text. The range of answers to these questions is likely to be narrow with less scope for subjectivity. Such questions are best used when we want to sustain a sense of momentum while reading.

Questions that analyse meaning provoke pupils to consider the ideas of a text more deeply, exploring authors' language choices and key themes (i.e. the big ideas an author explores through the text – see Chapter 10 for more on this). The range of answers to these questions is likely to be broad and provide opportunities to discuss and validate pupils' subjective views. Such questions are best used when we are returning to a text to probe aspects of it.

In practice, questions about texts cannot always be neatly divided into two types. These questions exist on a continuum with shades of grey between simple questions that check pupils' basic understanding and complex questions that elicit thoughtful analysis. The vital thing is to recognise how we want pupils to engage with a text and to match the questions we ask to this purpose.

HOW CAN WE ZOOM IN AND OUT OF TEXT WHEN WE ASK QUESTIONS?

As with effective explanation, effective questioning focuses on different levels within the text. We should ask questions that elicit thinking about words, phrases, sentences, paragraphs, chapters and aspects of the whole text. Lemov et al. (2016, p. 93) describe the process of moving between these levels of questioning as 'zooming in and out of text'. When we are questioning to help pupils grasp the basic meaning of a text, the level we focus on should be whatever is required to achieve this purpose. But when we are questioning to deeply explore a text, we should ensure that – over the longer term, at least – we are discussing texts at all levels, connecting them together. This might mean, for example, considering how individual words reflect the mood of a paragraph, how the repetition of a metaphor builds tension across a chapter or how the overarching themes of a text are expressed in specific sentence structures.

WHAT ROLE DO OPEN-ENDED QUESTIONS PLAY?

Beck et al. (2020, p. 8) encourage teachers to use open-ended questions that do not 'provide much directive information about what a correct response should be'. It is certainly the case that such questions (labelled 'queries' by Beck et al.) are of particular value. In contrast, questions that require little more than retrieval are less likely to stimulate pupils to think much about the meaning of the text although they might be a useful way to briefly assess pupils' understanding. For example, compare the following two questions:

'What words in the text tell us that Phoebe was happy to see the penguins?'

'How might Phoebe have felt when she saw the penguins?'

The first question guides pupils to a specific idea: *Phoebe was excited to see the penguins, and the text shows this*. The second question, in contrast, allows a wider range of responses, including some that may go beyond that which is directly suggested by the text. This is not to say that open-ended questions are always preferable. The former question might be useful as a quick check for understanding while the latter might be better at sparking dialogue. The crucial thing is to consider how we want pupils to engage with the text in that moment and to ask questions that align with this.

HOW CAN WE ADAPT OUR QUESTIONS TO INCREASE ENGAGEMENT?

Sometimes a question can fall flat simply because we have worded it in a way that is inaccessible to our pupils. Before moving on from a question that hasn't had the desired effect, consider how it can be reworded more simply or how further detail can provide guidance. For example, a teacher might ask, 'Why do you think the dragon is exhilarated?' and find that the class are not sure how to respond. To support their pupils, the teacher might then say, 'Exhilarated means happy and excited. Why do you think the dragon feels this way?' before adding helpful detail by asking, 'What things have happened to the dragon that might have caused this feeling?' The teacher has reacted to their class to make the question more accessible while building pupils' vocabulary knowledge. Rewording questions when required is an essential part of a teacher's repertoire that develops with practice.

WHAT MIGHT EFFECTIVE DIALOGUE LOOK LIKE?

Explanation and questioning are crucial components of effective dialogue. Explanation allows us to fill gaps in pupils' understanding so that dialogue is not held back by relatively trivial gaps in knowledge. And questions, mainly from the teacher but also from pupils themselves, are the sparks that ignite meaningful dialogue. Thus, it might seem odd to talk about dialogue as a separate entity. But there *is* something special about it. Dialogue is collaborative. It involves a shared search for meaning in which differences in opinion potentially contribute to a richer synthesis of ideas than could be achieved by any individual alone. While the best classroom dialogue can look almost effortless to an outside observer, creating and sustaining the conditions that allow it to flourish requires considerable pedagogical expertise.

And so it is no surprise that genuine classroom dialogue is not as common as we might hope. As discussed in Chapter 4, research focusing on classroom talk over the past fifty years has suggested that the most common form of classroom discussion consists of simple back-and-forths between a teacher and an individual pupil, often described as initiation-response-feedback. This involves a teacher asking a (usually closed) question, a pupil responding and the teacher giving feedback on their answer. This form of classroom talk has its place. It can be a useful way to check pupils' understanding, especially if there is an opportunity for all pupils to respond (e.g. using mini whiteboards). But genuine dialogue requires lengthy interactions, with the teacher keeping the discussion moving forward or guiding its direction.

There are three essential ingredients required for meaningful dialogue:

1   Questions that are asked should allow for a variety of responses (Nystrand, 2006). The majority of these should focus on themes and patterns within the text that the teacher has recognised, but pupils should also have opportunities to openly share their thoughts on a text, which might include what pupils liked, what confused them and what connections they spotted within and beyond the text (Chambers, 1993).

2   The teacher needs to recognise what might be valuable or interesting in pupils' responses so that they can purposefully guide pupils to build on each other's ideas. This means teachers need to do more than ask questions. They also need to explain things, encourage pupils to justify their ideas and, when necessary, re-word pupils' thoughts to allow the rest of the class to access them.

3   A supportive culture of trust must exist in the classroom between the teacher and the pupils and between the pupils themselves (Alexander, 2008).

While the first two points will be exemplified in subsequent chapters in Part III, let's turn our attention to the third essential ingredient.

HOW CAN WE CREATE AN ENVIRONMENT THAT SUPPORTS TEXT DISCUSSION?

It takes time to nurture an environment in which pupils listen to one another, express their thoughts freely and build on each other's ideas sensitively. It is much easier to create this atmosphere if expectations relating to classroom discussion are consistent across the school, but even then, such an environment is one that needs vigilant attention if it is to be sustained.

Pupils must trust that their responses will be listened to and respected by all in the class. This begins with the setting of clear expectations about how pupils should react to the thoughts of their classmates. In almost all circumstances, this will align with the behaviour expectations the school already holds, but clear reminders about how this applies to reading discussions are useful. This is likely to involve modelling how to build on the answer of a classmate and how to politely disagree. Sentence stems might be introduced to support this, for example:

- 'I agree with what Pupil X said because...'
- 'I'm not sure I agree with what Pupil X said because...'
- 'What I want to say connects to what Pupil X said...'

Then, if a pupil intentionally undermines this environment through the way they react to a classmate's answer, this must be treated as an unacceptable breach of classroom expectations. If the same thing happens but it is unintentional, then the classroom expectations should once again be made clear.

A key part of creating an environment that supports text discussion is to actively reduce the pressure pupils feel when responding to questions and offering ideas. There are a couple of ways we can achieve this:

- When asking questions with a variety of responses, consider using the word 'might'. 'Why did the author choose this metaphor?' feels like an assessment. In contrast, 'Why *might* the author have chosen this metaphor?' feels like an invitation.
- Be careful how you use praise. It can be tempting to lavish praise on responses, either because they are especially productive for the discussion or because they come from a pupil who is usually reluctant to contribute. But such praise often adds pressure to a discussion, and subsequent responses from you that are less effusive can feel demoralising to the pupils who receive them. In contrast, consistent warmth and gentle appreciation for all responses, even when ideas are corrected or challenged, stop pupils from chasing praise and worrying about whether their thoughts appear to be less well received than those of their peers.

WHY MIGHT IT BE USEFUL TO CENTRE THE AUTHOR IN OUR TEXT DISCUSSIONS?

In an approach to teaching reading comprehension called 'questioning the author', Beck et al. (1997) discuss the value of placing the author at the centre of questions (e.g. 'Why might the author have...?') They convincingly argue that this serves to 'depose the authority of the text', letting pupils know that 'the book's content is simply someone's ideas written down' (p. 18). The idea is that this reminds pupils of the inevitable fallibility of the author's communication and emphasises the role pupils must play in actively constructing meaning. It also has the advantage of eliciting discussion about authorial intentions, which can be a useful way to consider the array of devices at the author's disposal.

However, there are limits to the value of centring the author in our questions. Sometimes pupils' interpretations of texts go beyond what the author might have intended. Our discussions should often reflect what we think the author was trying to communicate, but we shouldn't be shackled by this, especially in the discussion of poetry and stories. There is much to be gained from discussions that temporarily ignore authorial intentions and explore purely what a text means to those reading it.

We might also want to avoid questions that centre the author when we are reading at pace and want to ask a question without removing pupils from the flow of the text. A question like 'How might Owen feel?' will pull pupils out of a story less than a question like 'What might the author be trying to show about Owen's feelings?' For this reason, questions that centre the author are most appropriate in close reading lessons rather than extended reading lessons. (See Chapters 9 and 10 for more on this.)

HOW MIGHT DISCUSSION VARY BASED ON THE TYPE OF TEXT WE ARE READING?

All types of text potentially offer the opportunity for worthwhile exploration through discussion. We can reflect on an author's choices and their impact just as well with an information text as with a poem or a story. However, text types that are traditionally considered to involve artistic expression tend to offer opportunities that are much less common in other forms of writing.

Discussions related to a story are likely to focus on the plot, setting and characters, including the conflict experienced by those characters that propels the story forward. Even brief discussion designed to check that pupils are making basic sense of the story will necessarily involve these elements. But deeper discussion of stories goes beyond this by addressing themes, the author's language choices and the interaction between these.

Poetry also offers unique opportunities for discussion. Again, themes can be identified and analysed in relation to the language choices made by the author. And there are concepts we might share with pupils to enhance these discussions (e.g. rhythm, alliteration, metre).

All of this can sound worryingly complex, the domain of secondary English teachers with the expertise required to do justice to such analysis of literature. And it is true that there is a tendency to import pedagogy and curricular ideas from secondary schools into the primary classroom without much thought as to how we will cope without the expertise of subject specialists. However, it *is* possible for us to facilitate increasingly sophisticated discussion of literature in a form that is appropriate to both our role as generalist teachers and to the developmental stage of our pupils. The unique ways we can explore stories and poetry are explored in Chapter 10.

———————————————— This Chapter in a Nutshell ————————————

- Text discussions are essential to teaching reading. They allow teachers to know what their pupils have understood; they ensure all pupils are thinking carefully about written language; they support pupils to react strategically to challenging text; they help build pupils' identities as readers; and they encourage pupils to interact with their peers in increasingly sophisticated ways.
- Text discussions contain three interconnected elements: explanation, questioning and dialogue.
- Effective explanations are usually succinct and, where possible, considered in advance. Often, explanation involves the teacher talking through their thought processes, especially when faced with challenging text.
- Effective questioning is directed at all pupils through strategies such as 'think-pair-share' and use of mini whiteboards. The questions we ask should look at texts on different levels, from the word level to the whole-text level, and they should frequently offer the opportunity for pupils to give a range of responses.
- Effective dialogue involves a shared construction of meaning, requiring teachers to recognise what might be interesting or valuable in pupils' responses.
- Text discussions work best when pupils trust that their responses will be listened to and respected by everyone in the class. Building this classroom culture requires modelling, clear expectations and patience. We can nurture this culture by using depressurising strategies, such as using 'might' in appropriate questions and being judicious in our use of praise.
- Centring the author in text discussions can encourage pupils to play an active role in making meaning and highlight the way writers consider their purpose and audience when writing. However, it is valuable for some discussion to temporarily put aside the role of the author so that pupils can focus on their own interpretations of a text and lose themselves in stories.
- All types of text offer opportunities for discussion. Deeper exploration of stories and poetry is supported by a basic understanding of the elements of story and the language of poetry.

————————————————— Further Reading ————————————————

- *Robust Comprehension Instruction with Questioning the Author* (Beck et al., 2020)
- *Reading Reconsidered* (Lemov et al., 2016)
- *Guiding Readers – Layers of Meaning* (Tennent et al., 2016)
- *Tell Me: Children, Reading and Talk* (Chambers, 1993)

─────────────────────────── Retrieval Quiz ───────────────────────────

- Define explanation, questioning and dialogue, including what might make each of these effective.
- What strategies might we use to ensure the questions we ask are being considered by all pupils?
- What role do depressurising strategies play in nurturing a classroom culture that encourages effective text discussion?

──────────── Questions for Professional Discussions ────────────

- In your current reading lessons, approximately what proportion of the questions you ask allow for a range of responses? If such questions are infrequently used, are there any reasons why this is the case (e.g. alignment of questions with the limited range used in reading assessments)?
- Are routines used across the curriculum in your school to ensure all pupils are thinking about their learning? If so, to what extent are these routines part of reading lessons?
- How often do pupils in your school ask questions as part of text discussions? Are they encouraged to do this as a routine part of sharing texts?

REFERENCES

Alexander, R. J. (2008). *Towards Dialogic Teaching: Rethinking Classroom Talk*. Routledge.

Beck, I. L., McKeown, M. G., Hamilton, R. L. & Kucan, L. (1997). *Questioning the Author: An Approach for Enhancing Student Engagement with Text*. International Reading Association.

Beck, I. L., McKeown, M. G. & Kucan, L. (2013). *Bringing Words to Life: Robust Vocabulary Instruction*. Guilford Press.

Beck, I. L., McKeown, M. G. & Sandora, C. A. (2020). *Robust Comprehension Instruction with Questioning the Author*. Guilford Publications.

Chambers, A. (1993). *Tell Me: Children, Reading and Talk*. Stroud: Thimble Press.

Lemov, D., Driggs, C. & Woolway, E. (2016). *Reading Reconsidered: A Practical Guide to Rigorous Literacy Instruction*. John Wiley & Sons.

Lyman, F. (1981). The responsive classroom discussion: The inclusion of all students. In A. Anderson (Ed.), *Mainstreaming Digest* (pp. 109–113). University of Maryland College of Education.

Hoover, W. A. & Tunmer, W. E. (2022). The primacy of science in communicating advances in the science of reading. *Reading Research Quarterly, 57*(2), 399–408.

Nystrand, M. (2006). Research on the role of classroom discourse as it affects reading comprehension. *Research in the Teaching of English, 40*(4), 392–412.

Oakhill, J., Hartt, J. & Samols, D. (2005). Levels of comprehension monitoring and working memory in good and poor comprehenders. *Reading and Writing, 18*, 657–686.

Tennent, W., Reedy, D., Hobsbaum, A. & Gamble, N. (2016). *Guiding Readers – Layers of Meaning: A Handbook for Teaching Reading Comprehension to 7–11-Year-Olds.* Trentham Books.

Zimmerman, L. & Reed, D. K. (2017). Attributes of effective explicit vocabulary instruction. Blog. Iowa Reading Research Center. https://irrc.education.uiowa.edu/blog/2017/10/attributes-effective-explicit-vocabulary-instruction

6

READING LESSON STRUCTURES INTRODUCED

WHAT DO I MEAN BY 'READING LESSONS'?

There are so many factors that contribute to reading development that it can be hard to pin down what someone means when they talk about 'reading lessons'. Do phonics lessons count as reading lessons? What about lessons across the curriculum that develop pupils' spoken language and their knowledge of the world – are these reading lessons as well? For the sake of simplicity, when I discuss reading lessons, I will *not* be talking about phonics lessons or reading that is done in science or history or geography, regardless of how much these contribute to reading development. Instead, I will use the phrase 'reading lessons' to refer to discrete slots in the timetable that focus upon pupils' reading capabilities through engagement with texts. It is possible to teach reading without discrete slots for reading lessons in the timetable, but this way of teaching reading is rare in primary schools. (See Chapter 11 for more on this.)

SHOULD READING BE TAUGHT THROUGH WHOLE-CLASS OR SMALL-GROUP TEACHING?

Classroom teaching generally takes place with one teacher (perhaps supported by another adult) and a class of around 30 children. This means there are unavoidable trade-offs between individualisation of learning and the time pupils get to spend being taught by a teacher. As soon as we divide pupils into groups, we drastically reduce the amount of time they spend being supported in their learning.

Some argue that this loss of teaching time is worth it because of what is gained by better differentiating the teaching to meet the needs of groups of pupils. However, putting pupils into groups to ensure they are reading texts that match their current attainment doesn't seem to improve learning (Shanahan, 2020). And there is no basis in evidence for the idea that pupils are demotivated by working with more challenging texts (Fulmer & Tulis, 2013; Gambrell et al., 1981). In fact, there is evidence that pupils learn more when supported by a teacher to access frustration-level texts (Brown et al., 2018).

And putting pupils into attainment-based groups disadvantages those who most need our support (Sørenson & Hallinan, 1986). This is no surprise because it is these pupils who are least equipped to gain from independent reading. (See Chapter 17 for more on this.) I have seen first-hand the impact on dysfluent readers who have been left to read independently or to get on with independent tasks for most of the week's reading lessons. Commonly, these pupils spend this time *pretending* to read, which reinforces their negative feelings about their potential to become readers. On several occasions I have heard a version of 'We read easy books because we're not on the clever table.' It is almost impossible to hear this and continue to think that habitually dividing the class into attainment-based groups is a good idea.

Nevertheless, there are some circumstances in which small-group teaching is advisable. Sometimes pupils require support with a particular aspect of reading, usually something most of their peers have already grasped. We might then use small-group interventions to address this, or – if such intervention time is unavailable – we might use occasional small-group teaching within reading lessons or as part of our wider curriculum. (This will be discussed in more detail in Chapter 12.) But wherever possible, we should seek to teach as many pupils at the same time as we can. This means starting with whole-class reading as a sensible default and only teaching small groups where this is absolutely necessary.

WHAT ARE WE TRYING TO ACHIEVE IN READING LESSONS?

As we saw in Chapter 2, the teaching of reading – beyond phonics and spoken language development – has three key aims:

1   Develop pupils' reading fluency
2   Increase pupils' understanding of written English and the world to which
    it relates
3   Nurture pupils' understanding of their subjective, strategic role in interpreting
    and appreciating texts.

I believe that *any* approach to reading lessons that targets and balances these three aims is likely to be effective. While this might seem obvious, in practice my experience suggests most primary schools do not adequately address these three aims. Often, fluency development is not a consideration; classes with many dysfluent readers use texts in ways that leave these pupils behind. Just as often, the need to build pupils' understanding of written English is disregarded, with the quantity and variety of texts used in reading lessons barely an afterthought. And schools frequently lack a clear idea of how they are helping pupils to understand their subjective, strategic role as readers, beyond well-meaning, scattergun initiatives aimed at developing reading for pleasure.

HOW DO WE ADDRESS THE THREE KEY AIMS OF READING LESSONS?

The components of reading development are intertwined. For example, anything that develops pupils' reading fluency is also likely to contribute to their understanding of written English and their understanding of themselves as readers, and vice versa. That said, there are aspects of reading pedagogy that *primarily* target each of the three aims:

1   Develop pupils' reading fluency… *by providing them with opportunities to reach fluency through modelling, practice and feedback.*
2   Increase pupils' understanding of written English and the world to which it relates… *by providing extensive, meaningful experiences with a variety of texts chosen for this purpose.*
3   Nurture pupils' understanding of their subjective, strategic role in interpreting and appreciating texts… *by planning and guiding discussions that analyse written language and explore pupils' own ideas.*

Or to put it more simply:

1   Build reading fluency through practice
2   Read plenty of thoughtfully chosen texts
3   Discuss texts in depth.

WHAT ARE THE ADVANTAGES OF USING DIFFERENT 'STRUCTURES' FOR READING LESSONS?

There are countless ways the three aspects of reading pedagogy described above could be used to achieve the three associated aims. However, I advocate one particular way of doing this that revolves around three different core lesson structures for the teaching of reading:

* **Fluency reading** primarily targets reading aim 1 (see Chapter 8)
* **Extended reading** primarily targets reading aim 2 (see Chapter 9)
* **Close reading** primarily targets reading aim 3 (see Chapter 10).

In addition to these core structures there is an introductory structure for use with younger classes, usually year 1, though it is sometimes useful with older pupils as well:

- **Scaffolded reading** primarily targets reading aim 1 while introducing pupils to whole-class reading (see Chapter 7).

Each reading lesson structure is, in effect, a different way to organise a whole-class reading lesson. I do not claim to have invented any of these reading lesson structures from scratch. They are merely my interpretation of methods of teaching reading that exist across the profession and have done so for decades.

Use of distinct reading lesson structures provides five advantages:

The first advantage of using different reading lesson structures is that it helps achieve a balance between the different priorities any approach to reading should address. It ensures time is dedicated to developing fluency, exploring plenty of texts and engaging pupils in discussions about written language.

The second advantage of using different reading lesson structures is that it allows teachers to be responsive to the needs of their class. For example, if almost all pupils in a class are relatively fluent readers, then some fluency reading lessons might be productively replaced with extended reading or close reading lessons. Those few pupils with fluency issues are likely to be best supported through an intervention under these circumstances. Conversely, if many pupils in a class appear to have issues with reading fluency that are unexpected for their age, the number of fluency reading lessons might be increased.

The third advantage of using different reading lesson structures is that these structures, once learned, can be used as tools across the wider curriculum and in interventions. If a teacher wants to explore a text in a history lesson, they can consider the specific way they want their class to engage with the text and apply the appropriate lesson structure. If a teaching assistant is asked to run a fluency intervention with a group of pupils, they can use the fluency reading lesson structure, something they will have seen the class teacher use many times.

The fourth advantage of using different reading lesson structures is that it allows teachers to develop their teaching of reading incrementally. Each reading lesson structure can be learned about, practised and implemented one at a time. This increases the chances that teachers will be able to make changes to their classroom practice without feeling overwhelmed or overworked. (The practicalities of professional development and implementing change across a school will be discussed in Part IV.)

The fifth advantage of using different reading lesson structures is that these provide a basis for innovation and individuality. The teaching of reading inevitably needs to work a little differently in different year groups and different schools, and a sense of agency is important to teacher motivation (Worth & Van den Brande, 2020).

It is tempting to think that adding shared structures to lessons necessarily conflicts with teacher agency, and this is true when taken to an extreme. But a certain degree of structure can also provide the foundation upon which a teacher can innovate and express their individuality. Reading lesson structures help teachers to understand which aspects of teaching are 'active ingredients' that need to be present and which aspects allow for greater personalisation.

WHAT NEEDS TO BE IN PLACE TO ALLOW A SCHOOL TO TEACH USING READING LESSON STRUCTURES?

To teach reading using these reading lesson structures, ideally there needs to be time dedicated to reading in the weekly timetable. These should be daily reading lessons of around 30 minutes (or more), but the approach is flexible enough to allow for other timetables to work. (This is discussed in detail in Chapter 11.)

These reading lesson structures are designed to be used with whole classes of pupils at the same time. It is *possible* to teach this way without class sets of texts, instead relying on a mixture of photocopying and texts displayed on screens using a document camera. However, as you will see in Chapters 9 and 10, class sets of texts allow the reading lesson structures to be used to their full potential. (The building of a reading curriculum and the role of class sets of texts is discussed in detail in Chapter 16.)

As with all teaching, the greater the spread of ages and attainment in a reading lesson, the greater the challenge of teaching all pupils at the same time. Where the spread of ages and attainment makes whole-class teaching impractical (e.g. in classrooms containing pupils from several year groups) adaptations will be required. Adaptations for the different lesson structures are discussed in each relevant chapter (and adaptations specific to mixed-year-group classes are discussed in Chapter 12). In some cases, support from a colleague (e.g. a teaching assistant) may be even more useful than usual. This being the case, and given the importance of reading development, school leaders should consider how teaching assistants might be made available for reading lessons in these classrooms. For example, this might mean changing when reading is taught in different classrooms.

Finally, all teaching depends on a sound approach to behaviour for learning. Ensuring pupils can learn in calm, predictable classrooms is the number one priority for any school where this isn't currently the case.

DOES TEACHING IN THIS WAY INCREASE TEACHERS' WORKLOAD?

No area of the academic curriculum warrants thoughtful planning and feedback more than the teaching of reading. However, any approach to teaching reading is doomed to failure if it places a heavy planning and marking burden on busy teachers.

These reading lesson structures are designed to maximise outcomes and experiences for pupils while keeping planning time to a reasonable minimum and entirely removing the need to provide written feedback. There is no reason why this approach should increase the planning burden placed on teachers. In fact, feedback from schools implementing this approach has suggested the opposite: planning time is mostly spent reading the text to be used and making brief notes, either on a copy of the text itself or elsewhere. (How to plan for each reading lesson structure is spelled out in Chapters 7, 8, 9 and 10.)

IS IT A PROBLEM THAT THIS APPROACH DOESN'T GENERATE PLENTY OF 'EVIDENCE' OF PROGRESS IN PUPILS' BOOKS?

The first thing to make clear is that, at opportune moments, pupils will still write in response to the texts they read. (See Chapter 10 for more on this.) However, it is true to say this approach to teaching reading may well involve children spending far more time actually reading, and thus less time writing, than your current approach. This is by design. The writing that pupils do in response to texts is valuable for consolidating and enhancing their understanding of a text, but it provides nothing that can be reliably used to make inferences about the pupils' underlying reading capability. And analysing pupils' written responses to texts is a highly inefficient way to guide next steps in teaching. In other words, pupils' writing is not 'evidence' in any productive sense of the word.

There is a common idea in the teaching profession that those responsible for inspecting schools in England want to see 'evidence' of reading progress in pupils' books. While it is impossible to account for the potential misconceptions of every school inspector, Ofsted (2018) has made it clear that no particular amount or frequency of work is expected in pupils' books. And this view has been reinforced by inspections undertaken in schools using reading lesson structures in the way advocated here. From this it can be safely concluded that there is no good reason why we should ask pupils to generate written 'evidence' based on fears of what school inspectors might think.

———————————— This Chapter in a Nutshell ————————————

- The key aims of reading lessons suggest three necessary aspects of reading pedagogy that can each be targeted by a different core reading lesson structure:

  o *Fluency reading*: Build reading fluency through practice

  o *Extended reading*: Read plenty of thoughtfully chosen texts

  o *Close reading*: Discuss texts in depth.

- A further introductory reading lesson structure can be used with younger pupils:

  o *Scaffolded reading*: Introduce pupils to whole-class reading.

- Using reading lesson structures has several advantages:
  - Balanced teaching priorities
  - Responsiveness to pupils' needs
  - Cross-curricular application
  - Efficient implementation across a school
  - A basis for innovation.
- Teaching using reading lesson structures works best with discrete reading lessons in the timetable and with access to class sets of texts (though it is still possible to teach this way without these).
- Adaptations to this approach are required where the spread of ages and attainments within a class is particularly wide.
- Where necessary, consider how teaching assistants might be made available to support reading lessons in classrooms with an especially broad range of reading capabilities.
- As with all teaching, reading lesson structures rely upon calm, predictable learning environments.

Further Reading

- *The Art and Science of Teaching Primary Reading* (Such, 2021)
- *The Behaviour Management Pocketbook*, 2nd Edition (Hook & Vass, 2011)

Retrieval Quiz

- What are the core reading structures? And which reading aim does each of these focus upon?
- What is the introductory reading structure? And what is its purpose?
- What are the advantages of using reading lesson structures?

Questions for Professional Discussions

- What are your experiences of whole-class teaching?
- This chapter makes the argument that a certain amount of structure can promote, rather than restrict, teacher agency. To what extent does this align with your experiences of classroom teaching and/or school leadership?
- Does your school currently have a discrete slot in the timetable for daily reading lessons? If so, how do these lessons work? If not, what might be the impediments to moving towards this sort of timetable in your context?

REFERENCES

Brown, L. T., Mohr, K. A., Wilcox, B. R. & Barrett, T. S. (2018). The effects of dyad reading and text difficulty on third-graders' reading achievement. *The Journal of Educational Research, 111*(5), 541–553.

Fulmer, S. M. & Tulis, M. (2013). Changes in interest and affect during a difficult reading task: Relationships with perceived difficulty and reading fluency. *Learning and Instruction, 27*, 11–20.

Gambrell, L. B., Wilson, R. M. & Gantt, W. N. (1981). Classroom observations of task-attending behaviors of good and poor readers. *Journal of Educational Research, 74*, 400–404.

Hook, P. & Vass, A. (2011). *The Behaviour Management Pocketbook*, 2nd Edition. Management Pocketbooks.

Ofsted (2018). Ofsted inspection – clarification for schools. https://assets.publishing. service.gov.uk/media/5b5b24c040f0b6339def5c5c/Ofsted_inspections_-_clarification_ for_schools_270718.pdf

Shanahan, T. (2020). Limiting children to books they can already read: Why it reduces their opportunity to learn. *American Educator, 44*(2), 13.

Sørensen, A. B. & Hallinan, M. T. (1986). Effects of ability grouping on growth in academic achievement. *American Educational Research Journal, 23*(4), 519–542.

Such, C. (2021). *The Art and Science of Teaching Primary Reading*. Sage Corwin.

Worth, J. & Van den Brande, J. (2020). *Teacher Autonomy: How Does It Relate to Job Satisfaction and Retention?* National Foundation for Educational Research.

7
SCAFFOLDED READING

WHAT IS SCAFFOLDED READING?

Scaffolded reading is a structure for teaching reading that is designed to give year 1 pupils plenty of decoding practice through repeated reading to begin to build fluency. Crucially, it also introduces year 1 pupils to some of the key routines of whole-class reading that are used from year 2 to year 6 in the three core reading lesson structures. Scaffolded reading primarily uses decodable books (i.e. books that match the grapheme–phoneme correspondences [GPCs] that pupils have learned). However, age-appropriate 'normal' books and texts (i.e. not decodable books) should ideally be used sometimes too, especially in the latter stages of year 1, to introduce pupils to words containing less-common or entirely unfamiliar GPCs and to model how to deal with these.

HOW DO I TEACH A SCAFFOLDED READING LESSON USING A DECODABLE BOOK?

* Arrange pupils in mixed-attainment pairs with a copy of the book shared between each pair.
* Briefly place the upcoming reading in a wider context. If you are starting a new book, show the front cover and the title. If you are continuing a book that was started in a previous lesson, summarise the part of the book that has already been read.
* Read a page of the decodable book aloud to pupils, modelling the decoding of the most challenging words. (A page of a decodable book is likely to be two or three sentences at most.) This is best done under a document camera, reading as slowly as possible while still maintaining a sense of fluency.
* Briefly explain the meaning of any words that are likely to be unfamiliar to pupils.
* Read the page again, this time asking the pupils to track the words in their own book as you read.
* Echo read the page with the class, one sentence at a time. This involves you reading a sentence aloud and then the class reading the sentence aloud in unison.

- Ask the pairs of pupils to take turns to read the page to each other. This is likely to only be for a minute or two although pupils should be encouraged to read the page more than once if they have time.
- Briefly discuss the page by posing a question for pupils to discuss with their partner before gathering a response from one or two of the pairs (i.e. think-pair-share).
- Once you finish a decodable book in this way, read the entire book aloud to pupils at a natural pace, and ask them to discuss with their partner what the entire book was about.
- A sensible length for a scaffolded reading lesson is ~15 minutes, but this lesson structure can still work well with shorter or longer lessons.

HOW DO I TEACH A SCAFFOLDED READING LESSON USING A 'NORMAL' BOOK OR TEXT?

Teach the lesson as described above with the following adaptation:

- If a page contains several sentences, limit the chunk being read by pupils to just three or four sentences.

HOW DO I PLAN A SCAFFOLDED READING LESSON?

- Choose a decodable book that matches the GPCs that pupils have already encountered in their phonics programme. As described above, a 'normal' text might sometimes be chosen instead. If this is the case, ensure the text is approximately age-appropriate.
- Read the book or text.
- Practise modelling the decoding of any particularly challenging words.
- Consider the questions you will pose to pupils for each page of the book. Try to ensure most of the questions relate to the text itself rather than any pictures. (For more on the value of picture books and how these might be explored, see Chapter 4.)

HOW DO I CHOOSE A TEXT FOR SCAFFOLDED READING?

Most of the time, the book chosen for scaffolded reading should focus on words with GPCs that pupils have already encountered at the point they are at in the phonics programme. The book is likely to also include 'common exception words' that pupils have already been introduced to in their phonics programme (i.e. words with relatively rare GPCs that pupils need to know at an early stage so they can begin engaging with decodable books, such as 'the', 'was', 'they', etc.). The book doesn't have to match the most recent GPCs that have been taught to pupils, but it makes sense to work with a book that matches a recent stage in the phonics programme. A sensible rule is to choose a book that focuses on the GPCs introduced in the previous few weeks, but don't worry if you use books that align with parts of the phonics programme further back than that.

As discussed above, you should ideally sometimes also use age-appropriate 'normal' books instead if class sets are available, especially in the later stages of year 1. Care should be taken to model the decoding of words that contain unfamiliar GPCs.

If class sets of decodable books are not available in your school, decodable texts can be found online. The sequence of GPCs may not match your phonics programme, but careful choice of texts should mean pupils are not overwhelmed by a lot of unfamiliar GPCs. However, using books that are aligned with your phonics programme is preferable.

A book might not be finished in any individual reading lesson. It is fine to pick up where you left off in a subsequent scaffolded reading lesson. Books can be read more than once across a week to build fluency. Equally, books can be re-read in subsequent weeks, especially if these offer experience with GPCs that pupils need more practice with or if the class particularly enjoy the book.

HOW DO I SUPPORT PUPILS WHO MIGHT STRUGGLE WITH SCAFFOLDED READING LESSONS?

Scaffolded reading is designed for pupils who are still at the early stages of decoding development but are ready for a whole-class approach to reading. The central requirement it places on pupils is the ability to decode words in the same way that they might in their phonics lessons. This means any pupil who can participate effectively in phonics lessons should be able to participate in scaffolded reading. However, pupils who struggle a little more should be paired with peers who are more likely to offer support when reading together.

HOW DO I STRETCH PUPILS WHOSE READING CAPABILITY MEANS THEY MIGHT FIND SCAFFOLDED READING LESS CHALLENGING THAN OTHER PUPILS DO?

Most pupils in scaffolded reading lessons will not yet be fluent readers. Through repeated reading, they might be able to read some sentences with a greater degree of fluency. More advanced readers can be encouraged to practise reading with prosody while ensuring that the decoding remains accurate.

HOW MIGHT MY TEACHING OF SCAFFOLDED READING CHANGE OVER TIME?

When scaffolded reading is first introduced in year 1, it is likely to be decodable text that is used. As the year progresses, however, opportunities can be taken to introduce pupils to some 'normal' texts (i.e. not decodable books). This should be undertaken with care to ensure pupils are not struggling with a lot of words that do not entirely consist of familiar GPCs. This does not mean decodable texts are no longer used in these lessons thereafter. It just means that slowly introducing pupils to a mixture of decodable and 'normal' texts prepares them for the reading they will do in the coming years. In particular, it prepares them to deal with unfamiliar GPCs and to begin learning about the complexities of English orthography by using the valuable knowledge and skills they acquired in phonics lessons.

As you become more confident in teaching scaffolded reading, give yourself more flexibility to sometimes just have fun with the book with the pupils in your class. Use the lesson structure to ensure pupils get supported decoding practice, but don't be afraid to move away from the routine in ways that allow pupils to enjoy the book you are reading. This might mean talking about the pictures, asking pupils about their favourite part of the book or reading aloud a funny part of a story multiple times because it makes your class laugh.

WHAT CAN GO WRONG WITH SCAFFOLDED READING? AND HOW CAN I FIX IT?

Table 7.1 Troubleshooting scaffolded reading

Problem	Solution
Some pupils might not look at the words in their copy of the book while you model reading a sentence.	Practise just this part of the lesson with pupils, building clear routines and expectations.
Pupils read too loudly when doing paired reading.	Explain to pupils that paired reading needs 'quiet voices', a volume that means their partner can hear them but not someone on the other side of the room.
There aren't enough copies of the book for pupils to undertake paired reading.	Place a copy of the book under a document camera and ask pupils to read from there. (This should only be done occasionally as it is important for pupils to get used to the feel of real books and the routines involved in sharing a real book with a peer.)
Implementation of our phonics programme already includes something quite similar to scaffolded reading.	If pupils are already engaging in whole-class repeated reading of decodable texts, then scaffolded reading may be unnecessary. However, it might be worth considering how you are intentionally introducing pupils to whole-class reading lessons with 'normal' texts.

An Example from a Scaffolded Reading Lesson

Here is a page from a decodable text that will be referred to in the example that follows:

It was not cold, so Toad took off his coat and hung it on a branch. He went to float a stick on the moat, but he fell in. He was soaked!

And in Table 7.2 is an example of the dialogue for this part of the lesson. This lesson is with a class who have participated in a scaffolded reading lesson before. Italics are used to show where reading aloud is taking place.

Table 7.2 A transcript from a scaffolded reading lesson

Teacher:	'Let's continue with our story from yesterday. Everybody turn to page 7. We saw so far that it is Toad's birthday, and he has decided to take a walk to see his friends.'
	(The teacher shows the page under the document camera and begins to read at a careful pace, using their finger to point at each word as it is read.)
	'It was not cold, so Toad took off his coat and hung it on a branch.'
	'Let's sound out this word together: b-r-a-n-ch, branch.'
	'He went to float a stick on the moat, but he fell in. He was soaked!'
	'A moat is a ditch around a building that can be filled with water. It is used to protect the building. You can see the moat on the picture, just here.'
	'I'm going to read the page again. This time follow along with your partner in your copy of the book. Ready? Let's go.'
	'It was not cold, so Toad took off his coat and hung it on a branch. He went to float a stick on the moat, but he fell in. He was soaked!'
	'Now let's echo read the text.'
	'It was not cold, so Toad took off his coat and hung it on a branch.'
Pupils:	*'It was not cold, so Toad took off his coat and hung it on a branch.'*
Teacher:	*'He went to float a stick on the moat, but he fell in.'*
Pupils:	*'He went to float a stick on the moat, but he fell in.'*
Teacher:	*'He was soaked!'*
Pupils:	*'He was soaked!'*
Teacher:	'Excellent! Now it's your go. Take it in turns to read the page with your partner. Partner A will read this page first while partner B listens, and then you will swap over. Ready? Off you go.'
	(The pupils read in pairs for about two minutes while the teacher moves around the room, listening and supporting.)
	'Well done, everybody. Why did Toad take off his coat? Tell your partner.'
	(The pupils briefly talk to their partner about the question.)
	'Why did Toad take off his coat… Veronica?'

(Continued)

Table 7.2 (Continued)

Veronica:	'We thought it was because it was warm enough.'
Teacher:	'How do we know it was warm enough for Toad to take off his coat? With your partner find the words that tell us this?'
	(The pupils briefly talk to their partner about the question.)
	'I can see that you've spotted the words 'not cold' in your books. That's right! It's not a cold day, so that tells us it was probably warm enough for Toad to remove his coat.'
	'Let's move on to the next page...'

This Chapter in a Nutshell

- Scaffolded reading is a lesson structure designed to introduce year 1 pupils to whole-class reading while offering decoding practice, brief text discussion and some repeated reading for fluency.
- Scaffolded reading involves a gradual release of responsibility for reading a page of a decodable book:
  o Teacher reading
  o Echo reading
  o Paired reading
  o Brief discussion.
- Scaffolded reading is designed to be relatively brief (i.e. ~15 minutes).
- The bottom line is that if pupils in year 1 are given whole-class opportunities for echo reading and repeated reading after the modelling of fluent reading by the teacher, then this is likely to benefit their decoding proficiency and lay the groundwork for whole-class reading in subsequent year groups.

Further Reading

- *Understanding and Teaching Primary English: Theory into Practice* (Clements & Tobin, 2021)

Retrieval Quiz

- How does the gradual release of responsibility work in scaffolded reading?
- What kind of texts should be used for scaffolded reading? Why?
- What is a sensible duration for a scaffolded reading lesson?

──────────── Questions for Professional Discussions ────────────

- Ideally, scaffolded reading introduces whole-class reading to year 1 pupils. However, some schools may choose to use scaffolded reading with small groups, at least initially. What might be the advantages and disadvantages of this?
- It is common for year 1 pupils, when attempting the reading with their partner, to take a turn each and then begin to chat about the book in front of them. Why might this still be beneficial?
- Some phonics programmes include whole-class reading of decodable books as a component of instruction. If this is the case with your school's phonics programme, does your school's use of decodable readers in this way include the key aspects of scaffolded reading? Would scaffolded reading be an unnecessary extra component in your context?

REFERENCE

Clements, J. & Tobin, M. (2021). *Understanding and Teaching Primary English: Theory Into Practice*. Sage.

8

FLUENCY READING

WHAT IS FLUENCY READING?

Fluency reading is a structure for teaching reading that is designed to target pupils' reading fluency through successful decoding practice and repeated reading. In an ideal world, all pupils at the start of their journey to reading fluency would practise decoding through one-to-one reading with a well-trained adult on a daily basis. However, this is rarely a possibility. One of the key advantages of fluency reading is that it offers regular, successful decoding practice to all pupils in a way that doesn't rely on one-to-one reading. (For more on the best use of one-to-one reading, see Chapter 22.)

Through repeated reading of texts, pupils also observe the modelling of fluent reading and then explicitly practise it. There is a robust body of evidence to suggest that repeated reading supports fluency development, which in turn frees up the cognitive resources that pupils can then dedicate to comprehending the text in front of them (Pikulski & Chard, 2005; Rasinski et al., 2011). There is still uncertainty as to whether it is merely accurate decoding practice or focused repetition specifically that is the 'active ingredient' in repeated reading (Ardoin et al., 2016). Regardless, repeated reading provides a vehicle for whole-class accurate decoding practice, so the fluency reading lesson structure is a practical way to build fluency.

There are advantages to fluency reading that go beyond those suggested by research. Throughout my career, I have met countless pupils who were mortified at the prospect of reading aloud. These negative feelings were, I believe, often the result of pupils' first experiences of reading aloud, in which they desperately struggled to read unfamiliar texts in front of their peers. (Imagine how you might feel about an activity if the first 20 times you had been asked to do it, you had failed in front of most of your peers, many of whom appeared to succeed effortlessly at the same activity.) In contrast, fluency reading maximises the chances that pupils' first experiences of reading aloud are successful. Pupils only read aloud after fluent reading of the text has been modelled and after they have had the chance to practise reading it with some degree of fluency in a low-stakes environment. Many pupils who you might think would never read aloud actually grow to relish the prospect when their first experiences of reading in front of an audience are positive rather than embarrassing and demotivating.

HOW DO I TEACH A FLUENCY READING LESSON?

- Arrange pupils in mixed-attainment pairs with a copy of the text between them. Consider pupils' current attainment and their ability to support their peers when deciding on productive pairings.

- Choose a chunk of text that takes the average pupil in your class approximately one to two minutes to read on their first attempt following modelling.

- Briefly place the upcoming reading in a wider context. If you are using an extract, explain how this relates to the rest of the text. If you are using a complete text (e.g. a poem or short information text), explain what kind of text it is.

- Model reading the text fluently, emphasising slightly the natural prosody of your voice (i.e. the rhythm and intonation).

- Explain up to five words or phrases in the text that are likely to be unfamiliar to pupils. Draw attention again to the pronunciation of these words if necessary. Then, briefly summarise the text. Don't take more than a couple of minutes over this.

- Model reading the text again, this time asking pupils to follow the text as you read it aloud. If at this point you are not confident that pupils are ready for paired rehearsal of the text, you can echo read the text, sentence by sentence. This involves you reading the first sentence aloud before the class do the same in unison while looking at the words. You then repeat this with the second sentence, and so on.

- Get pupils to take it in turns to read the text to their partner. As one pupil reads, their partner should track the text. A ruler or finger might be used to support this. (It is useful for this expectation to be consistent across a school with exceptions made for individual pupils where appropriate.)

- Allow time for pupils to read the text three times each although further repetition is fine. With each read, pupils should aim for their reading to flow a little more like the way modelled by you. However, accurately recognising each word by paying attention to all the letters within it remains an essential first step towards this. Emphasise the idea that pupils are not merely reading aloud; they are *rehearsing* the text in a way that helps them to understand it better. Also, emphasise the appropriate volume for reading which is slightly more than a whisper. The aim is for each pupil to be heard clearly by their partner but not by someone on the other side of the room. This repeated reading is likely to take 10–15 minutes. Circulate around the classroom to offer support and encouragement.

- Support pupils to read the text aloud to the class. This might be a whole-class choral read, pupils volunteering to read or individual pupils selected to read. This depends on the confidence of the class and the extent to which a relationship of trust has been nurtured. This performance of the text should give the earlier rehearsal a sense of purpose.

- For the final 5–10 minutes of the lesson, discuss the content of the text with pupils. This is likely to involve a small number of questions being asked about the text and some explanation if necessary.
- A sensible length for a reading fluency lesson is ~30 minutes. Lessons much shorter than 30 minutes are less likely to allow for an adequate amount of repeated reading. Lessons much longer than 30 minutes are less likely to maintain pupils' concentration as they undertake repeated reading.

HOW DO I PLAN A FLUENCY READING LESSON?

- Choose the chunk of text that will be used for fluency reading. (See below for more details.)
- Decide which words and phrases you will explain to pupils and consider how you will summarise the chunk of text. Find pictures to support the explanation of any words or phrases that are otherwise much more difficult to explain. (This might not be necessary for many of the words you identify.)
- Consider the questions and explanation you will ask towards the end of the fluency reading lesson. The aim of these questions should be to get pupils to think about the content of the text. If it is impossible to think of such questions, then this might be a sign that the text isn't worth repeated reading and thus isn't suitable for a fluency reading lesson.

HOW DO I CHOOSE A TEXT FOR A FLUENCY READING LESSON?

Any text we put in front of pupils should be one worth reading. This might mean it contains fascinating information that complements a part of the academic curriculum or goes beyond it. It might contain a key extract from a story the class already enjoyed. It might be a poem that offers a sense of rhythm we want pupils to experience. What matters is that the text has been chosen because of what it offers to pupils.

The first challenge is to find a text that is an appropriate length to allow for three or more rehearsals by both pupils of a pair in around 10–15 minutes. A text that takes the average pupil in your class approximately one to two minutes to read the first time through is suitable. It is likely to take a little experimentation to get this right.

The second challenge is to find a text that is roughly appropriate for the current reading attainment of your class. There is likely to be a wide distribution of current reading attainment in your class. A sensible idea is to pitch the choice of text a little above the average reader in the class. This pitch can be intentionally varied across fluency lessons. Less challenging texts build the confidence of weaker readers while more challenging texts offer greater challenge to stronger readers. It can be tempting to try to use different texts in the same fluency lesson, but this reduces opportunities for modelling, feedback and shared discussion, so it is generally best avoided.

HOW DO I SUPPORT PUPILS WHO MIGHT STRUGGLE WITH FLUENCY READING LESSONS?

Some pupils in your class may still struggle with the very basics of decoding (i.e. they are still working their way through the early stages of the school's phonics programme). If this is the case, fluency reading – even with the support of a high-attaining peer – might be unproductive. There are different ways to adapt the lesson in cases like this.

Assuming these pupils constitute a small group (eight or fewer), a sensible choice is to echo read the text with them while others read in pairs. This involves you reading a sentence aloud before the pupils read the same sentence aloud in unison. It is important that pupils are looking at the words in the text as they do this. Alternatively, if you are fortunate enough to have the support of a teaching assistant, pupils at the early stages of decoding are likely to benefit from decoding practice using a decodable book or a phonics intervention during this part of the day. If support via interventions is logistically unachievable in your context, then it might be necessary to find time in the week to offer small-group support to these pupils while other pupils work independently. This might be for short bursts each day or during an entire reading lesson once a week. (See Chapters 12 and 21 for more on this.)

Some pupils may be unable to engage with fluency reading in the way described above due to issues relating to special educational needs and disabilities (SEND; e.g. speech dysfluency, social and emotional issues). It is essential that these pupils are given the opportunity to engage with the lesson in a way that works for them. This method is most likely to be specific to the child and found through a conversation with the SEND coordinator (SENDCo), the pupil's parents/carers and, most importantly of all, the pupil.

There is not one correct way to support pupils whose current reading capabilities mean they struggle with fluency reading. The key thing is to ensure the majority who can benefit from fluency reading are able to do so and that those who cannot yet benefit instead receive support with initial decoding.

HOW DO I STRETCH PUPILS WHO MIGHT FIND FLUENCY READING LESSONS LESS CHALLENGING THAN OTHER PUPILS DO?

While it might seem that relatively fluent readers have little to gain from fluency reading, this is not the case. Unless a pupil is displaying the reading fluency of an exceptionally fluent reader (i.e. what we might expect of a teacher), then fluency reading offers the opportunity for them to work on their prosody, emphasising the rhythm and intonation of expert readers.

However, rare cases do exist in which a pupil clearly has little to gain from practising their reading fluency while their peers still stand to benefit from such practice. Here, by definition, the pupil is a strong enough reader to benefit from independent reading, and they can be offered the opportunity to do so while others take part in fluency reading. As a general rule, though, wherever possible all pupils should be part of the same reading lesson.

HOW MIGHT MY TEACHING OF FLUENCY READING LESSONS CHANGE OVER TIME?

Fluency reading is particularly reliant on the development of productive routines. Pupils need to learn the role they play when working with a peer, and they need to be encouraged to maintain their focus while reading aloud, trying each time to read with a little more fluency.

For the first few lessons, your focus is likely to be on establishing these routines. You might benefit from staying at the front of the room and watching pupils engage with the reading aloud rather than moving around the room to support. With young pupils in particular, it is a good idea initially to keep the repeated reading brief – perhaps just long enough for pupils to read once or twice each – and then build this up over time. At this early stage, once the pupils have rehearsed the text in pairs, it is best to read the text chorally (i.e. the whole class in unison) or allow pupils to volunteer to read parts.

Once productive routines are established, you can move around the room while pupils are reading, positioning yourself to give the best view of the rest of the class. You can also begin to discuss elements of rhythm and intonation that pupils can attempt to mirror, such as the rising intonation of a question or the stress of a particular word or phrase. And once pupils have rehearsed the text, you can begin to choose pupils to read aloud, giving less confident readers a little advance warning and being sensitive to those who may need more time to build up the required confidence.

SHOULD I HELP PUPILS TO READ WITH GREATER PROSODY BY GETTING THEM TO MAKE NOTES ON THE TEXTS THEY ARE READING?

Sometimes I have found it useful to ask pupils to underline words they might need to emphasise or circle bits of punctuation they might otherwise miss. However, having tried to engage different classes with extensive annotation of texts, I have found the negatives outweigh the positives. What are these negatives? First, annotation requires us to undertake the reading on a sheet of paper that is most likely then discarded rather than with a book or a text that will be used in subsequent years. Second, the process of annotation uses valuable time that could be used in modelling, practice and discussion. Third, on the first reading of a text, pupils who benefit most from fluency practice (i.e. relatively dysfluent readers) sometimes focus more on the marks on the text than the accurate decoding of the words.

That said, you or other teachers in your school might find the annotation of texts to be a profitable part of fluency reading lessons. Assuming this process isn't taking more than a minute or two, there is no definitive reason to discourage this. However, it can be regarded as an optional extra that can be safely left out of fluency lessons.

SHOULD I ENCOURAGE PUPILS TO SIMPLY READ MORE QUICKLY?

While speed is a component of fluency, we should avoid asking pupils to merely focus on reading at a higher rate in fluency reading lessons. A key ingredient of building reading fluency is accurate decoding practice, and a focus purely on pace sometimes discourages pupils from accurately decoding each word as they first read the text. We should encourage pupils to start by accurately recognising each word by paying attention to every letter. Increased reading speed and prosody can then follow as pupils repeatedly practise the text.

WHAT CAN GO WRONG WITH FLUENCY READING? AND HOW CAN I FIX IT?

Table 8.1 Troubleshooting fluency reading

Problem	Solution
There is an odd number of pupils in the class, which means that pairs can't be formed.	Create one group of three consisting of stronger readers.
Despite reading the text repeatedly, pupils don't seem to read the text with increased fluency.	The difficulty of the text is likely to be too high. In subsequent lessons, try using texts with simpler sentence structures and vocabulary.
Most pupils read the text completely fluently on the first attempt.	The difficulty of the text is likely to be too low. In subsequent lessons, try using texts with more complex sentence structures and vocabulary. Equally, if your class consists predominantly of very fluent readers, their time might be better spent on other reading lesson structures.
The classroom is too noisy during paired reading.	Explain to pupils that paired reading needs 'quiet voices', a volume that means their partner can hear them but not someone on the other side of the room.
Pupils are not following as their partner reads.	Stay at the front of the room, actively observing pupils while this routine is embedded. Use shorter chunks of text initially to help pupils build these routines. If all else fails, consider asking pupils to alternate the sentences that they read, swapping who reads the first sentence each time.
Some pairs only have time to read the text once or twice in the time that other pairs are reading three or four times.	Ensure that the slowest readers are paired up with the quickest. If necessary, consider providing the slowest readers with experience of the text before the lesson begins (e.g. as part of an intervention or through a brief pre-teach at any moment in the day when the rest of the class is working silently).

An Example from a Fluency Reading Lesson

Here is a brief text from a science curriculum used in a fluency reading lesson in year 3:

Plants

Plants are made up of different parts that perform different functions. Most plants have roots, a stem and leaves. Some plants also have flowers.

Roots anchor a plant to the ground. They also absorb water and nutrients from the soil.

The stem holds up the leaves so that they can gather light to make food, and it holds up the flowers so that they can receive pollen and disperse their seeds. The stem also transports water and minerals from the roots to the other parts of the plant.

The leaves make food by trapping light and using its energy to turn carbon dioxide and water into carbohydrates.

In Table 8.2 is an example of the dialogue for part of the lesson. This lesson is with a class accustomed to the fluency reading lesson structure. Italics are used to show where reading aloud is taking place.

Table 8.2 A transcript from a fluency reading lesson

Teacher:	'Today, we are going to practise our reading fluency and learn more about plants, building on our science topic that we started yesterday. This is an information text that tells us interesting things about plants. We can see that this information text is about plants from the title at the top. I will read the text to you. I just want you to listen this time.'
	'Plants are made up of different parts that perform different functions. Most plants have roots, a stem and leaves. Some plants also have flowers...' (to the end of the text).
	'There are some words in here that we started to learn yesterday like "root", "stem", "leaves" and "pollen". And there are some words that you might not have heard before.'
	(The teacher writes the words 'function', 'absorb' and 'disperse' on the whiteboard.)
	'The word "function" means "something that a thing does". In this case, the function of a part of a plant is the job that it does for that plant.'
	'The word "absorb" means "suck up" or "take in". For example, a sponge absorbs water.'
	'And the word "disperse" means "spread out". For example, we saw in our science lesson yesterday how the wind disperses seeds from some plants.' ...
	'We will learn more about these words, and some of the other unfamiliar words in this text, in our science lessons.'
	'I'm going to read the text a second time. This time I'd like you to look at the words on your copy of the text as I read aloud:

(Continued)

Table 8.2 (Continued)

	(The teacher shows the page under the document camera, and begins to read, using their finger to point at each word as it is read.)
	'Plants are made up of different parts that perform different functions. Most plants have roots, a stem and leaves. Some plants also have flowers...' (to the end of the text).
	'Now it's your turn. Today, I'd like Partner B to rehearse the text first while Partner A follows along in the text. Don't forget to use your quiet voices for this. Ready... off you go.'
	(For the next 10 minutes approximately, the teacher moves around the room listening to pairs reading and offering support, focusing more attention on pairs with any readers who need a little more help. One or two pupils have written words on their mini whiteboards that neither partner knows how to decode, so the teacher models decoding these words for them. The teacher praises pupils who are helping each other with words where one partner gets stuck.)
	'I'm just going to give you 20 seconds to get to the end of the sentence... Excellent. I heard some brilliant reading. I especially liked the way that you used the punctuation to show you when to pause. I also really liked how the reading flowed a little more each time you rehearsed it.'
	'Today, I'd like us to show what we've learned by reading the text all together. Ready? Let's go...'
Teachers and pupils:	*'Plants are made up of different parts that perform different functions. Most plants have roots, a stem and leaves. Some plants also have flowers...'* (to the end of the text).
Teacher:	'Now that we can read the text fluently, it's much easier for us to understand it. With your partner, I'd like to you to write down on your mini whiteboards three facts about plants that you have learned from the text.'
	(The teacher gives pupils two minutes to write three facts about plants using information from the text.)
	'Let's gather some of the fascinating things we have learned about plants. Share one fact with the class... Jasmine.'
Jasmine:	'We wrote down that the job of the stem is to hold up the leaves and flowers of a plant.'
Teacher:	'Thank you, Jasmine. The stem does hold up the leaves of a plant. I think the stem does other jobs too. Does anyone want to build on Jasmine's answer... Bilal?'
Bilal:	'We wrote down that the stem also carries water to the rest of the plant.'
Teacher:	'Thank you, Bilal. In the third paragraph, the author uses a different word to say that water is carried through the plant. With your partner, see if you can find what that word is and point to it.'
	(The teacher gives the pupils 20 seconds to look back in the text.)
	'I can see that most of you are pointing at the word "transport". You are right. When we see "trans" in a word, this often means "across" or "through". And when we see "port" in a word, this sometimes relates to "carrying" in some way. In this case, water is being carried through the plant. It is being transported.'

─────────────── This Chapter in a Nutshell ───────────────

- Fluency reading is a structure for teaching reading that targets fluency through successful decoding practice and repeated reading.
- This lesson structure involves the modelling of fluent reading of a short text (1–2 minutes), repeated oral rehearsal in pairs by pupils, performance of the text and discussion.
- Planning a fluency reading lesson involves finding a text worth reading, considering which words and phrases to explain and deciding on a few questions to provoke deeper thinking and discussion towards the end of the lesson.
- Adaptations to suit weaker readers might involve echo reading and/or support from a teaching assistant.
- Fluency reading relies on productive routines, so focus on getting these embedded with the simplest version of the lesson you can manage. Once these routines are secure, you can consider discussing aspects of prosody (i.e. stress and intonation) and selecting pupils to read aloud after the repeated reading.
- The bottom line is that if pupils are rehearsing reading a text a few times while aiming for a higher degree of fluency, then this is likely to be of benefit to all readers, but especially those who are not yet fluent.

─────────────── Further Reading ───────────────

- A synthesis of research on reading fluency development: Study of eight meta-analyses (Padeliadu & Giazitzidou, 2018)
- Fluency matters (Rasinski, 2014)

─────────────── Retrieval Quiz ───────────────

- Approximately how long should it take pupils to read a well-chosen text the first time through in a fluency reading lesson?
- How many times should each pupil read the text aloud with their partner?
- How can you support pupils who otherwise might struggle with fluency reading?

─────────────── Questions for Professional Discussions ───────────────

- What might be the disadvantages of teaching fluency in this way if this were the *only* reading lesson structure pupils experienced each week?

(Continued)

- What I have described is not the only way to organise repeated reading. Look back at the final bullet point in 'This chapter in a nutshell' above. How else might fluency practice be organised to align with this 'bottom line'?
- Think about some of the classes you have taught and individual pupils who may have been reluctant to read aloud due to lack of confidence. How might you have used fluency reading over time to give them the confidence to try reading aloud in front of an audience?

REFERENCES

Ardoin, S. P., Binder, K. S., Foster, T. E. & Zawoyski, A. M. (2016). Repeated versus wide reading: A randomized control design study examining the impact of fluency interventions on underlying reading behavior. *Journal of School Psychology, 59*, 13–38.

Padeliadu, S. & Giazitzidou, S. (2018). A synthesis of research on reading fluency development: Study of eight meta-analyses. *European Journal of Special Education Research*, 3, 4, https://oapub.org/edu/index.php/ejse/article/view/2052/4689

Pikulski, J. J. & Chard, D. J. (2005). Fluency: Bridge between decoding and reading comprehension. *The Reading Teacher, 58*(6), 510–519.

Rasinski, T. (2014). Fluency matters. *International Electronic Journal of Elementary Education, 7*(1), 3–12.

Rasinski, T. V., Reutzel, D. R., Chard, D. & Linan-Thompson, S. (2011). Reading fluency. In M. L. Kamil, P. D. Pearson, E. Birr Moje & P. Afflerbach (Eds), *Handbook of Reading Research*, Volume *IV* (pp. 286–319). Routledge.

9
EXTENDED READING

WHAT IS EXTENDED READING?

Extended reading is a structure for teaching reading that is designed to give pupils plenty of experience of the written English language. It is a lesson that recognises that the breadth of our pupils' reading experiences is as important as the depth of their exploration of individual texts. In an extended reading lesson, pupils engage with a lot of text, either with support or independently. This reading is interspersed with explanations and questions that don't overly interrupt the flow of the lesson, allowing pupils the chance to feel immersed in texts while teachers track and support pupils' comprehension.

When pupils in a class are still at an early stage of developing reading fluency, it is unrealistic to expect them to independently read a lot of text. At this stage, which usually continues into the start of year 3 at least, extended reading involves the teacher reading aloud while pupils (a) follow the words in their own copy of the text, or (b) follow the words under a document camera, or (c) just listen. In other words, the exact way extended reading works will depend on the current reading capabilities of the class being taught.

HOW DO I TEACH AN EXTENDED READING LESSON WITH LESS-DEVELOPED READERS?

By less-developed readers, I mean a class in which fewer than 80% of pupils are confident independent readers.

- Briefly place the upcoming reading in a wider context: if you are starting a new text, show the title and front cover (if there is one); if you are continuing a text that was started in a previous lesson, summarise the part of the text that has already been read.
- Read the text aloud to pupils, asking the class to follow the words as you read in their own copy. You might ask them to use a ruler or finger to show they are following the text. (It is useful for this expectation to be consistent across a school with exceptions made for individual pupils where appropriate.)

- Pause to explain anything essential that pupils might not understand and ask questions that encourage pupils to make sense of the text as it is progressing. Keep explanations brief. Give all pupils time to think about the questions being asked, but do not let these discussions drag on; a minute or two is plenty. The aim is not to deeply explore the text through these discussions, but to ensure pupils are making basic sense of the text. Only a small amount of the lesson, approximately a third or less, should be spent discussing text. The rest of the time should be spent reading at pace.
- Use a routine to transition swiftly between reading and discussion. The routine should ensure pupils keep their place in the text (e.g. you might say, 'Finger freeze – eyes on me' when preparing pupils to listen to an explanation or consider a question).
- Where the text is particularly challenging, point this out to pupils and model effective strategies to tackle such text by re-reading potentially confusing parts, asking relevant questions about the text and summarising sections or chapters. Talk through your reasoning as you do this (e.g. 'That paragraph was quite complicated. I think we should slow down and read it again to ensure we make sense of it'). As pupils become familiar with these strategies, ask them to briefly do this for themselves.
- A sensible length for an extended reading lesson of this sort is ~30 minutes. However, this form of reading can still work well with lessons considerably shorter or longer than 30 minutes.

HOW DO I TEACH AN EXTENDED READING LESSON WITH MORE-DEVELOPED READERS?

By more-developed readers, I mean a class in which 80% or more of pupils are confident independent readers.

- Initially, teach extended reading as described above (i.e. taking charge of the reading, discussing the text briefly and teaching pupils how and when to use strategies to deal with challenging text).
- Once pupils are confident with this reading lesson structure, begin to ask pupils to quietly read short chunks of text for themselves, no more than a few sentences, with a clearly defined stopping point. Tricky vocabulary or background knowledge required to comprehend the chunk of text might be briefly introduced to pupils before pupils begin reading. Make it clear that if a pupil finishes reading, they should write a one-sentence summary of the chunk of text. If they finish this, they should re-read the chunk of text again to ensure their one-sentence summary accurately represents it. Make this a routine so that pupils know what to do if they finish reading before others have done so.

- After pupils have independently read a chunk of text, explain anything essential that pupils might not understand and ask questions that encourage pupils to make sense of the text. This should be done in the same way as when you are in charge of the reading. Encourage pupils to ask their own questions about any words or phrases they didn't understand.
- Where the chunk of text pupils have independently read is particularly challenging, point this out to pupils and teach effective ways to tackle such text by re-reading potentially confusing parts, asking relevant questions about the text and summarising sections or chapters. Again, this should be done in the same way as when you are in charge of the reading.
- Month by month, gradually increase the length of the chunks of text you ask pupils to read independently. By the end of year 6, the aim is for pupils to find it normal to read multiple pages before briefly discussing them to clarify their understanding.
- Use a mixture of the two ways of reading in your extended reading lessons: sometimes take charge of the reading, and sometimes ask the pupils to read chunks independently. Start with pupils independently reading short chunks once or twice in the lesson while you take charge of the reading for the remainder. Gradually build up the time pupils spend reading chunks of text independently until the reading is shared roughly evenly between you and the pupils. Balance your reading aloud with pupils' reading independently to maintain a sense of momentum in the lesson (i.e. where the pace of the lesson lulls, take charge of the reading to re-establish momentum).
- A sensible length for an extended reading lesson of this sort is ~30 minutes. However, this form of reading can still work well with lessons considerably shorter or longer than 30 minutes.

HOW DO I PLAN AN EXTENDED READING LESSON?

- Choose the text to be read. It is likely you will often use the same text for many lessons (e.g. a story might last several weeks).
- Read the text. Ideally, you should read the whole text before you begin to teach with it. Where this is not possible, ensure you grasp an outline of the whole text and you have read ahead of the text that will be used in your extended reading lesson.
- Make notes about the text, specifically parts you think will need explaining and questions you will ask at key points. These notes can be written directly on the text or somewhere else, using a key to relate each note to a part in the text.
- If you are working with pupils who are confident independent readers, decide which parts of the text you intend them to read for themselves and which parts you intend to read aloud.

HOW DO I CHOOSE A TEXT FOR AN EXTENDED READING LESSON?

Extended reading lessons work best when pupils each have a copy of the text being read so they can follow the words or read independently although one text between two pupils can also work if necessary. This means the text for extended reading should ideally be one the school has selected to be part of its reading curriculum, with class sets available as a result. Alternatively, teachers could read the text under a document camera or teach extended reading without opportunities to read chunks of text independently. This misses opportunities to build pupils' 'reading stamina' and develop their view of themselves as capable independent readers. However, where class sets of texts are not available, this is an acceptable – though ideally temporary – alternative.

Extended reading lessons involve a lot of reading, so fiction books can be read in their entirety over many lessons. For example, a single story might be read in extended reading lessons for several weeks. (Aspects of this text might subsequently be explored more deeply in close reading lessons. See Chapter 10 for more on this.) Equally, other kinds of texts, such as information texts, speeches, biographies, etc. can all work too, assuming the text is long enough to be read for at least one extended reading lesson.

As with any reading lesson, the most important thing is that you have chosen the text because of what it offers to pupils.

HOW DO I SUPPORT PUPILS WHO MIGHT STRUGGLE WITH EXTENDED READING LESSONS?

The version of extended reading in which you read aloud to pupils rarely needs much adaptation. However, pupils with listening comprehension difficulties are likely to benefit when you summarise a section of text or explain unfamiliar words or phrases. They can also be supported at the start of reading lessons by summaries of the entire text read so far.

Most pupils should be encouraged to follow the words in the text as you read aloud, but some might find this too challenging, especially those still struggling with the basics of decoding. It makes sense to allow these pupils just to listen as you read until their increasing capabilities allow them to follow the text with the rest of the class. Reading the text under a document camera can allow these pupils to choose when to follow the words and prepare them for following along at a later point in their reading development. If many pupils in a class struggle to follow along (as may be the case at the start of year 2, for example), then it might be preferable to simply allow all pupils the choice of whether to follow along or just listen. Pupils can then be gently encouraged to try following along with their own copy of the text when they feel ready to do so.

More adaptation is likely to be needed when teaching the version of extended reading in which pupils are sometimes asked to read independently. There might be some pupils who are still at the earliest stages of decoding who find such independent reading impossible. While other pupils are reading quietly, you (or a teaching assistant) can read the same chunk of text aloud to these pupils in a small group. These pupils still require active decoding practice through reading fluency lessons and/or suitable interventions, depending on their barriers to reading development. (For more on assessing and addressing reading difficulties, see Chapter 21.)

HOW DO I STRETCH PUPILS WHO MIGHT FIND EXTENDED READING LESSONS LESS CHALLENGING THAN OTHER PUPILS DO?

A central part of the challenge in extended reading lessons comes from the texts themselves. You should ensure the texts you read with pupils delve into language and concepts that are new to all pupils.

Most of the questions you ask in extended reading lessons should be designed to ensure pupils are making basic sense of the text rather than eliciting deeper exploration, which is more appropriate in close reading lessons (see Chapter 10). However, you can use questions to stretch pupils who will benefit from a greater degree of challenge. You might, for example, ask an overarching, open-ended question before you read a chapter, something for pupils to consider as the chapter progresses. You might then give pupils an opportunity to offer their thoughts on this question towards the end of the lesson, perhaps even asking pupils to put their ideas into writing.

HOW MIGHT MY TEACHING OF EXTENDED READING LESSONS CHANGE OVER TIME?

Extended reading benefits from the development of productive routines. This means ensuring pupils understand your expectations about following words in a text and transitioning between reading and discussion. For the first few lessons, focus primarily on establishing these routines.

Regardless of the age and reading capabilities of pupils, it makes sense for the teacher to take charge of all the reading when first introducing pupils to extended reading lessons. Once this version of extended reading is familiar to pupils, classes with more capable readers can undertake extended reading lessons with some independent reading, as described above.

The most important way extended reading can change over time is in how it responds to pupils' changing reading capabilities. As discussed above, extended reading lessons initially work best with pupils accessing the text entirely through the teacher's reading aloud. Schools and classes vary, but generally this form of extended reading predominates between years 2 and 4. In year 5 and above, almost all pupils tend to be ready for extended reading in which they are also sometimes expected to read chunks of text independently. However, pupils might be ready for this transition to a different form of extended reading considerably earlier or later than this. As soon as 80% or more of pupils are confident, independent readers, you can begin handing over some of the responsibility for reading the text to them. (This figure is chosen as it leaves a maximum of 20% of the class needing teacher support during independent reading, which is a manageable proportion.)

Pupils read at different speeds. At first, it can be difficult to judge how long you should give pupils when asking them to read a chunk of text independently. A rough rule is to give pupils twice as long as it takes you to read the text at a relaxed pace. This is one of the reasons why it is best to start with just a few sentences and then build up over time. If in doubt, at first give pupils a little more time than you think is necessary for all to have read the chunk of text, and then tighten up in subsequent lessons. Again, make clear the expectation that pupils who finish should write a one-sentence summary of the chunk of text and then read the chunk again to check the accuracy of their summary.

Sometimes it is necessary to reach the end of a text before a deadline. Perhaps you only have access to the class set of books for a half term or you need to move on to another text to align with the wider curriculum. Don't be afraid to take a lesson or two to simply read aloud the remainder of the book to your class. This is always preferable to leaving a book unfinished.

SHOULD PUPILS BE FREE TO JUST LISTEN WHEN A TEACHER IS READING ALOUD?

The question of whether pupils should follow the words in a text as another person reads aloud, something we might call passive decoding, is a complicated one. The meagre research that exists on the subject suggests that passive decoding while a *dysfluent* reader reads aloud causes weaker comprehension compared to just listening to the text read aloud by a teacher (Lynch, 1988). And it can be argued that passive decoding while a teacher reads aloud might impede comprehension because pupils are asked to deal with similar information in two different modes, an example of what is known as the redundancy effect (Sweller et al., 2011).

However, there are important differences in the information provided by written text and spoken language (Rastle, 2019). Text potentially provides information that goes beyond a spoken version, and vice versa. And the few studies that have explored the suggested redundancy effect when written text and speech are used simultaneously show mixed findings (Trypke et al., 2023), including some instances where comprehension *improved* when readers listened and followed the words simultaneously (Moreno & Mayer, 2002).

Even if there *were* reason to believe that comprehension is impaired by following the words in a text as it is fluently read aloud, pupils' immediate understanding of text is not the only thing we care about. When pupils undertake this passive decoding, they are exposed to the associations between the sounds of words and how these words are spelled. Evidence for the potential benefits of this is currently seen in studies of how 'precocious readers' appear to pick up the basics of decoding from such experience (Olson et al., 2006) and studies that look at the effect of television subtitles on reading development (Linebarger et al., 2010).

It is reasonable to suspect that pupils' recognition of the patterns of the English writing system is supported by passive decoding experience. However, it would be wrong to suggest there is certainty over whether it is beneficial. And it would be irresponsible to assume that passive decoding could replace active decoding practice, in which pupils work out words for themselves. However, on the assumption that pupils *are* undertaking plenty of active decoding practice (through lessons like fluency reading), then it seems a sound approach to sometimes include passive decoding as part of pupils' reading diet when teachers are reading aloud.

In the unlikely event that robust evidence emerges to suggest pupils should not follow text as it is read aloud to them by a teacher, then this aspect of extended reading can be ignored. Equally, if this practice is simply one that doesn't fit with your school context, again it can be ignored without negating all the benefits of extended reading lessons.

WHAT CAN GO WRONG WITH EXTENDED READING? AND HOW CAN I FIX IT?

Table 9.1 Troubleshooting extended reading

Problem	Solution
Most of the lesson is spent discussing text instead of reading.	Be strict with how much time you spend explaining aspects of the text and asking questions. Use brief paraphrasing and timely summaries to maintain pupils' understanding as the text moves at pace.
Some pupils struggle to follow the text as it is read aloud.	Encourage pupils to follow the text if they can but allow others just to listen where necessary. Read with a text under a document camera so that pupils can choose to follow only sometimes. As pupils' reading fluency develops, encourage them to try following texts again.
Exceptionally fluent readers are reading ahead in the text, leading them to struggle to follow when you pause to discuss the text.	In almost all cases, pupils can learn to follow as you read, but if this is not possible, ask these pupils to just listen as you read aloud.

(Continued)

Table 9.1 (Continued)

Problem	Solution
When asking pupils to read chunks of text independently (i.e. part of the lesson with a class of more-developed readers), you suspect some pupils are not reading the text.	Ask pupils to summarise the chunk of text they have read on mini whiteboards or in exercise books. (This is a good routine to embed regardless.)
Pupils have a question about an aspect of the text.	This is a good thing! Discuss the question briefly. If the question requires more time and would slow the pace of the reading down more than you would like, consider using this chunk of text for a close reading lesson and referring back to the questions asked by pupils.

Example Planning Extracts from an Extended Reading Lesson

As described above, planning for an extended reading lesson requires the teacher to have read the text and to have made notes for key stopping points to explain things and ask questions. These should mostly be used to ensure pupils are making basic sense of the text. The priority is for most of the time in extended reading lessons to be spent absorbed in reading. In the example below, the teacher has underlined words/phrases they want to briefly explain or ask questions about, making relevant notes in the margin. While only an extract is shown in Tables 9.2 and 9.3, a teacher would use much more text than this for an extended reading lesson, often continuing reading an entire book across several lessons.

Table 9.2 Planning extract for a year 4 extended reading lesson using Chapter 3 of *The Hidden Legacy* by Cindy Katz

"What are you doing in this house?" said Torval. "Do you know what my father would do to you?"

Usually, any stranger in Farleth Manor would be regarded as a thief, which was dangerous enough. But on the night when the council met, this wild-eyed girl would doubtless be treated as a spy.

"Wait… You're the child who sought payment from us yesterday. I will tell you again: your mother is mistaken. We owe you nothing."

The girl stared at Torval. Echoing footsteps from the adjacent hall punctured the silence. She turned to run, but Torval grabbed her firmly by the arm.

"If you want to see your mother again, you have to come with me now."

The girl hesitated. She glanced at Torval's hand on her arm, and he loosened his grip. The rapid breathing of the girl reminded Torval of the injured robin he had nursed back to health as an infant. He remembered his father's disgust at his soft-heartedness, and his determination to spare this girl grew. "This way. Now."

Define: 'Pause because not sure'

The pair tore down the dimly lit corridors, watched by Torval's ancestors represented in oil in gilded frames. They reached a wooden hatch with an iron ring. Torval yanked it open to reveal a damp stone staircase descending into total darkness. The girl opened her mouth to speak, but the words did not come.

"Down there," commanded Torval. "It's just a cellar. They will send me to fetch wine, and I will check on you. Once everyone is too drunk to notice, I will get you home."

Quick think-pair-share: 'Why do you think the words did not come?'

He lifted a candle holder from the wall and passed the flickering light to the girl. "You'll be okay. I promise."

The girl stepped cautiously into the dark, but turned back when Torval began to close the hatch. "You have to trust me," he said.

"Sigrun," she said. "My name is Sigrun."

Torval nodded and gently closed the hatch.

End of chapter: ask pupils to summarise on mini whiteboards

Table 9.3 Planning extract for a year 6 extended reading lesson using a biography taken from a history curriculum topic focusing on human rights and civil rights icons

Malala Yousafzai

Malala Yousafzai is an activist for female education and the youngest winner of the Nobel Peace Prize.

Define: 'Prestigious international prize for someone promoting peace'

Yousafzai was born in 1997 in the Swat District of north-western Pakistan. She was mostly educated by her father, who was a school owner and an educational activist. At this time, the Taliban – a movement and a military organisation – threatened people who did things that they thought were wrong, including the seeking of an education by girls.

At the age of just 11, Yousafzai began speaking about education rights, making a speech that was reported upon by local newspapers and television channels. In the speech she asked, "How dare the Taliban take away my right to an education?" As part of the BBC World Service, BBC Urdu sought someone to create an anonymous blog about life as a girl in the Swat province. Yousafzai began writing the blog for the BBC to publish, detailing how her

Define and relate to 'synonym' and 'antonym'

(Continued)

Table 9.3 (Continued)

classmates were increasingly not attending schools due to fear of what the Taliban would do.	
Yousafzai was then approached with an opportunity to film a documentary about her life and about the difficulties in getting an education where she lived. Following the documentary, Yousafzai began appearing on television to advocate girls' right to an education. The increase in Yousafzai's profile led to the Taliban deciding that she should be killed. While riding a bus, a Taliban gunman shot her, and she was seriously wounded. She survived thanks to cooperation between doctors in different countries. This attempted murder sparked outrage and sympathy across the globe, with protests taking place in many cities across Pakistan. As a result, a Right to Education bill was signed by over two million people across Pakistan, and the bill was signed into law.	Pose-pause-pounce-bounce: 'What do you think 'advocate' might mean?'
After months of rehabilitation following her ordeal, Yousafzai continued her own education in England, including attendance at Oxford University. In 2014, Yousafzai won the Nobel Peace Prize, becoming the youngest Nobel Laureate in history. She has since authored books about her experiences and has continued to be a globally recognised advocate for girls' education and a campaigner for other causes relating to human rights. The Malala Fund, to which people around the world donate, is used to pay for the building of schools and the provision of education for those without access to it.	After end of paragraph: On mini whiteboards: 'Write three adjectives that describe Malala Yousafzai.

This Chapter in a Nutshell

- Extended reading is a structure for teaching reading that is designed to give pupils plenty of experience of the written English language.
- With less-developed readers (i.e. fewer than 80% of a class are confident independent readers), this lesson structure involves you reading aloud to pupils. This is interspersed with explanations and questions to ensure pupils construct a basic understanding of the text.
- With more-developed readers (i.e. 80% or more are confident independent readers), this lesson combines you reading aloud to pupils, *and* pupils independently reading chunks of text quietly. This is interspersed with explanations and questions to ensure pupils construct a basic understanding of the text. Over time, the chunks of text pupils read independently should be increased in length. Balance your reading aloud with pupils' independent reading to maintain a sense of pace in the lesson (i.e. if the pace of the lesson lulls, take charge of the reading to re-establish momentum).
- Planning an extended reading lesson involves choosing the text, reading the text, making notes about what to discuss with pupils and deciding which chunks of text – if any – you will ask pupils to read independently.
- Extended reading works best with class sets of texts, but it can work with just you reading aloud if necessary.

- When pupils are reading a chunk of text independently, support weaker readers by reading the chunk of text aloud to them.
- There is scant evidence about the benefits or impediments associated with pupils following the words in a text as a teacher reads. Based on the currently available evidence, a reasonable approach is to ask most pupils to follow words in a text as you read aloud. However, this is not essential to extended reading. Schools can choose to ignore this aspect of extended reading if they prefer, or they can allow pupils to choose whether they follow the words in their own copy of the text.
- The bottom line is that if pupils experience and appreciate many varied texts, then this is likely to be of benefit to all readers.

Further Reading

- *Robust Comprehension Instruction with Questioning the Author* (Beck et al., 2020)
- Matthew effects in reading: Some consequences of the individual differences in the acquisition of literacy (Stanovich, 2009)
- Two types of redundancy in multimedia learning: A literature review (Trypke et al., 2023)

Retrieval Quiz

- How would you know if a class were ready for the version of extended reading for more-developed readers?
- How might pupils who are still struggling to read independently be supported when others are reading a chunk of text independently?
- How might we challenge high-attaining pupils in an extended reading lesson?

Questions for Professional Discussions

- What might be the disadvantages of teaching extended reading in this way if this were the *only* reading lesson structure pupils experienced each week?
- What I have described is not the only way to ensure pupils experience plenty of reading. Look back at the final bullet point in the section above headed 'This chapter in a nutshell'. How else might extended reading be organised to align with this 'bottom line'?
- Think about the most recent class of pupils you taught. Which form of extended reading would be most suitable for them based on what you know about their reading capabilities?

REFERENCES

Beck, I. L., McKeown, M. G. & Sandora, C. A. (2020). *Robust Comprehension Instruction with Questioning the Author*. Guilford Publications.

Linebarger, D., Piotrowski, J. T. & Greenwood, C. R. (2010). On-screen print: The role of captions as a supplemental literacy tool. *Journal of Research in Reading, 33*(2), 148–167.

Lynch, D. J. (1988). Reading comprehension under listening, silent, and round robin reading conditions as a function of text difficulty. *Reading Improvement, 25*(2), 98.

Moreno, R. & Mayer, R. E. (2002). Verbal redundancy in multimedia learning: When reading helps listening. *Journal of Educational Psychology, 94*(1), 156.

Olson, L. A., Evans, J. R. & Keckler, W. T. (2006). Precocious readers: Past, present, and future. *Journal for the Education of the Gifted, 30*(2), 205–235.

Rastle, K. (2019). EPS mid-career prize lecture 2017: Writing systems, reading, and language. *Quarterly Journal of Experimental Psychology, 72*(4), 677–692.

Stanovich, K. E. (2009). Matthew effects in reading: Some consequences of individual differences in the acquisition of literacy. *Journal of Education, 189*(1–2), 23–55.

Sweller, J., Ayres, P. & Kalyuga, S. (2011). The redundancy effect. In J. Sweller, P. Ayres & S. Kalyuga, *Cognitive Load Theory* (pp. 141–154). Springer.

Trypke, M., Stebner, F. & Wirth, J. (2023). Two types of redundancy in multimedia learning: A literature review. *Frontiers in Psychology, 14*, 1148035.

10
CLOSE READING

WHAT IS CLOSE READING?

Close reading is a structure for teaching reading that is designed to engage pupils in deeper exploration of texts. The aim is to carefully consider the ways authors use language and the impact this language has on different readers. Through the discussion of texts, pupils can also gain an understanding of themselves as readers. This means encouraging them to see that texts can be interpreted in different ways – some shared, some personal – and that these interpretations are worth investigating.

The analysis of texts that characterises close reading has existed for centuries and until recently was associated with academic literary criticism (Byron, 2021). The use of this phrase in education rose to prominence due to a focus on it as part of the 'Common Core State Standards' in the United States in 2009, primarily to describe literary analysis undertaken with older pupils (Brown & Kappes, 2012). This means there are risks in using 'close reading' as a label for a reading lesson structure designed for primary classrooms. It could be argued that close reading, as usually understood, is not meant for young children or that applying this label to something more specific might lead to confusion. However, the aim of this chapter is to show how the deeper exploration of language used in a text can be structured at primary level – 'close reading' seems like a sensible label for this as it is already familiar to many teachers.

HOW DO I TEACH A CLOSE READING LESSON?

- Briefly place the upcoming reading in a wider context. If you are using an extract, explain how this relates to the rest of the text. If you are using a complete text (e.g. a poem or short speech), explain what kind of text it is.
- Read the text and discuss it. Only a small amount of the lesson, approximately a third or less, should be spent actually reading text. The rest of the time should be spent discussing what has been read.
- A close reading lesson might focus on one or two chunks of text (anywhere between a paragraph and a few pages). It might also focus on a particular pattern of language choices that can be explored in small bursts of reading through a text (e.g. an author's use of figurative language across multiple chapters).

- Use different methods of reading text with pupils that match the part of the text being explored (i.e. you read aloud, pupils read in pairs or pupils read independently). You can use different methods of reading within the same lesson or stick with one method.

- Discuss the text with pupils, using a mixture of explanation where required and dialogue in response to questions you ask. Explanations should focus on anything essential that pupils might not understand and that they cannot profitably work out for themselves with guidance. Questions should explore themes and language choices made by the author that you have identified in your planning. They should also provide opportunities for pupils to express their opinions and share observations.

- Ensure all pupils are actively thinking about the questions you ask by using strategies that promote this, such as 'pose-pause-pounce-bounce', 'think-pair-share', use of mini whiteboards and written responses. Written responses can allow pupils to consolidate or extend what was discussed in the lesson. You may want pupils to have an exercise book to write in for this purpose, but this writing should not be done for the purposes of gathering 'evidence'. Trying to determine a pupil's reading capabilities from such 'evidence' is a waste of time because of the inherent inaccuracy of this as a method of assessment.

- Encourage pupils to ask questions and use discussions to explore their thoughts that go beyond the themes and language choices you planned to address. This includes pupils' personal reflections on a text that go beyond any reference to authorial intentions. Having explored these thoughts, return to the themes and language choices you identified in your planning.

- Where part of a text is particularly challenging, point this out to pupils and model effective strategies to tackle such text by re-reading potentially confusing parts, asking relevant questions about the text and summarising sections or chapters. Talk through your reasoning as you do this (e.g. 'That paragraph was quite complicated. I think we should summarise it to check we have understood it.') As pupils become familiar with these strategies, ask pupils to briefly do this for themselves.

- A sensible length for a close reading lesson is ~30 minutes. However, this form of reading will work well with lessons considerably shorter or longer than 30 minutes.

HOW DO I PLAN A CLOSE READING LESSON?

- Ensure you are familiar with the text you will explore with your pupils. A close reading lesson can address an entire short text or part of a longer text. However, it is difficult to explore part of a longer text if you are not familiar with it in its entirety. For this reason, it is often most effective to use close reading to explore (a) shorter texts, or (b) parts of texts you and your class have already read.

- Identify themes and language choices you want to explore with your class. (See below for more on this.)
- Make notes on the part of the text you wish to explore. Identify things you will explain and the questions you will ask. These questions should mainly explore the themes and/or language choices you have identified and provide pupils with opportunities to express their opinions and share observations. (Again, see below for more on this.) You might also find it useful to prepare slides to display some or all of the questions you will ask, but this is not a necessity.
- Decide how the chosen text will be read (i.e. you read aloud, pupils read in pairs or pupils read independently).

HOW DO I CHOOSE A TEXT FOR A CLOSE READING LESSON?

Close reading lessons work best when pupils each have a copy of the text being read so that they can follow the words or read independently. However, one text between two pupils can work if necessary. Sharing the text using a document camera can also work, but ideally this should be a temporary measure.

The text for a close reading lesson needs to be worth the deeper exploration this lesson structure affords. Stories, poetry and speeches generally offer suitable opportunities for exploring important themes of the text and the language choices of the author. Other forms of text may also offer such opportunities, but this is less common. As a general rule, a text is suitable for a close reading lesson if the author has attempted to use words, phrases and sentences that communicate ideas in ways that might not be immediately apparent to pupils. Ideally, there will also be identifiable themes running through the text that can be discussed. The best discussions in close reading lessons often look at ways the author's language choices relate to the themes of the text.

Often the deepest discussions in close reading lessons come about when pupils return to parts of a text that has already been read in its entirety in extended reading lessons or as part of shared reading. Returning to a text in this way allows pupils to better understand an author's language choices, especially those that are in service of themes that are explored in a text. For example, authors often introduce a protagonist at the beginning of a story in ways that accentuate the subsequent character development the protagonist undergoes. Likewise, a description of a setting that seems incidentally atmospheric upon first reading might foreshadow later events in ways that are not immediately apparent. By re-exploring aspects of texts that pupils have already read in their entirety, we provide them with opportunities to better understand the craft of writing.

HOW DO I IDENTIFY THE THEMES OF A TEXT?

The themes of a story are the big ideas – the underlying meanings or morals – that are explored through the unfolding events. A theme can be identified by recognising the journey of the protagonists in the story and how the conflicts in the story resolve.

There are various themes that can be identified in any story. What defines a theme is that it is a generalised idea about human experience of the world that goes beyond the specifics of the narrative. For the purposes of exploring texts with primary pupils, it is not usually productive to think of themes as merely one-word concepts like 'power' or 'jealousy' or 'reinvention'. Instead, themes are more usefully constructed as sentences or questions the author explores. However, what the author says or thinks about these themes may be far from straightforward. And we do not necessarily have to agree with a theme or know for sure what the author thinks about it for us to explore it. To understand this better, let's look at a few examples.

Shakespeare's *Romeo and Juliet* is not particularly suitable for the primary classroom, but as one of the most well-known stories of all time, it makes a useful starting point for understanding how we might derive potential themes from a text. In this play, the eponymous duo are kept apart by the ongoing feud between their families and the resulting expectations placed upon them. This triggers a seemingly irrevocable chain of events that climaxes with the young lovers opting to take their own lives rather than face existence without each other. From this basic description of the play, here are some themes we might identify:

- Love is a powerful force, and trying to stand in its way can lead to tragedy.
- Individual desires sometimes collide with familial responsibilities.
- People's lives are controlled by fate.

In *Charlie and the Chocolate Factory*, a young boy earns riches beyond his wildest dreams as a result of his kind-heartedness. Other potential young beneficiaries of this wealth receive nothing due to their obvious vices, which are implicitly attributed to the way the children have been raised. Here are some themes we might identify in this story:

- People tend to get what they deserve.
- Adults determine the virtuousness of the children they are responsible for.

In 'The Three Little Pigs', the main characters are terrorised by a wolf who tries to assail them by blowing down their houses. It is only the painstakingly built house of bricks that saves the three pigs from disaster. Here, as with most fairy tales, the central theme is immediately apparent:

- Hard work pays off.

Themes are not always as obvious as those found in fairy tales. With more complex texts, themes may well be better expressed as questions (e.g. How should we balance individual desires and social responsibilities? To what extent are adults responsible for the actions of the young people they have raised?) Often, the most valuable explorations of a text's theme require us to acknowledge the complexity of the theme, rather than try to find a simple answer.

Themes can be identified in texts other than stories. One way to do this is to look for repeated ideas. For example, Martin Luther King Jr's 'I Have a Dream' speech from the steps of the Lincoln Memorial in Washington, D.C. in 1963 was a call for civil and economic rights and an end to racial discrimination. Here are some themes we might identify in this speech:

- Embracing non-violent protest in the face of physical force is powerful, dignified and challenging.
- One must maintain hope in the possibility of a future based on equality and opportunity for all, despite past and present failures to enact these ideals due to racial discrimination.

Identifying the most important themes of a text is a subjective process, and not all texts have themes that are worth exploring. For example, it is much rarer to find worthwhile themes in information texts because the purpose of these texts is usually to communicate ideas explicitly rather than to explore them more subtly. We are not secondary English teachers, and our pupils should not be expected to engage in the level of textual analysis that is expected of 16-year-olds. But we *can* productively identify themes within texts and use these as a focus for the discussions we have with pupils to guide them in exploring texts in a deeper way. Over time, pupils should be encouraged to identify for themselves themes in texts they have read.

HOW DO I EXPLORE THE LANGUAGE CHOICES MADE BY AN AUTHOR?

Each author writes in their own style and brings their own thoughts to the themes they explore. Part of our job as teachers is to identify the ways an author has used language and to discuss the effect the author might have intended to produce. This means considering how and why an author has used individual words, phrases, sentence structures (e.g. punctuation, sentence length, ordering of sentence components), metaphors, paragraphing and typography (e.g. italics, bold, capitalisation) in a text. These might be individual instances or patterns across a text. There is no need to try to explore texts with pupils by looking for all these things as if you are ticking off a list. The idea is to read a text together while noticing interesting language choices, something that requires you to have read the text with an analytical eye before a close reading lesson. Many of the best questions to spark discussion will be variations of 'What has the author done here?' and 'Why might they have done it?' (i.e. 'What impact on the reader might they have wanted to achieve?').

Discussions in close reading lessons can work perfectly well without introducing pupils to a wide range of technical vocabulary relating to authors' language choices. However, these few words can be helpful:

- *Mood*: The overall atmosphere or the emotion invoked in a reader by the author's language choices (e.g. a story might be sombre or jovial).
- *Tone*: The attitude an author appears to have towards ideas in a text, conveyed by their language choices (e.g. an author might imply that they view the characters they are portraying as admirable or that the events they are portraying are absurd).
- *Motif*: A repeated object, idea or phrase that points to something more significant within a text such as a theme.

These terms hint at something important: themes and language choices are both worth exploring for their own sake, but the most fascinating discussions are often those in which these two things interact, where we explore how the author's use of language has contributed to the bigger ideas of a text.

HOW DO I PROVIDE OPPORTUNITIES FOR PUPILS TO SHARE THEIR OPINIONS AND OBSERVATIONS RELATED TO A TEXT?

Pupils should be encouraged to share their thoughts about any aspect of a text being read by putting up their hand to express an idea or ask a question. It is a good idea to also provide explicit opportunities for all pupils to do this. Occasional questions of the following sort can generate deep discussion (Chambers, 1993):

- What did you like or not like about what we have read?
- Was there anything we read that you found confusing?
- What connections did you spot between what we have read and anything else you have learned about?

Questions of this sort can be asked at any apposite moment, but they tend to work best after key points in a text, such as the end of a section, the end of a text or after a major plot point in a story.

HOW MIGHT I ASK PUPILS TO RESPOND TO TEXTS IN WRITING?

Writing has an important role to play in reading development, and vice versa (Graham & Harris, 2017). However, English primary schools tend to allocate more time to writing instruction than reading instruction, typically 45–60 minutes per day for writing and 30 minutes per day for reading. This means that significant periods of writing in response to text are better placed in writing lessons than in reading lessons.

If, however, a school's timetable allocated 45–60 minutes per day to reading and 30 minutes per day to writing – a reverse of the typical school timetable – it would be advisable to include more writing in response to text in reading lessons.

Regardless, older pupils writing in response to text in *some* close reading lessons is still beneficial. The most obvious benefits are the potential to deepen pupils' thinking about texts and the opportunity to informally assess their understanding. We might ask pupils to jot down their thoughts onto a mini whiteboard in response to a question. This relatively casual form of writing can be used whenever it might be convenient for pupils to express their thoughts in a written medium or whenever we want to assess understanding of the class in this way.

We might also ask pupils for a lengthier written response to a question – several sentences or perhaps a whole paragraph. In most cases, it is best to ask pupils to write at length only when the classroom discussion has primed them with things to express. Of course, pupils' written responses may well go beyond the exact contents of classroom discussions as they share their own ideas. However, before we ask pupils to write carefully constructed sentences, it is best to have already explored the relevant ideas in the classroom. We can think of pupils' writing as a chance for them to summarise a text discussion or paraphrase elements of it. Such practice means writing is specifically done to consolidate what has been learned, showing pupils that writing is an aid to thought rather than merely a means of a teacher assessing a pupil's comprehension. This also has the added benefit of highlighting to pupils the importance of listening carefully to their peers and to the teacher when texts are being discussed.

When we first ask pupils to write multiple-sentence responses to questions, we should explicitly model how we might go about doing this well. At first, sentence starters can be a useful scaffold (e.g. 'The author wanted to show us that Bradley was... They did this so that...') Equally, pupils' answers can be shared and discussed so that they gradually build up their understanding of how to respond to different sorts of questions (e.g. questions that require a justification from the text or questions that seek a subjective viewpoint).

Pupils can also be occasionally introduced to specific question formats they are likely to face in standardised assessments. The central purpose of this is to ensure they feel confident and comfortable when they face such assessments. (See Chapter 20 for more on this.)

HOW DO I SUPPORT PUPILS WHO MIGHT STRUGGLE WITH CLOSE READING LESSONS?

As discussed above, in close reading lessons we can use different ways of engaging with text. Reading aloud to pupils allows all of them to access the text. However, when most pupils are asked to read in pairs as they might in a fluency reading lesson, pupils still at the early stages of learning to decode can be supported in this through echo reading.

(See Chapter 8 on fluency reading for further detail.) And where pupils are expected to read a chunk of text independently, dysfluent readers can be supported by listening as you read aloud. (See the section on extended reading lessons in Chapter 9 for further detail.)

As discussed in Chapter 5, open-ended questions provide an opportunity for all pupils to think and respond to text. When we explore texts in depth with pupils and ask meaningful questions, there are likely to be parts of the discussion that leave some pupils confused. To support these pupils, it makes sense to wrap up discussions with summaries in simple language before moving on.

HOW DO I STRETCH PUPILS WHO MIGHT FIND CLOSE READING LESSONS LESS CHALLENGING THAN OTHER PUPILS DO?

One of the central advantages of close reading lessons is the opportunity these lessons afford to stretch high-attaining pupils. Meaningful, open-ended questions about authorial intentions and language choices allow pupils to share ideas that might not be apparent to others and to open their peers' minds to different perspectives. This relies on questions that allow for a variety of responses, but, crucially, it also relies on you choosing texts that are worth exploring in depth.

HOW MIGHT MY TEACHING OF CLOSE READING LESSONS CHANGE OVER TIME?

Close reading lessons are always evolving. The way these lessons work will depend greatly on the environment that has been nurtured in the classroom and across the school to support discussion of texts. Initially, even the most inviting questions about the most intriguing texts are unlikely to lead to pupils offering their views or building on each other's ideas. The following situation is common when you first teach close reading lessons: You read together, and you ask an interesting question, ensuring all pupils are engaged in thinking about an answer (using the sort of strategies described in Chapter 5). You then seek responses, but pupils' answers are short or undeveloped. They look to you to validate what they have said, in the hope they have given you the 'right' answer. And pupils don't yet think to put their hand up to ask questions or to respond to their peers' ideas.

But don't be alarmed. It takes time to build the trust that allows pupils to share their ideas. If you keep reading interesting texts, asking probing questions that invite a variety of responses and being consistently warm and gently appreciative, then the discussions in close reading lessons will gradually become more complex and rewarding.

WHAT CAN GO WRONG WITH CLOSE READING? AND HOW CAN I FIX IT?

Table 10.1 Troubleshooting close reading

Problem	Solution
Pupils are initially reluctant to offer answers to questions.	Consider eliciting responses from a few pupils at a time, jotting down notes on the whiteboard based on what they say. Then discuss what has been said rather than any individual's response. As pupils grow accustomed to answering questions, you can rely on this strategy less.
Pupils' answers are consistently brief and undeveloped.	Ask pupils to build on their answers by asking them how they reached a conclusion (e.g. 'That's interesting. What led you to think that?') When pupils do expand on their answers by justifying what they think or by offering multiple ideas, gently point out that you liked how they did this. Developing a classroom environment in which this is the norm takes time and persistence.
Pupils rarely build on each other's answers.	Ask questions of the class relating to answers that individual pupils have given. This should be done sensitively, encouraging pupils to explain why they might agree or disagree or partially agree.
Pupils don't ask their own questions about the text.	Create opportunities for pupils to ask questions. Once a trusting atmosphere has been developed, some of the best discussions can begin with the simple request, 'Do you have any questions about what we read?' or 'Were you curious about anything in that paragraph?'

Example Planning Extracts from a Close Reading Lesson

Planning for close reading lessons requires teachers to search for interesting language choices made by an author, especially those that contribute to the themes in a text. It is important to recognise that the questions are the impetus for discussion and should be asked one at a time. It is also essential to note that the questions being asked in the examples below are not the 'correct' ones. There are different themes and language choices that could be explored here, as there are with all other texts worth exploring in close reading lessons. What matters is that pupils are learning that such exploration can reveal depths to an author's use of language that might otherwise go unnoticed.

In the first example (Table 10.2) words and phrases the teacher will explain are in the margin. The second example (Table 10.3) includes a simplified translation of the poem. (This does not mean every aspect of the poem is explained to pupils in such terms from the outset.) Questions that will be used to guide the lesson are beneath the extract. The planned questions and ways for pupils to respond have been written out in detail for illustrative purposes. A teacher planning their own close reading lesson would be able to save time by making much less detailed notes. Depending on the discussions these questions provoke, the planning seen here might be used for more than one lesson.

Table 10.2 Planning extract for a year 4 close reading lesson using Chapter 7 of *The Hidden Legacy* by Cindy Katz

---

Identified themes explored in this lesson:

- People's actions and personality can be radically different depending on the situation.

- It is noble to take risks to protect the vulnerable.

'Don't dawdle,' said Sigrun. 'If we don't reach the other side before nightfall, we won't live to see the dawn.'

'You're exaggerating again,' replied Torval.

Torval knew of local folk who claimed to have spent the night in Ostika Forest and lived to share their story. He had listened to such people in the musty taverns near his home as they repeated the same tales every month with the full moon, each new retelling <u>embellished</u> just enough to keep the regulars amused. But he also recalled the scars that each storyteller had displayed at the climax of their account, and he felt his step quicken to ensure he kept pace with Sigrun. He may have been the one carrying the sword, but she knew the terrain. She was like the forest, at one with it: isolated, <u>inscrutable</u>, untamed. Enchanting. Torval realised that he had never truly known danger until now. Here was the one place in the kingdom where his father's reputation for vicious reprisals was of no consequence. Here he sought protection instead of offering it. Here he had to follow, despite a life spent being readied for leadership.

Define: 'Make something more interesting or decorative by adding unnecessary detail'

Define by relating to the idea of scrutiny: 'Adjective meaning that it's hard to work someone or something out; mysterious'

Sigrun slowed and then came to a halt. She held up her hand as a silent command for Torval to stop, the urgency in her gesture clear. Without the sound of their feet disturbing the undergrowth, the forest was now almost silent. Sigrun scanned in every direction before her gaze settled on the path directly behind them.

'We are being followed,' she whispered.

'Wolves? Already?'

'I hope so, but perhaps worse. We need to leave this path and take our chances another way.'

'What's worse than wolves?' asked Torval. 'What's behind us?'

He caught a hint of something in Sigrun's expression that he preferred to not interpret as fear. She knelt down and studied the ground, saying nothing, deep in calculation.

'I'm not taking another step unless you tell me what you're thinking,' bluffed Torval.

Sigrun rose to her feet and strode away from the forest path. Torval stood still momentarily, hoping his defiance would force an explanation, but Sigrun was almost out of sight already. He had no choice but to chase behind her.

1   Think back to Chapter 4 when the author first introduced Sigrun in Farleth Manor. What was she like in that situation? And how is she different in this chapter? Why do you think this is? (Use 'think-pair-share' for this with pupils jotting thoughts on mini whiteboards too. Ask a few pupils to share their responses.)

2   a   When Sigrun was introduced in Chapter 4, at first the author just called her *the girl'*. This changed when Sigrun told Torval her name. What does this tell us about whose perspective the author is writing from? (Use 'pose-pause-pounce-bounce' to get a quick answer: this is a limited third-person perspective focusing on Torval.)

    b   Can you find any other evidence of this perspective in the last three paragraphs of this extract? (Give pupils three minutes to re-read these paragraphs and note down what they find before sharing with their partners. Ask a few pupils to share their responses.)

3   In this extract we see Sigrun guiding Torval through Ostika Forest, probably saving his life. She does this even though Torval should be a sworn enemy of her family. What might the author want us to know about Sigrun? (Use 'think-pair-share'.)

4   Look at this sentence: '"*We are being followed," she whispered.*'

    How might this sentence feel different if the author had used 'said' instead of 'whispered'? What effect do you think the author wanted to have on the reader? (Use 'pose-pause-pounce-bounce'.)

5   Look at this sentence from the extract: *She was like the forest, at one with it: isolated, inscrutable, untamed. Enchanting.*

    What has the author done with this list of adjectives? Why do you think the last one is on its own? (Use 'pose-pause-pounce-bounce'.)

6   Does this part of the story remind you of any other stories that you have experienced before? Did you notice any other connections to something you have learned about elsewhere? (Pupils to use mini whiteboards to write their answer before discussing with their partner. Ask a few pupils to share their responses.)

Table 10.3   Planning extract for a year 6 close reading lesson using 'The Tyger' by William Blake (Stevenson, 2007)

Identified themes explored in this lesson:

• Life's creations are majestic.

• There is deep mystery in the motives and powers of the universe's creator.

Tyger Tyger, burning bright, In the forests of the night; What immortal hand or eye, Could frame thy fearful symmetry?	Translation: The author considers the tiger and wonders which immortal being could have created it.
In what distant deeps or skies. Burnt the fire of thine eyes? On what wings dare he aspire? What the hand, dare seize the fire?	The author considers further where and how such a creature was created.

(Continued)

Table 10.3 (Continued)

And what shoulder, & what art, Could twist the sinews of thy heart? And when thy heart began to beat. What dread hand? & what dread feet?	Bearing in mind the power of the tiger, the author wonders at the power required to create such a beast.
What the hammer? what the chain, In what furnace was thy brain? What the anvil? what dread grasp. Dare its deadly terrors clasp?	The creator is compared to a blacksmith, and the author wonders again about the power of such a creator.
When the stars threw down their spears And water'd heaven with their tears: Did he smile his work to see? Did he who made the Lamb make thee?	The author considers whether this creator was pleased at its accomplishment and whether the same creator could be responsible for a symbol of gentleness.
Tyger Tyger burning bright, In the forests of the night: What immortal hand or eye, Dare frame thy fearful symmetry?	Finally, the author wonders what kind of creator would even dare to create the tiger.

1   What did you like or not like about the poem? And is there anything that you found confusing? (Pupils to use mini whiteboards to write their answer before discussing with their partner. Ask a few pupils to share their responses.)

2   What is the rhyming pattern of this poem? Are there any lines that seem to break this pattern? (Use 'pose-pause-pounce-bounce'.)

3   In the English of William Blake's time, 'thy' means 'your'. Re-read the first stanza. Who might the speaker of the poem be talking to? (Use 'think-pair-share'.)

4   What do you think the speaker of the poem feels about the tiger based on the first stanza? (Discuss the translation of the stanza. Ask pupils to write down on mini whiteboards words that led them to a conclusion, e.g. 'fearful'. Ask a few pupils to share their responses.)

5   Who might William Blake have been considering as the creator in this poem? Why might he have not stated this explicitly? (Use 'pose-pause-pounce-bounce'.)

6   In the penultimate stanza, the speaker of the poem wonders whether the creator of a creature such as a tiger could also possibly have created a creature such as a lamb. Think about the differences between a lamb and a tiger. Why might the speaker ponder this question? (Use 'think-pair-share'.)

7   Compare the first stanza to the last stanza. At the start of the poem, the speaker seemed merely amazed at the existence of the tiger. What has changed through the course of the poem? What might have led to this change? (Pupils to use mini whiteboards to write their answer before discussing with their partner. Ask a few pupils to share their responses.)

8   In the poem 'The Tyger', William Blake uses the existence of the tiger to consider the world we live in and what it says about the creator of such a world. What might William Blake be suggesting about this creator and the world they created? (Ask pupils to answer this independently in writing based on the rest of the discussion.)

--------------- This Chapter in a Nutshell ---------------

- Close reading is a structure for teaching reading that is designed to engage pupils in deeper exploration of texts.
- This lesson structure involves reading texts (or chunks of texts) in a variety of ways and spending the majority of the lesson discussing the text through responses to questions. Pupils might also respond to texts in writing, consolidating or extending what was discussed in the lesson.
- Planning a close reading lesson begins with choosing the text, reading it and deciding how it will be read. You will need to identify themes in the text and language choices made by the author. You can then create questions (and consider explanations) that allow pupils to explore these themes and language choices.
- Close reading lessons require texts where language choices and/or themes are worth exploring. Stories, poetry and speeches almost always offer these although other forms of text can as well.
- The themes in a story are the big ideas – the underlying morals or meanings – that are explored through the unfolding events. Identifying a theme in a story means finding a generalised idea about human experience of the world that is examined through the protagonists' journeys and conflicts. In other texts, themes are repeated ideas that are central to the text's purpose.
- Exploring the language choices of an author means considering how and why they have used individual words, phrases, sentence structures, metaphors, paragraphing and typography in a text.
- Because English primary schools typically dedicate more time to writing lessons than reading lessons, lengthy written responses to texts in close reading lessons should be used sparingly. When you do ask pupils to craft answers into multiple sentences, this should most often be used as an opportunity for pupils to consolidate what has been discussed.
- Readers who might struggle with close reading lessons can be supported to access the text in the same ways as seen in fluency reading (see Chapter 8) and extended reading (see Chapter 9). Summarising discussions of texts can support those who might otherwise lose track of the key ideas that have been shared.
- Readers who might find close reading lessons less challenging can be stretched through the open-ended questions that are central to this reading lesson structure.
- Close reading lessons depend on the nurturing of low-pressure environments that allow pupils to discuss texts and understand how they might build on the answers of their peers and ask questions of their own. This takes time.

--------------- Further Reading ---------------

- *Guiding Readers – Layers of Meaning* (Tennent et al., 2016)
- *Tell Me: Children, Reading and Talk* (Chambers, 1993)
- *Robust Comprehension Instruction with Questioning the Author* (Beck et al., 2020)
- *Reading Reconsidered* (Lemov et al., 2016)
- Teaching kids to interpret theme – you really can teach comprehension (Shanahan, 2016)

---------- Retrieval Quiz ----------

- Approximately what fraction of a close reading lesson should be dedicated to reading?
- What do you need to bear in mind when choosing a text for a close reading lesson?
- How might you identify the theme in a story?

---------- Questions for Professional Discussions ----------

- Imagine tomorrow you will begin teaching close reading lessons with your class (or the class you most recently taught). How ready would your pupils be to discuss questions about a text? Why?
- How similar are the discussions of a close reading lesson to aspects of your pedagogy in other parts of the curriculum? How might this affect how long it would take pupils to acclimatise to the expectations of close reading lessons?
- Think of a story you have read with a class. Consider what themes you might identify in this story to explore with pupils. If the text is available to you, consider what questions you might ask about parts of the text that examine these themes.

REFERENCES

Beck, I. L., McKeown, M. G. & Sandora, C. A. (2020). *Robust Comprehension Instruction with Questioning the Author*. Guilford Publications.

Brown, S. & Kappes, L. (2012). *Implementing the Common Core State Standards: A Primer on 'Close Reading of Text'*. Aspen Institute.

Byron, M. (2021). Close reading. In *Oxford Research Encyclopedia of Literature*. Oxford University Press.

Chambers, A. (1993). *Tell Me: Children, Reading and Talk*. Thimble Press.

Graham, S. & Harris, K. R. (2017). Reading and writing connections: How writing can build better readers (and vice versa). In C. Ng & B. Bartlett (Eds), *Improving Reading and Reading Engagement in the 21st Century* (pp. 333–350). Springer.

Lemov, D., Driggs, C. & Woolway, E. (2016). *Reading Reconsidered: A Practical Guide to Rigorous Literacy Instruction*. John Wiley & Sons.

Shanahan, T. (2016). Teaching kids to interpret theme – you really can teach comprehension. Blog. www.shanahanonliteracy.com/blog/teaching-kids-to-interpret-theme-you-really-can-teach-comprehension

Stevenson. W. H. (Ed) (2007). *Blake: The Complete Poems,* 3rd edition. Pearson Longman.

Tennent, W., Reedy, D., Hobsbaum, A. & Gamble, N. (2016). *Guiding Readers – Layers of Meaning: A Handbook for Teaching Reading Comprehension to 7–11-Year-Olds*. Trentham Books.

11

HOW AND WHEN TO USE DIFFERENT READING LESSON STRUCTURES

WHAT IS THE RIGHT BALANCE OF READING LESSON STRUCTURES?

When considering how to balance the different priorities of reading instruction, one statement can be made with absolute certainty: pupils at the early stages of fluency development *need* regular active decoding practice. Some pupils get this at home, but others do not, so it must be provided as a central part of a reading curriculum. This means it is essential to provide regular fluency reading lessons at the start of a pupil's journey to reading fluency.

Primary school pupils at all stages of development benefit from lessons that focus on explicit fluency development, lessons that focus on reading breadth and lessons that focus on deeper discussion of texts. The ideal balance between these lessons changes over time. As pupils become more fluent, the value of lessons that explicitly target fluency development decreases. Equally, the extent to which pupils can undertake lengthy discussions about texts increases as pupils mature. This means it makes sense to gradually replace fluency reading lessons with close reading lessons. A default timetable with five reading lessons per week might look like the timetable in Table 11.1:

Table 11.1 Default timetable for reading lesson structures

	Monday	Tuesday	Wednesday	Thursday	Friday
most pupils still learning the basics of decoding (usually year 1)	scaffolded reading	scaffolded reading	scaffolded reading	scaffolded reading	scaffolded reading

(Continued)

Table 11.1 (Continued)

	Monday	Tuesday	Wednesday	Thursday	Friday
most pupils at early stages of fluency (usually year 2)	fluency reading	extended reading	fluency reading	extended reading	fluency reading
most pupils approaching fluent reading (usually years 3–4)	fluency reading	extended reading	fluency reading	extended reading	close reading
most pupils relatively fluent readers (usually years 5–6)	fluency reading	extended reading	close reading	extended reading	close reading

It doesn't matter which specific days are used for each reading lesson structure. What matters is that the balance of reading lesson structures ensures pupils are developing fluency, reading broadly and discussing text in proportions that are roughly appropriate for their stage of development:

- Pupils who are still learning the basics of decoding, but who are ready for some experience of whole-class reading, are likely to benefit most from scaffolded reading each day.
- Pupils who are at the earliest stages of reading fluency are likely to benefit most from regular fluency reading lessons alongside some extended reading lessons.
- Pupils who are approaching reading fluency are likely to benefit most from a roughly 50:50 split between fluency lessons and extended reading lessons with occasional close reading lessons.
- Pupils who are relatively fluent readers are likely to benefit most from a roughly 50:50 split between extended reading and close reading lessons with occasional fluency reading lessons.

HOW MIGHT TEACHERS CHANGE THIS BALANCE IN RESPONSE TO THE PUPILS IN THEIR CLASS?

While the timetable in Table 11.1 represents a reasonable default in most cases, every class of pupils is unique and should be treated as such.

For example, a year 6 teacher might have a class of pupils who are all so fluent that fluency reading lessons are no longer an effective use of time. Thus, the suggested timetable for year 6 shown above might not be a good fit, and the fluency reading lesson might be best replaced with another extended reading or close reading lesson.

Even if a small group of pupils in the class still requires support with fluency, it might be deemed more useful to support them with an intervention rather than through a whole-class reading lesson. Likewise, a year 6 teacher might have a class of pupils where reading fluency is commonly far below age-related expectations. Here, teaching two or even three reading fluency lessons per week might represent a better balance.

We can also respond to younger pupils' needs by changing the balance between reading lesson structures. A year 2 class might already be well on their way to reading fluency, or a year 4 class might need more support in this area. Teachers and school leaders should discuss the current needs of each class and change the balance of reading lesson structures accordingly.

As in every area of teaching, finding the right balance in reading lessons is harder in classes with an especially wide spread of attainment. Struggling pupils stand to lose more than high-attaining pupils from a balance that doesn't quite meet their needs. Where compromises need to be made – and they almost always do – prioritise the needs of those who, without effective support, are less likely to become fluent readers. This might sound like an unfair deal for high-attaining pupils, but in the long run these pupils benefit from being in classrooms where fewer of their peers have been left to fall further and further behind.

HOW MIGHT THE LESSON STRUCTURES BE ADAPTED IF I WANT GREATER FLEXIBILITY?

The reading lesson structures I have discussed in the preceding chapters are just one way to meet the three key aims of reading lessons. Let's remind ourselves of these aims and how they can be met through our teaching:

1   Develop pupils' reading fluency... *by providing them with opportunities to reach fluency through modelling, practice and feedback.*
2   Increase pupils' understanding of written English and the world to which it relates... *by providing extensive, meaningful experiences with a variety of texts chosen for this specific purpose.*
3   Nurture pupils' understanding of their subjective, strategic role in interpreting and appreciating texts... *by planning and guiding discussions that analyse written language and explore pupils' own ideas.*

As previously stated, any approach to teaching reading that achieves these aims is sensible, assuming it allows for adaptation to meet the needs of pupils as they develop. You might use elements of fluency reading, extended reading and close reading in every lesson, either in the same order or more flexibly. You might decide that a hybrid of extended reading and close reading with a roughly 50:50 split of reading and discussion works better in your context alongside fluency reading. Once you are familiar with the reading lesson structures and the rationale behind each of them, there is nothing to stop you from using them as you see fit. That said, my experience suggests that using the reading lesson structures as I have described is a reliable way to build teachers' expertise in teaching reading that also provides useful clarity on how reading is taught across a school.

HOW MIGHT A SCHOOL USE READING LESSON STRUCTURES IF THEIR TIMETABLE DOESN'T INCLUDE DISCRETE READING LESSONS?

Primary schools' timetables usually include discrete reading lessons, but there is nothing to say a reading curriculum can't be equally effective without them, in theory at least. The title of a lesson on a timetable is unimportant. What is important is whether pupils are getting the balance of explicit fluency development, reading experience breadth and discussion of texts that matches their stage of development.

However, in schools without discrete reading lessons, it can be difficult to know whether pupils *are* getting enough of what is required for their reading to develop effectively. It is all too easy for reading to become something that is done every now and then, especially given the challenges of engaging relatively dysfluent readers.

If your classroom or school doesn't have discrete reading lessons, you and your colleagues will need a clear idea of how much explicit fluency development, reading breadth and discussion of texts should be taking place on average each week. Regardless, reading lesson structures can be used across the wider curriculum, both in schools that use discrete lessons and those that don't.

HOW CAN READING LESSON STRUCTURES BE USED ACROSS THE WIDER CURRICULUM?

The core reading lesson structures (fluency reading, extended reading and close reading) can be used to engage with text in any lesson. A creation myth in an RE lesson might be read using a fluency reading structure because you want pupils to feel the rhythm of the words for themselves. A short story in an English lesson might be read using an extended reading structure because you want pupils to quickly grasp the plot. A historical source might be analysed using a close reading structure because you want pupils to dig into the author's language choices and what this conveys about their point of view. Choose the reading lesson structure that best matches your reading purpose.

Once reading lesson structures are embedded across the curriculum, they can also be adapted for use in interventions. (See Chapter 21 for more on this.)

——————————— This Chapter in a Nutshell ———————————

- Finding the right balance between reading lesson structures involves responding to the needs of individual classes, but the default timetable (Table 11.1) is a sound starting point.
- As pupils' reading fluency develops, fluency reading lessons can be gradually replaced by close reading lessons.
- Extended reading lessons are valuable no matter the pupils' level of reading fluency.
- Without discrete reading lessons, it is much more difficult to know whether pupils are getting enough of what is required for their reading to develop effectively.
- The core reading lesson structures (fluency reading, extended reading and close reading) are tools that can be used across the curriculum to read text with pupils. The key is to match the purpose of the reading to the lesson structure based on what it offers.

——————————— Further Reading ———————————

- One-stop shop for @Suchmo83 resources (Such, 2019)

——————————— Retrieval Quiz ———————————

- What reading lesson structure is most appropriate for pupils still learning the basics of decoding?
- Why might close reading play a more prominent role for older pupils?
- When might it be most appropriate to use the close reading lesson structure across the wider curriculum?

——————————— Questions for Professional Discussions ———————————

- To what extent does your current approach to teaching reading allow teachers to adapt to the needs of the class?
- To what extent are pupils in your school provided with explicit fluency teaching, reading experience breadth and opportunities for deeper discussion of texts?
- To what extent is reading a part of the wider curriculum in your school?

REFERENCE

Such, C. (2019). One-stop shop for @Suchmo83 resources. https://primarycolour.home.
    blog/2019/11/02/one-stop-shop-for-suchmo83-resources

12
SMALL-GROUP READING

WHAT IS SMALL-GROUP READING?

By definition, small-group reading is not a structure for whole-class teaching of reading like the core reading lesson structures (fluency reading, extended reading and close reading) and the introductory reading lesson structure (scaffolded reading). Put simply, small-group reading is any attempt to teach a small group of pupils as part of classroom teaching while other pupils are working independently. Naturally, pupils will also work in small groups if they are part of an out-of-classroom intervention. (See Chapter 21 for more on this.)

ISN'T THIS GUIDED READING?

Guided reading was originally associated with a reading scheme in the US (Shanahan, 2016). It then became associated with the teaching of small attainment-based groups in New Zealand (Simpson, 1966) and Australia (Holdaway, 1979) before gaining popularity as such in the US (Fountas & Pinnell, 1996) and England (Beard, 2000; Bodman & Franklin, 2014; Department for Education and Employment, 1999; Tennent et al., 2016). More recently, the label 'guided reading' has arguably lost any coherent meaning in schools: some educators insist guided reading simply means any form of small-group instruction while others say they teach 'whole-class guided reading'. For the sake of clarity, I will dispense with the label and instead talk about small-group reading.

WHEN MIGHT SMALL-GROUP READING BE NECESSARY?

Teaching pupils in small groups is a method to be employed when whole-class teaching cannot meet a crucial reading need of some pupils in a class. There are two circumstances when this might occur:

1   A small group of pupils are struggling with decoding or fluency considerably more than their peers, and an out-of-classroom intervention is unavailable to address this need.

Here, it can be sensible to work on decoding (via phonics) or fluency (via the fluency reading lesson structure) with these pupils while others are learning independently. If independent reading is part of your school timetable, this might provide an opportunity for small-group reading with pupils with significant decoding or fluency issues because these pupils are unlikely to benefit from independent reading.

2   Your class has pupils of a range of ages that make whole-class reading impractical.

Classes containing two different year groups that are both ready for core reading lesson structures (i.e. a year 2/3 class, a year 3/4 class, a year 4/5 class or a year 5/6 class) are almost always still conducive to whole-class reading. However, if a class contains pupils across three or more year groups, it is rarely appropriate to teach whole-class reading because the content of the texts being read is unlikely to be suitable for the entire class. However, it still makes sense to try to teach as many pupils at a time as possible. For example, a class with year 3 to year 6 pupils can be more productively divided into two groups than into three or more. Then, whole-class reading structures can still be employed with one half of the class while the other half work independently or are supported by another adult.

Classes containing two different year groups that include either reception or year 1 (i.e. a reception/year 1 class or a year 1/2 class) tend to not be suited to whole-class teaching as the difference in decoding ability is so pronounced. Again, classes like this can be more productively divided into two groups than into three or more. Whole-class reading lesson structures can still be employed with one half of the class while the other half work independently or are supported by another adult. At these ages it is sensible to divide the pupils based on their year group because the phonics and other reading teaching they require will differ considerably.

In short, the presence of mixed-age classes in your school might mean you need to consider teaching reading in groups rather than using whole-class teaching. However, it is best to minimise the number of groups to maximise efficiency.

──────────────── This Chapter in a Nutshell ────────────────

- Small-group reading is any attempt to teach a small group of pupils while the rest of the class are working independently.
- The phrase 'guided reading' is currently used in education to mean various things, some of them contradictory.
- Small-group teaching is useful when:
  o   A small group of pupils is struggling with decoding or fluency, and an intervention is unavailable
  o   A class has pupils with a range of ages that prevent whole-class reading.
- Small-group teaching as an alternative to intervention might be undertaken while relatively fluent pupils read independently.
- Small-group teaching in mixed-age classrooms should still try to minimise the number of groups into which pupils are divided.

─────────────── Further Reading ───────────────

- *Guiding Readers – Layers of Meaning* (Tennent et al., 2016)

─────────────── Retrieval Quiz ───────────────

- What are the different ways in which the phrase 'guided reading' is used?
- When might small-group reading be necessary?
- How might the pupils in a mixed reception/year 1 class be divided for the teaching of reading?

─────────────── Questions for Professional Discussions ───────────────

- Is the phrase 'guided reading' used in your school? If so, what is meant by the term?
- Do any of the classes in your school meet the conditions that might make small-group teaching necessary?
- If you have ever worked in mixed-age classrooms, what were the challenges and advantages of this?

REFERENCES

Beard, R. (2000). Research and the National Literacy Strategy. *Oxford Review of Education*, *26*(3–4), 420–436.

Bodman, S. & Franklin, G. (2014). *Which Book and Why: Using Book Bands and Book Levels for Guided Reading in Key Stage 1*. Trentham Books.

Department for Education and Employment (1999). The National Literacy Strategy: Additional Literacy Support. Module 1., Phonics and Spelling; Reading (Guided and Supported). DfEE.

Fountas, I. C. & Pinnell, G. S. (1996). *Guided Reading: Good First Teaching for All Children*. Heinemann.

Holdaway, D. (1979). *The Foundations of Literacy* (Vol. 138). Ashton Scholastic.

Shanahan, T. (2016) Should we stop using guided reading because of Common Core? www.shanahanonliteracy.com/blog/should-we-stop-using-guided-reading-because-of-common-core

Simpson, M. M. (1966). *Suggestions for Teaching Reading in Infant Classes*. Methuen.

Tennent, W., Reedy, D., Hobsbaum, A. & Gamble, N. (2016). *Guiding Readers – Layers of Meaning: A Handbook for Teaching Reading Comprehension to 7–11-Year-Olds*. Trentham Books.

PART IV

IMPLEMENTING CHANGE ACROSS A SCHOOL

13

LEADING PROFESSIONAL DEVELOPMENT

HOW CAN WE CONCEPTUALISE PROFESSIONAL DEVELOPMENT FOR TEACHERS?

By definition, any significant change to teaching across a school requires teachers to do something in a different way. In almost all cases, this in turn requires professional development for those teachers and anyone else who has a role in implementing that change. High-quality professional development for teachers is associated with better pupil outcomes, alongside other desirable outcomes such as teacher wellbeing (Mccrea, 2023; Sims & Fletcher-Wood, 2021; Wiliam, 2016).

In her discussion of teacher education, Kennedy (2016) argues that a useful way to conceptualise the development of teacher expertise is to focus on 'persistent problems' faced by teachers and how knowledge and practices might address these problems. In particular, she reminds us that teachers need to understand the purpose of professional development and how it is relevant to their own goals. And she reminds us that professional development is likely to run into trouble if it addresses one challenge teachers face without consideration of the impact this might have on other challenges.

WHAT DOES RESEARCH SUGGEST ABOUT PROFESSIONAL DEVELOPMENT FOR TEACHERS?

Academics in the field of education have tried to identify characteristics of professional development that make it more effective, focusing on aspects of teacher development that appear to lead to improved pupil outcomes (Dunst et al., 2015; Timperley et al., 2007). However, the accuracy of their conclusions has been scrutinised and questioned (Sims & Fletcher-Wood, 2021). The complexity of professional development for teachers allows for only the most tentative of recommendations, but the Education Endowment

Foundation (EEF) provides advice for those delivering professional development that is worth considering (Collin & Smith, 2021). As part of their report on the subject, they categorise mechanisms of professional development:

- *Build knowledge*: manage cognitive load; revisit prior knowledge.
- *Motivate staff*: set and agree goals; present information from a credible source; provide affirmation and reinforcement after progress.
- *Develop teaching techniques*: provide instruction; offer social support; model techniques; monitor and offer feedback as these techniques develop; include opportunities for rehearsal.
- *Embed practice*: provide prompts and cues; prompt action planning; encourage monitoring; prompt context-specific repetition.

The report suggests that professional development is more likely to be effective if it includes mechanisms from each of these categories, something they term a 'balanced design' (Collin & Smith, 2021, p. 27).

Anyone with a responsibility for teacher development would be well served by taking the time to read the EEF's guidance report on professional development for teachers. For now, it suffices to say we should have sound answers to the following questions before engaging teachers in professional development:

- What concepts do we want teachers to understand that underpin a change in their teaching? How will we ensure these concepts are more likely to be connected to prior knowledge and thus understood?
- How will we motivate our colleagues by ensuring they understand the purpose of professional development in addressing the challenges faced in the classroom? And how will we sustain that motivation when new techniques meet the complex reality of day-to-day teaching?
- How will we ensure teachers understand new techniques, including *why* these techniques work, and are confident in putting them into practice?
- How will we ensure new techniques are embedded through thoughtful practice and, over time, the development of useful habits?

WHEN DOES PROFESSIONAL DEVELOPMENT NEED TO BE PERSONALISED?

Every experienced teacher can recall whole-school professional development sessions that were irrelevant to their needs. It's tempting to think that trying to support multiple teachers at the same time is always doomed to failure, not least because coaching teachers on a one-to-one basis can be so powerful (Goodrich, 2024). However, the same principles of efficiency we apply to pupil learning apply to teachers: teach as many as you can at a time and personalise only where required.

When it comes to making changes to reading provision across a school, a reasonable idea is to share the theory and grapple with new teaching techniques on a whole-school basis and provide an opportunity to share successes and difficulties. However, once teachers are implementing new techniques in their own classroom, it is best to offer feedback and support on a one-to-one basis where possible. This might mean offering support as part of a coaching cycle if one is already employed in your school. Or it might mean leaders finding time to monitor the outcomes of professional development. The next chapter will discuss how this might be achieved as part of whole-school implementation of change.

WHAT DOES ALL THIS LOOK LIKE IN PRACTICE?

In Chapter 15, we will explore how professional development forms part of whole-school change by looking at how to introduce reading structures across a school.

─────────────── This Chapter in a Nutshell ───────────────

- A useful way to conceptualise teacher professional development is as an attempt to address persistent problems of teaching (Kennedy, 2016).
- Research into professional development only allows tentative conclusions. However, a sound approach is to ensure attempts to develop teachers' expertise contain the following aspects (Collin & Smith, 2021):
  o Building teachers' knowledge
  o Motivating teachers through goal-setting and support
  o Developing teaching techniques through instruction, modelling, rehearsal and feedback
  o Embedding practice so that new techniques are integrated into everyday teaching.
- When supporting teachers to improve their teaching of reading, the sharing of theory and the initial learning of new teaching techniques often works best on a whole-school basis. Once teachers are putting these new techniques into practice in their own classroom, one-to-one feedback and support works best.

─────────────── Further Reading ───────────────

- *Effective Professional Development: Guidance Report* (Collin & Smith, 2021)
- Parsing the practice of teaching (Kennedy, 2016)
- *Developing Expert Teaching* (Mccrea, 2023)
- Identifying the characteristics of effective teacher professional development: A critical review (Sims & Fletcher-Wood, 2021)
- *Responsive Coaching* (Goodrich, 2024)

--------------------- Retrieval Quiz ---------------------

- What is a helpful way to conceptualise professional development according to Kennedy (2016)?
- What does the EEF's (Collin & Smith, 2021, p. 27) guidance report into effective professional development mean by a 'balanced design' to professional development?
- When supporting teachers' understanding of teaching techniques related to reading, when might it be effective to offer support on a whole-school basis? And when might one-to-one support be required?

--------------- Questions for Professional Discussions ---------------

- Think back to your own experiences of professional development relating to the teaching of reading. Did it lead to changes in your classroom practice? If so, why? If not, why not?
- Consider times when you have attempted to offer professional development to other teachers. To what extent did this include mechanisms from the four different categories identified by the EEF as contributing to a 'balanced design' for professional development (Collin & Smith, 2021, p. 27)?
- Think back to points in your career when you were less open to professional development. What professional and personal factors contributed to this? What could your school have done to support you?

REFERENCES

Collin, J. & Smith, E. (2021). *Effective Professional Development: Guidance Report.* Education Endowment Foundation.

Dunst, C. J., Bruder, M. B. & Hamby, D. W. (2015). Metasynthesis of in-service professional development research: Features associated with positive educator and student outcomes. *Educational Research and Reviews, 10*(12), 1731–1744.

Goodrich, J. (2024). *Responsive Coaching: Evidence-Informed Instructional Coaching That Works for Every Teacher in Your School.* John Catt.

Kennedy, M. (2016). Parsing the practice of teaching. *Journal of Teacher Education, 67*(1), 6–17.

Mccrea, P. (2023). *Developing Expert Teaching.* Self published.

Sims, S. & Fletcher-Wood, H. (2021). Identifying the characteristics of effective teacher professional development: A critical review. *School Effectiveness and School Improvement, 32*(1), 47–63.

Timperley, H., Wilson, A., Barrar, H. & Fung, I. (2007). *Teacher Professional Learning and Development: Best Evidence Synthesis Iteration [BES].* Ministry of Education, New Zealand.

Wiliam, D. (2016). *Leadership for Teacher Learning: Creating a Culture Where All Teachers Improve So That All Students Succeed.* Learning Sciences International.

14

IMPLEMENTING CHANGE ACROSS A SCHOOL

HOW MIGHT IT BE BEST TO STRUCTURE IMPLEMENTATION OF CHANGE ACROSS A SCHOOL?

Schools are complex organisations, so implementing whole-school change is always a challenge. There is never likely to be a single correct way to implement a new initiative across every possible school. However, research into effective implementation in various settings seems to suggest it can be useful to consider implementation as having distinct phases with their own areas of focus (Aarons et al., 2010). The Education Endowment Foundation's (EEF) guidance report on implementation suggests four phases for implementation in schools (Sharples et al., 2024):

1   *Explore*: Define the problem and identify potential solutions.
2   *Prepare*: Create a plan (including identifiable outcomes to assess whether the implementation has worked), ensure the school is ready, prepare colleagues and prepare required resources.
3   *Deliver*: Put the change into effect in classrooms, offer support to colleagues and adapt as necessary.
4   *Sustain*: Ensure change is embedded through continued support and acknowledgement of good practice and scrutinise the impact of the change based on outcomes chosen in advance.

The EEF's report (Sharples et al., 2024, p. 21) states that implementation 'doesn't occur in a neat and linear fashion: strategies and phases overlap and are revisited over time'. (We will see in Chapter 15 how the boundaries between implementation phases can be blurry in practice.) It also makes clear that implementing change across a school should be seen as an ongoing process rather than a one-off event.

The EEF's report also suggests there are three key behaviours that increase the chances implementation will be successful. Schools need to:

> Engage people so they can shape what happens while providing overall direction.
>
> Unite around what is being implemented, how it will be implemented and why it matters.
>
> Reflect, monitor and adapt to improve implementation.
>
> (Sharples et al., 2024, p. 4)

While it is essential for school leaders to have a clear vision of what they want to achieve, everyone in the school who will be part of the implementation needs to be involved in shaping its direction. This means the perspectives and expertise of all colleagues should be sought and should inform implementation so that everyone is pulling in the same direction. It means collaboration between colleagues should be encouraged. And it means all colleagues need to reflect on the 'fit and feasibility' of the implementation from the outset and on the necessary flexible adaptation as implementation proceeds (Sharples et al., 2024, p. 11). In other words, implementation is most likely to succeed if all involved feel it is something being done *with* them rather than something done *to* them.

WHY DOES IMPLEMENTATION OF WHOLE-SCHOOL CHANGE OFTEN GO WRONG?

Implementation of change can go wrong for countless reasons: a lack of preparation, unpredictable events (e.g. an unexpectedly high number of colleagues leaving the school), change that is poorly matched to a school's needs or a culture that means colleagues do not feel safe to try new things. But there are two especially common reasons why implementation goes wrong:

1   Teachers don't have a clear idea of what to do or why they are being asked to do it.
2   School leaders do not adequately monitor how the proposed changes have been translated by teachers into actual classroom practice.

To address the first of these potential issues, school leaders need to explain precisely what is being aimed for, including the purpose behind it, and they need to ensure teachers see changes to classroom practice clearly modelled. As part of this, teachers should be shown which aspects of modelled classroom practice are essential and which can be adapted.

To address the second of these potential issues, school leaders need to recognise that making changes in a school is always messy. If you are a school leader, monitoring implementation means getting a clear view of the various ways you should have done things differently. It means hearing teachers tell you why some of the assumptions you made were incorrect. It means watching your ideal vision become something inevitably imperfect. However, perfection is not the aim. The aim is improvement, and although it is important to plan carefully to avoid unnecessary mistakes, improving anything involves errors and regrets that can take a bite out of a person's self-esteem.

Equally, school leaders often feel incentivised to make changes at pace. Rather than focus on a single key priority (or a few key priorities where capacity allows for this), it is tempting to change a lot of things quickly, especially if accountability pressures incentivise school leaders to be able to say they've done something, even if the impact was minimal. But successful implementation requires school leaders to postpone other lower-priority changes and to accept that their plans are unlikely to work exactly as they first intended. What is required, in other words, is focus and humility.

WHAT DOES THIS LOOK LIKE IN PRACTICE?

In the next chapter, we will explore how professional development and implementation interact by looking at how to introduce reading structures across a school.

———————————————— This Chapter in a Nutshell ————————————————

- It is useful to consider implementation of change across a school as composed of four phases (Sharples et al., 2024):
  - *Explore*: Choose a solution in response to a priority problem.
  - *Prepare*: Make a plan and get ready to deliver it.
  - *Deliver*: Enact the changes in classrooms, offering support and adapting where required.
  - *Sustain*: Continue to offer support and scrutinise the impact against intended outcomes.
- When implementation fails in primary schools, commonly it is the result of a weak shared understanding of what changes to classroom practice should look like and a lack of monitoring, which prevents necessary adaptation.

———————————————— Further Reading ————————————————

- *A School's Guide to Implementation: Guidance Report* (Sharples et al., 2024)
- *The ResearchED Guide to Leadership* (Lock, 2020)

—————————————————— Retrieval Quiz ——————————————————

- What are the four phases of implementation identified by the Education Endowment Foundation (Sharples et al., 2024)?
- Which of these phases involves choosing identifiable outcomes against which success of the implementation can be assessed?
- What are two common reasons why primary school leaders might not monitor and adapt whole-school changes they have begun to implement?

—————————— Questions for Professional Discussions ——————————

- Think back to your own experiences of whole-school changes relating to the teaching of reading. How were these changes monitored?
- In relation to the above question, what opportunities were you given to highlight problems that could be addressed through adaptations?
- Consider times when you have attempted to make whole-school changes to reading. How closely did the process follow the four stages identified by the EEF (Sharples et al., 2024)?

REFERENCES

Aarons, G., Hurlburt, M. & McCue Horwitz, S. (2010). Advancing a conceptual model of evidence-based practice implementation in public service sectors. *Administration and Policy in Mental Health and Mental Health Services Research. 38*(1), 4–23.

Lock, S. (2020). *The ResearchED Guide to Leadership: An Evidence-Informed Guide for Teachers.* John Catt.

Sharples, J., Eaton, J. & Boughelaf, J. (2024). *A School's Guide to Implementation: Guidance Report.* Education Endowment Foundation.

15

INTRODUCING READING LESSON STRUCTURES ACROSS A SCHOOL: PROFESSIONAL DEVELOPMENT AND IMPLEMENTATION IN PRACTICE

HOW DO I EXPLORE MY SCHOOL'S CURRENT CIRCUMSTANCES TO DECIDE WHETHER IMPROVING THE TEACHING OF READING IS AN IMMEDIATE PRIORITY?

Teaching reading effectively is one of the most important things a school can do, but this doesn't mean that potentially making it more effective is automatically an *immediate* priority. For example, if behaviour for learning is not at least adequate, then every aspect of pedagogy is undermined, and the introduction of a new structure for teaching reading (or teaching anything, for that matter) is likely to fail. Appropriate classroom behaviour is the foundation upon which everything else is built. Until pupils feel safe, and their learning can progress relatively uninterrupted, it is a waste of time to focus on the pedagogy of any particular area of the curriculum.

Equally, even though reading development is arguably the most important part of the academic curriculum, this does not mean that improving the teaching of reading is automatically more important than other areas. You must consider both the importance of the subject and the current standard of teaching of that subject. This can be hard to judge, but it is the responsibility of school leaders to live with this uncertainty and to make decisions regardless. For example, if you believe that the teaching of reading is merely adequate, then it might be tempting to introduce reading lesson structures immediately. However, what if many teachers across the school do not assess pupils' understanding in lessons across the curriculum and respond accordingly (i.e. formative assessment isn't an embedded part of classroom teaching)? Or what if the mathematics curriculum and related pedagogy are clearly inadequate? Under such circumstances, it is probably wiser to postpone the introduction of reading lesson structures and to focus on higher priorities.

It can be tempting to make changes just because you find a person's arguments convincing. You might have read this book so far and thought, 'This all sounds sensible, but my school already achieves excellent outcomes for all pupils, including those who initially struggle to learn to read.' If this is you, please consider leaving in place whatever way of teaching reading is currently used in your school. Your colleagues' time and attention are likely better devoted to other areas of their teaching. You might still find ideas in this book that can be used to supplement what is already working so well, but it is obviously a bad idea to make wholesale changes to anything that is demonstrably excellent. Ultimately, what matters is that pupils are becoming capable, confident readers.

HOW DO I JUDGE WHETHER READING LESSON STRUCTURES ARE A GOOD FIT FOR MY SCHOOL?

The reading lesson structures in this book have been designed to be flexible enough to work in the vast majority of contexts. In fact, these structures are already used effectively in a diverse range of primary schools. However, you might think the use of reading lesson structures wouldn't work well in your context. Perhaps your school has committed to teaching all subjects through small-group instruction. Or perhaps your school is keen to avoid classroom instruction in which the teacher plays a central role in guiding pupils, instead opting to rely on pupils almost always learning without such guidance. While these circumstances are rare (and almost always inadvisable), it would be foolish to assume that reading lesson structures are suitable for *every* school. It is up to you to decide whether whole-class reading in this form fits your context.

While the rest of this chapter will assume your school has discrete timetable slots for the teaching of reading (ideally, but not necessarily, on a daily basis), it is possible to use reading lesson structures in other ways. (See Chapter 11 for more on this.)

WHAT SHOULD I DO IF I THINK MOST OF MY COLLEAGUES WOULD BENEFIT FROM USING READING LESSON STRUCTURES, BUT A FEW ALREADY TEACH READING EXCEPTIONALLY WELL?

One of the challenges of school leadership is that you are responsible for seeing the bigger picture and acting accordingly. As a classroom teacher, I tended to dislike any prescribed methods that I felt prevented me from teaching in the way I considered to be most effective. But as a school leader, I saw that the strategic use of some prescribed whole-school methods was necessary to ensure every pupil in the school was receiving adequate teaching as a bare minimum. Regardless, the introduction of new methods frequently improved my teaching despite my initial scepticism. With the benefit of hindsight, I was often glad I had been asked to teach out of my comfort zone.

It can be challenging to ask highly competent colleagues to try to teach in a different way. Getting to grips with new methods almost inevitably makes teachers feel less effective at first, especially expert teachers who may have honed their current methods to a fine art. And there might be circumstances where it is wiser as a school leader to show a little discretion and allow a teacher to continue using their tried-and-tested methods. However, as a general rule, reading lesson structures work best as part of a consistent, whole-school approach for a number of reasons:

First, a consistent approach allows pupils to become accustomed to specific ways of being taught so that from the very beginning of the school year they can focus their attention on the text in front of them rather than the teacher's instructional idiosyncrasies. There will, of course, be plenty of differences between teachers, but a consistent approach provides pupils with a useful degree of stability when they move to a new year group. Each year of teaching is not an isolated stage but part of a chain of learning for pupils. Teachers are part of a team working together to maximise outcomes for their pupils. This works best when the responsibilities we have to our colleagues are part of our thinking.

Second, when implementing reading lesson structures across a school, experienced teachers are likely to provide the most helpful feedback on what might need to be adapted to increase the chances of success. They are also more likely to be able to provide a model for less-expert teachers. By exempting them from the professional learning being undertaken by their colleagues, an experienced teacher's expertise remains confined to a single classroom.

Finally, reading lesson structures provide plenty of scope for teachers to teach in ways that align with their own values and personality. There is no reason why the techniques and knowledge that expert colleagues have accumulated cannot be incorporated into their use of reading lesson structures.

When introducing new methods to teachers, especially expert teachers, it pays to be honest about the inherent trade-offs. Explain that trying something new is likely to make teaching harder for a while, but you believe the long-term benefits for pupils and teachers alike are worth the short-term difficulties. Where necessary, speak to expert teachers in your school on a one-to-one basis so that you can acknowledge that their current teaching is already effective, but you see benefits to the wider school team of them being part of the changes. In short, be honest about what you are asking of teachers. Reassure them that they will be given the space to learn without fear of judgement, and acknowledge the effort making changes will require.

HOW DO I PREPARE TO IMPLEMENT READING LESSON STRUCTURES ACROSS MY SCHOOL?

The first step in preparing for implementation of reading lesson structures is to create an implementation plan. This means specifying what will be done and in what order. You need to specify the 'active ingredients' of each lesson structure so that you are clear which elements are essential and which can be adapted to different classes of pupils (Sharples et al., 2024, p. 30). And you need to decide on the outcomes you will monitor. However, an implementation plan should not prevent you from altering course where necessary. As Sharples et al. (2024, p. 28) suggest, implementation plans are 'living documents that are developed iteratively and revised over time.'

Below is the outline of an example implementation plan for introducing reading lesson structures across a school. Any implementation plan should be scrutinised by the school's leadership team before implementation begins.

―――――――――――――― Implementation Plan ――――――――――――――

Stages 1 to 5 of the implementation plan might be undertaken with a small number of 'scout' teachers before being repeated with the whole school. This is likely to include the school leader responsible for reading and other teachers with the capacity to experiment with the lesson structures in advance of whole-school implementation.

The introduction of fluency reading, extended reading, close reading and scaffolded reading does not have to follow the order described in this plan. However, experience suggests this is an effective order. You might also consider it beneficial to focus purely on the core reading lesson structures (i.e. to not introduce scaffolded reading).

1 Prepare

Via an anonymous feedback form, give colleagues the opportunity to share their views on the current method of teaching reading.

Lay the groundwork by justifying the need for change in how reading is taught based on the difference between current outcomes and desired outcomes. Respond to colleagues' current views, emphasising that a different approach will try to incorporate the aspects that are valued about the current approach. Explain that the aim is a structure that affords the benefits of whole-school consistency while allowing colleagues to maintain their own teaching style and respond to the individual needs of their class.

Deliver a professional development session that builds teachers' understanding of reading development and justifies an approach that ensures:

o   Fluency is explicitly developed
o   Reading is broad and varied
o   Texts are discussed in depth.

This might involve shared reading and discussion of Chapter 1 of this book or another resource that introduces colleagues to the key information about reading development.

Assess the readiness of colleagues to begin experimenting with different reading lesson structures.

Select medium-term outcome measures against which the implementation of reading lesson structures will be judged over the first year following implementation:

o   Teacher satisfaction based on an anonymous survey
o   Pupil feedback based on pupil interviews
o   Effectiveness of reading lessons based on observation.

Decide upon long-term outcome measures against which the implementation of reading lesson structures will be judged:

o   Tracked pupil reading fluency assessment scores
o   Tracked standardised comprehension scores
o   Key stage 2 attainment data.

2   Deliver – fluency reading

Deliver a professional development session on fluency reading, modelling the 'active ingredients' (or sharing a video of this being modelled with a class):

o   Modelling of the extract by the teacher (twice)
o   Repeated paired reading by pupils (3+ times)
o   'Performance' of the text
o   Brief discussion of the text.

(Continued)

Give teachers in years 2 to 6 at least two weeks to experiment with fluency reading in their own classroom. During these initial experiments with the lesson structure, teachers might find it useful to use a shorter fluency reading lesson (e.g. 15 minutes), building this up as pupils become accustomed to the routines involved.

Ensure teachers know that these first attempts are low stakes, an opportunity for them to get comfortable with the lesson structure and to work out how it might need to be adapted to overcome any logistical difficulties (e.g. sharing of teaching assistants across different year groups, sourcing of texts).

Teachers might wish to continue teaching reading as normal for some of the week and only practise fluency reading in one or two lessons.

Take feedback from teachers and discuss any current impediments to the use of fluency reading. Make adaptations in response to these impediments.

3   Deliver – extended reading

Once teachers are accustomed to fluency reading, deliver a professional development session on extended reading, modelling the 'active ingredients' (or sharing a video of this being modelled with a class):

o   Reading at pace (majority of lesson spent reading)

o   Brief explanation where required and questioning to ensure a basic grasp of the text for all pupils

o   Progression through longer texts across multiple lessons.

Give teachers in years 2 to 6 at least two weeks to experiment with extended reading in their own classroom.

Encourage teachers initially to only use extended reading in which they read aloud while (most) pupils follow along.

Ensure teachers know that these first attempts are low stakes, an opportunity for them to get comfortable with the lesson structure and to work out how it might need to be adapted to overcome any logistical difficulties.

Teachers might wish to continue teaching reading as normal for some of the week and only practise extended reading in one or two lessons.

Encourage teachers to continue practising fluency reading alongside extended reading if they prefer but explain that it is also fine for them to focus purely on extended reading for the time being.

Take feedback from teachers and discuss any current impediments to the use of extended reading. Make adaptations in response to these impediments.

4   Deliver – close reading

Once teachers are accustomed to extended reading, deliver a professional development session on close reading, modelling the 'active ingredients' (or sharing a video of this being modelled with a class):

o   Deeper discussion based on themes in the text and language choices

o   Strategies to ensure all pupils think about questions asked and participate in discussion (e.g. use of mini whiteboards, pose-pause-pounce-bounce, think-pair-share).

Give teachers in years 2 to 6 at least two weeks to experiment with close reading in their own classroom.

Ensure teachers know that these first attempts are low stakes, an opportunity for them to get comfortable with the lesson structure and to work out how it might need to be adapted to overcome any logistical difficulties.

Teachers might wish to continue teaching reading as normal for some of the week and only practise close reading in one or two lessons.

Encourage teachers to continue practising fluency reading and extended reading alongside close reading if they prefer but explain that it is also fine for them to focus purely on close reading for the time being.

Take feedback from teachers and discuss any current impediments to the use of close reading. Make adaptations in response to these impediments.

5   Deliver – scaffolded reading

Once teachers are accustomed to close reading, deliver a professional development session on scaffolded reading in year 1, modelling the 'active ingredients' (or sharing a video of this being modelled with a class):

o   Modelling of the page by a teacher (twice)

o   Echo reading of the page

o   Repeated paired reading of the page

o   Brief discussion of the page

o   Repeat with subsequent pages.

Give teachers in year 1 at least two weeks to experiment with scaffolded reading in their own classroom. During this time, teachers in years 2 to 6 should continue to familiarise themselves with the three core reading lesson structures (fluency reading, extended reading and close reading).

Ensure teachers know that these first attempts are low stakes, an opportunity for them to get comfortable with the lesson structure and to work out how it might need to be adapted to overcome any logistical difficulties.

Teachers in year 1 might wish to continue teaching reading as normal for some of the week and only practise scaffolded reading in one or two lessons.

Take feedback from teachers and discuss any current impediments to the use of scaffolded reading. Make adaptations in response to these impediments.

(Continued)

6 Deliver – implementation of all reading lesson structures

Teachers in years 2 to 6 begin to implement the weekly timetable using the core reading lesson structures.

Teachers in year 1 begin to use scaffolded reading as part of their daily timetable.

Monitor the introduction of reading lesson structures, including this as part of each teacher's coaching/individual professional development if this is deemed a priority for the teacher in question.

7 Sustain – implementation of all reading lesson structures

In the half-term after implementation, lead a professional development session that looks at how the implementation of reading lesson structures is progressing. Offer shared feedback on observed good practice and areas for improvement. Express gratitude for teachers' willingness to try new things.

Via an anonymous feedback form, give colleagues the opportunity to share their views on the use of reading lesson structures. Where necessary, address any continuing difficulties.

If possible, film videos of good practice for each of the core reading lesson structures and scaffolded reading to support future newly employed members of staff.

Assess the effectiveness of the implementation against chosen medium-term and long-term outcome measures at appropriate intervals.

HOW DO I DELIVER AND SUSTAIN IMPLEMENTATION OF READING LESSON STRUCTURES ACROSS A SCHOOL?

The implementation plan above gives an overview of how reading lesson structures can be implemented across a school. Let's explore some of the key aspects of each stage of the development plan:

At the beginning of the implementation plan, we see that each of the reading lesson structures might be employed by a small group of 'scout' teachers before whole-school implementation begins. If there is scope to do this, it should include the teacher leading the whole-school professional development, alongside one or two teachers from different year groups. This is not always possible due to time constraints, but it is useful for at least one teacher to act as an advocate for the reading lesson structures, having used them already in their own classroom. A key part of this is that it allows 'scout' teachers to talk honestly about the teething problems and potential solutions that are an inevitable part of any implementation.

1   *Prepare*:

This stage involves gathering information about teachers' current perceptions of the teaching of reading, using this to support teachers to understand the rationale and the method for the upcoming changes and then choosing outcome measures against which the implementation will be judged.

2   *Deliver – fluency reading*:

Fluency reading is the most methodical of the reading lesson structures, so it is usually the simplest to implement. The 'active ingredients' of fluency reading should be modelled with teachers acting as a class of pupils, but there is no need for detailed role play. The idea is not to simulate the exact classroom experience. The idea is for the teacher leading the professional development to have an opportunity to talk through the different stages of a fluency reading lesson. Alternatively, if the technology is available, the 'scout' teachers might film themselves delivering a fluency lesson. This can be watched and discussed in this professional development session.

Following the professional development session, teachers across the school in the relevant year groups should be given the opportunity to experiment with fluency reading and offer feedback on their experiences and any related difficulties. Trying new things in the classroom is always tricky, so it is likely teachers will benefit from plenty of reassurance, especially from anyone who already has more experience with the reading lesson structures.

There might also be adaptations that need to be considered, assuming these do not undermine the 'active ingredients' of fluency reading. For example, a teacher in year 2 might find they would benefit from the support of a teaching assistant as their pupils begin to familiarise themselves with the routines of fluency reading, so you might see if a teaching assistant can be redeployed from another classroom for this lesson. Likewise, the teachers in year 3 might find that introducing this reading lesson structure immediately after lunch is leading to pupils being a little less settled than they had hoped. As a result, the teachers might temporarily teach reading at a point in the school day that differs from the usual timetable. Naturally, such adaptations are not always possible, and what is logistically feasible is different in every school. This means the solutions to some initial issues are likely to be specific to your context.

3   *Deliver – extended reading*:

The same principles that were followed for teachers' first experiences of fluency reading also apply to extended reading. However, extended reading requires more teacher judgement in terms of when to explain parts of a text, when to ask questions, what questions to ask, etc. If the teachers haven't taught reading in an interactive fashion involving the whole class before, then this might be a steep learning curve. This means it is again important to prepare teachers to expect initial difficulties and to reassure them that this is valuable as part of their development as a teacher of reading.

4   *Deliver – close reading*:

The same principles that were followed for teachers' first experiences of fluency reading and extended reading also apply to close reading. Close reading is the least methodical of the reading lesson structures. It requires teachers to ask questions about themes in the text and the language choices made by the author in order to guide pupils towards a deeper appreciation of the text. This challenge might mean teachers are initially best served by simplifying close reading. This can be achieved by reading a chunk of text to start the lesson and then spending the rest of the lesson discussing related questions. As teachers' confidence develops, they can be encouraged to begin to move between reading the text and discussion in whatever way they think best suits the text and the aims of the discussion.

5   *Deliver – scaffolded reading*:

The same principles that were followed for teachers' first experiences of the core lesson structures in years 2 to 6 also apply to scaffolded reading in year 1. Due to the age of the pupils, teachers might find it works best to introduce scaffolded reading in short bursts to begin with (e.g. five minutes) before gradually building up to the required lesson length.

6   *Deliver – implementation of all reading lesson structures:*

Teachers should only move on to this stage once they are confident with each of the reading lesson structures. This is the stage at which the reading lesson structures simply become how your school teaches reading lessons. Offer professional development support to those who need it. This might take place through coaching if this is part of how teachers are supported in your context. Where some teachers struggle more than others, it is often practical to focus on securing just one of the reading lesson structures at a time.

7   *Sustain – implementation of all reading lesson structures:*

This is the stage of implementation that is most often ignored. Even if everything appears to be going well, it is essential that the continued use of reading lesson structures is monitored. At appropriate intervals, judge implementation against the predetermined outcome measures. Use these to decide whether adaptations are required. Assuming implementation has progressed satisfactorily, create resources that will help newly employed teachers to incorporate the teaching of reading lesson structures into their own pedagogy. They will have the advantage of being able to observe other teachers across the school teaching in this way, but other resources such as model lesson videos and documents explaining the underlying theory can be useful too.

———————————— This Chapter in a Nutshell ————————————

- The *explore* phase of introducing reading lesson structures involves:
  - Deciding whether improving the teaching of reading is the highest priority
  - Deciding whether reading lesson structures are right for your school
  - Deciding whether you want to consider any timetable changes to facilitate this way of teaching reading.

- The *prepare* phase of introducing reading lesson structures involves:
  - Creating an implementation plan, which might involve adapting the implementation plan exemplified in this chapter
  - Finding out your colleagues' views about the way reading lessons are currently taught
  - Supporting colleagues to understand the rationale for using reading lesson structures through a shared understanding of key aspects of reading development and pedagogy
  - Checking colleagues are ready to begin experimenting with different reading lesson structures
  - Selecting outcome measures against which the implementation will be assessed.

- The *deliver* phase of introducing reading lesson structures involves:
  - Delivering professional development on fluency reading by sharing the 'active ingredients' and modelling them
  - Giving teachers in years 2 to 6 at least two weeks to experiment with fluency reading in their own classroom in a low-stakes environment
  - Taking feedback from teachers on this reading lesson structure and adapting it where necessary, only moving on to the next reading structure when teachers begin to feel comfortable with fluency reading
  - Repeating the above three steps for extended reading, close reading and scaffolded reading, the last of these lesson structures being used only by year 1 teachers and only where required
  - Beginning to use all lesson structures in a set timetable, which can be adapted by teachers to the needs of their class with oversight from school leaders
  - Monitor the use of reading lesson structures, ideally offering support to teachers who need personalised support (e.g. coaching).

- The *sustain* phase of introducing reading lesson structures involves:
  - Leading a professional development session that reinforces good practice and expresses gratitude to teachers for their willingness to try new things

(Continued)

- o Surveying colleagues' views about reading lesson structures and making necessary adaptations in response
- o Creating resources to support future new members of staff
- o Assessing the effectiveness of the changes using predetermined outcome measures.
- o Consider being part of a small team of 'scout' teachers who experiment with the different reading lesson structures before they are introduced to the rest of school.

Further Reading

- *A School's Guide to Implementation: Guidance Report* (Sharples et al., 2024)
- *Effective Professional Development: Guidance Report* (Collin & Smith, 2021)

Retrieval Quiz

- What might be used as outcome measures for the implementation of reading lesson structures across a school?
- Why is it essential that teachers are given opportunities to offer feedback on their use of reading lesson structures?
- What are the steps in the 'sustain' phase of introducing reading lesson structures across a school?

Questions for Professional Discussions

- To what extent is behaviour for learning in place that would allow the implementation of new pedagogical methods to be successful in your context?
- What adaptations would there need to be to the implementation plan in this chapter for it to be used in your context?
- Why might it be problematic to use assessment results to determine the success of implementation soon after it has taken place?

REFERENCES

Collin, J. & Smith, E. (2021). *Effective Professional Development: Guidance Report*. Education Endowment Foundation.

Sharples, J., Eaton, J. & Boughelaf, J. (2024). *A School's Guide to Implementation: Guidance Report*. Education Endowment Foundation.

PART V

BUILDING A READING CURRICULUM AND NURTURING A READING CULTURE

16

BUILDING A READING CURRICULUM

WHAT *IS* A READING CURRICULUM?

A sensibly defined reading curriculum is more than just a list of what pupils will learn and when this will happen. It is also valuable to have a clear idea of the expected capabilities that will be developed by the end of primary school and, where appropriate, within specific year groups. However, there are limits to what can be usefully listed in a curriculum, especially relating to the integrated bodies of knowledge that underpin reading comprehension. To understand this better, we need to consider the relationship between curriculum and pedagogy.

The knowledge and skills we want pupils to develop are intimately connected to how we teach them. This means the contents of a reading curriculum must be informed by our understanding of what reading is and how it develops. To this end, it is helpful to consider reading as consisting of capabilities that exist on a spectrum, with those that are most constrained at one end and those that are least constrained at the other (Dougherty Stahl, 2011; Paris, 2005; Snow & Matthews, 2016).

Constrained capabilities are, in effect, those that consist of a relatively *limited* set of items while **unconstrained capabilities** are those that consist of an effectively *unlimited* set of items. Aspects of reading that relate to constrained capabilities benefit from being written down in a clearly defined progression. In contrast, aspects of reading that relate to unconstrained capabilities can only be described indirectly in a reading curriculum, as we will see.

Initial decoding is a constrained capability. It consists of the initial grapheme–phoneme correspondences (GPCs) to be learned through a systematic phonics programme and the related phonemic skills required to begin to recognise and spell words (i.e. blending and segmenting). This relatively limited set of items needs to be clearly listed so that teachers know what to teach and when to teach it. Systematic phonics programmes, by definition, specify the progression of this set of knowledge and skills.

Use of the most effective comprehension strategies is another constrained capability. We can usefully write down when pupils will first be taught to re-read, summarise and use self-questioning in response to challenging texts. The modelling, guided practice and independent practice used to teach these strategies is likely to be an integrated part of discussions of texts (see Chapters 5, 9 and 10). However, teachers might still benefit from knowing when to start being more explicit in teaching this.

Beyond the teaching of initial decoding and comprehension strategies, every other aspect of reading development is best considered as an unconstrained capability. The development of reading fluency depends on pupils' ever-increasing grasp of the English writing system and its connection to spoken language. Equally, the ability to comprehend text is an unconstrained capability. As discussed in Chapter 2, it is pointless to try to write a list of the knowledge of the written English language we want pupils to develop during their time at primary school. However, we can still make thoughtful decisions about the parts of the curriculum that support the development of this body of knowledge. Pupils' reading fluency and comprehension will develop through the experiences we give them. This means that, beyond initial decoding and comprehension strategies, by far the most important part of curriculum development is choosing the texts pupils will experience.

In short, an effective reading curriculum is likely to contain the following:

- A general statement of end-of-school expectations (i.e. that pupils will become capable, confident readers who understand their own reading preferences and recognise the individual and social aspects of interpreting texts).
- A scope and sequence relating to the chosen systematic phonics programme.
- A list of the comprehension strategies to be introduced and details of when these are likely to become more explicit in reading lessons.
- A list of the texts that pupils will experience in different ways and the text structures, themes, tenses, perspectives, familiarity of content and other language choices of these texts.

DO WE NEED TO USE WHOLE TEXTS OR WILL EXTRACTS SUFFICE?

An unfortunate consequence of misconceptions about reading comprehension is that engagement with whole texts has often been deprioritised in favour of random extracts. After all, if teaching comprehension merely means teaching pupils how to answer different types of questions, then what need is there for pupils to read entire texts? In contrast, when we understand that teaching comprehension primarily involves increasing pupils' understanding of written English through meaningful experiences with texts, we can't help but see things in a more productive light.

If we want pupils to grasp the patterns of narratives, then they need to explore entire stories. If we want pupils to understand the organisational features of information texts, then they need to see how these fit together across complete pieces of writing. If we want pupils to recognise how themes are woven into speeches, then pupils need to see how these speeches are organised as whole entities. Only by seeing texts in their entirety can we fully understand the choices an author has made and the conventions of the text type they have employed or subverted.

Beyond the need to ensure pupils grasp how texts work as coherent wholes, there is also the issue of motivation to consider. A crucial part of teaching pupils to read is helping them to recognise the value of reading. A reading diet that consists predominantly of disconnected chunks of text sends a message to pupils that reading is little more than a potentially useful way to extract information and answer questions. But reading is also a way to explore the world we inhabit and our relationship to that world. It can be joyous, scary, hilarious, bewildering and enlightening. We must offer pupils meaningful experiences with texts. We must show them that reading has the power to change how we think and feel, not least because we hope ultimately to inspire them to continue reading when we are not there to guide them. And this is much easier to achieve when pupils explore texts in the way the author intended, from start to finish.

None of this means that extracts serve no purpose in a primary reading curriculum. On the contrary, we can sometimes help pupils to find greater meaning in the whole texts they are reading through thoughtful use of extracts from other texts. For example, a story opening from a book being read in its entirety might be contrasted with another opening from a different book in the book corner or library. And information books are often *designed* to be read without much attention to the exact sequence in which they are printed, so extracts from such books can act as meaningful whole texts. What matters is that for much of the reading pupils do in reading lessons, there is the chance to see how texts are organised and to experience the satisfaction of seeing an entire text unfold.

HOW SHOULD WE DECIDE ON THE VARIETY OF TEXTS IN OUR READING CURRICULUM?

There is no definitive list of texts that should be included in every primary curriculum. The decision to include or exclude any text is subjective. However, there are a list of considerations that can guide our decision-making:

The evidence base that exists provides little detail on how we might balance fiction and non-fiction in our reading curriculum. Some argue that fiction is uniquely useful in helping pupils to recognise the perspectives of other people (Mar et al., 2009; Oatley, 2011). Others argue that interventions that include non-fiction tend to be particularly beneficial in supporting comprehension outcomes (Filderman et al., 2022). Regardless, the picture is far too complicated to reach many definitive conclusions. What *can* be said with certainty is that pupils should experience plenty of both fiction and non-fiction and they should experience a wide variety of text types and genres during their time in primary school. If in doubt, a good starting point is to think of storybooks as comprising approximately half of your reading curriculum, and all other forms of texts (information texts, biographies, speeches, letters, newspaper articles, etc.) as comprising the other half. If your reading curriculum veers a little from this general rule, then that is not a problem. As long as your aim is to introduce pupils to the joy and utility of written English, and you have in mind the importance of both quality and variety, then you won't go far wrong. Of course, what defines the quality of a text is subjective, but this does not mean that anything goes. The pupils in our schools deserve a collection of reading experiences that have been carefully curated, and we should be ready to justify the choices we have made.

HOW DO WE ENSURE THE COMPLEXITY OF LANGUAGE IN TEXTS INCREASES IN A WAY THAT SUPPORTS LEARNING?

We do not need to worry that every aspect of every text in a reading lesson is more complex than the one that preceded it. Texts are too complicated for such an analysis. Some stories pair simple narrative structures with tortuous sentence formations and vocabulary that would have almost any reader reaching for a dictionary. Equally, some stories pair mind-boggling plot sequences with the simplest of language. And this mixture of difficulties within a text is just as evident in non-fiction. In other words, we can't simply think of a text as being uniformly more or less complex than another. There is little to be gained from trying to ensure the complexity of each text in a reading curriculum outstrips the one that came before. Providing we aim to include a variety of texts at an age-appropriate level, then much of the job of selecting texts for a reading curriculum is done.

However, there certainly are decisions we can make to consciously increase the variety of texts experienced by pupils and, crucially, to help teachers find connections between the text being read and others that pupils have read previously. A reasonable starting point to achieve this is to identify important aspects of texts: text structure, theme, tense, perspective, familiarity of content and other language choices. Knowing about these aspects allows you to decide whether the texts are a good fit for your curriculum. And if a text *is* given a place in your school's curriculum, sharing details of these aspects with teachers can support them when they plan lessons. Let's look more closely at these aspects of texts:

- *Structure*: The key parts of the structure to consider are type/genre, overt structural choices (e.g. subheadings, tables, chapter length) and, in the case of stories, the sequencing of the narrative.
- *Theme*: The identification of themes was discussed in Chapter 10. Where overarching ideas are explored in a text, sharing these with teachers helps them consider the discussions they might have with pupils. The subjective nature of identifying themes should be taken into consideration when detailing themes in a curriculum.

- *Tense*: Texts are written predominantly in the past, present or future tense, or a combination of these. In most cases, the tense used matches the purpose of the text (or the purpose of the individual sentence within that text). As such, while tense might be something worth exploring, there is little point in noting this down in your curriculum. The exception is the use of tense in stories. Most stories are written in the past tense, but not all of them are. Where a story in your curriculum is written primarily in the present tense, this is information that can be useful for teachers. For example, if this is perhaps the first story pupils have read in the present tense, a teacher can draw pupils' attention to this. Likewise, if an earlier text in the curriculum has used the present tense, a teacher who is aware of this can draw pupils' attention to their prior experience, enhancing their grasp of the potential impact of this choice by an author.

- *Perspective*: Texts are written from different points of view. In non-fiction, we can recognise the stance of the author in the text and the role they play. Are they trying to be objective? Are they clearly expressing an opinion? Might they be biased? In fiction, we can categorise the point of view of the narrator as first person, second person or third person.

  o A *first-person* narrative is a story being told from the perspective of a character using pronouns such as 'I' and 'me'. First-person texts tend to provide the most interesting opportunities for discussing the extent to which a narrator's version of events can be trusted (i.e. whether they may be an 'unreliable narrator').

  o In a *second-person* narrative – the rarest point of view by far – the narrator uses 'you' in the story, drawing the reader in as a character.

  o A *third-person* narrative is the most common perspective used in fiction, and it involves pronouns such as 'he', 'she' or 'they'. There are variations on a third-person point of view. Most important of these are third-person limited (where the narrator only has access to the thoughts and emotions of one character, usually a central protagonist) and third-person omniscient (where the narrator has access to the thoughts and emotions of all characters). However, if we choose to explore these differences, it is likely to be with the oldest pupils in primary school only.

  Non-fiction can also be considered in terms of point of view, especially the way this relates to different types of text (e.g. autobiographies are written from a first-person perspective by definition).

- *Familiarity of content*: Some texts are closer to pupils' life experiences than others, and comprehension relies on background knowledge some pupils are less likely to have. Naturally, all pupils know different things about the world, but it can still be useful to note the extent to which a text *on average* is likely to be more challenging to grasp due to its content. Doing this can allow you to stagger such texts in your curriculum so that a text requiring rarer background knowledge is followed by something more familiar (and perhaps challenging in different ways). It can also allow teachers to consider in advance how they might familiarise pupils with some of the background knowledge that will support comprehension.

- *Other language choices*: Every aspect of a text could in theory be described as a language choice. However, what I am specifically referring to here is the length and complexity of sentence formation and the use of stylistic choices such as repetition, evocative description, humour, archaic language, etc. If something clearly contributes to the author's style, it is worth noting this in your curriculum.

Let's look at a couple of examples of the sort of information we might note down in our reading curriculum to help us make curricular decisions and to support teachers in their classroom practice (DiCamillo, 2009; Zephaniah, 2000).

The Miraculous Journey of Edward Tulane by Kate DiCamillo

- *Text structure*: story with elements reminiscent of fairy tales (especially Hans Christian Andersen's 'The Steadfast Tin Soldier'); 27 chapters – approximately 8–10 pages per chapter; straightforward time sequence; illustrations every few pages
- *Possible themes*: loss and suffering can lead to a greater understanding of love and the possibility of self-discovery and redemption; life can be unpredictable and cruel, even to those who are least able to withstand it; all love is impermanent, but it is no less valuable for this fact
- *Tense*: past
- *Perspectives*: third-person (limited – narrator focuses on experiences and thoughts of Edward Tulane, the central protagonist)
- *Familiarity of content*: relatively familiar settings (homes, shops, farms, trains) but somewhat removed from pupils' immediate experience due to 1930s American context; sensitive content warning – child mortality, extreme poverty and homelessness
- *Other language choices*: relatively normal sentence complexity for a book used in year 4-6; occasional challenging vocabulary, e.g. 'tremulous', 'surmised', 'kerosene', 'surpassingly'; some Americanisms, e.g. 'garbage', 'hobo', 'dang', 'motel'.

'The British' by Benjamin Zephaniah

- *Text structure*: poem written in the style of a recipe; stanzas used but without a clear pattern
- *Possible themes*: migration from across the world is central to the story of modern Britain; the cultural and linguistic diversity of Britain should be valued; unequal treatment of groups of people has negative consequences

- *Tense*: present
- *Perspectives*: second-person (through implied 'you' in the imperative verbs)
- *Familiarity of content*: potentially unfamiliar names of ancient Britons and modern nationalities; pupils' understanding of the role of migration in the story of modern Britain might be different depending on pupils' individual family histories; discussion of Roman Britain and the Anglo Saxons might connect to school's history curriculum
- *Other language choices*:
  - Imperative verbs to match recipe analogy. However, in recipes, imperative verbs usually separate us from the person writing the instructions; here, in contrast, they lead us to consider who is writing these instructions and how their experiences might have contributed to their perspective
  - Extensive (but not comprehensive) list of nationalities who have made Britain their home emphasises the diversity of modern Britain
  - Short lines for some key phrases (e.g. 'Serve with justice').

HOW DO WE INCREASE THE CHANCES THAT OUR READING CURRICULUM IS APPROPRIATE FOR OUR PUPILS?

One way to think about the value of diversity in our reading curriculum is by considering three interconnected dimensions: diversity of perspective, diversity of content and diversity of language.

Diversity of perspective in our reading curriculum is an ethical necessity. Pupils are entitled to see themselves and their communities reflected in the texts they experience in school. Equally, reading should allow pupils to learn more about the diversity of the world they inhabit. This idea is famously expressed through Rudine Sims Bishop's idea of texts offering mirrors, windows and doors to pupils (Bishop, 1990): mirrors that reflect their own experiences, windows that offer views of other worlds and doors that suggest pupils can explore those worlds for themselves through their imagination.

To begin to do justice to this idea, we need to consider the protagonists of the stories that pupils experience. We must ask ourselves whether the characters in these narratives reflect both the pupils' own cultural experiences and the diversity of wider society. For example, since 2017 there has been an overall – if worryingly inconsistent – upward trend in the representation of racially minoritised characters in children's books (Centre for Literacy in Primary Education, 2024). As a result, including recently published fiction in a reading curriculum is likely to play a critical role in ensuring a diversity of perspectives is represented.

We must also think about the aspects of the wider world we are exploring through the rest of the texts in our curriculum. In particular, we must ask ourselves what impression of different parts of the world pupils are getting from the reading we offer them. And we must consider whether this impression is a complex enough representation of that reality.

The diversity of content in our reading curriculum is an expression of the breadth of what we hope children will learn from their reading. It is not the end of the world if every story is set in the last half century, but if we can introduce pupils to characters and ideas from different parts of history, then why wouldn't we? Equally, why wouldn't we try to include stories that are set in different parts of the world and that build on pupils' understanding of different nations and cultures?

Pupils' reading experiences provide an opportunity to complement pupils' learning from the rest of the curriculum. For example, if pupils in year 5 learn about ancient Greece in history, this can be complemented by reading versions of famous Greek myths. Or if pupils in year 3 learn about light in the science curriculum, this can be complemented by reading about the scientific achievements of Hasan Ibn al-Haytham and Isaac Newton.

Reading experiences can also supplement your wider curriculum. If there just isn't room in your history curriculum for pupils to learn about the Kingdom of Benin, for example, pupils can read an information text in reading lessons that details its fascinating history and the importance of oral traditions in historical understanding.

The diversity of language in our reading curriculum is addressed when we provide pupils with varied experiences relating to the aspects of texts described above: text structure, theme, tense, perspective, familiarity of content and other language choices.

We must also consider whether the texts we are sharing with pupils are age-appropriate. Despite the common use of standards that measure word frequency and sentence complexity, there is no reliable, objective standard for what counts as an age-appropriate text in terms of language or content. The most sensible way to judge whether a text is appropriate for a given year group is to use professional judgement, discussing potential text choices with colleagues and looking at the texts chosen by other schools.

IF WE DECIDE WHICH TEXTS PUPILS WILL EXPERIENCE IN OUR READING CURRICULUM, DOES THIS REDUCE TEACHER AGENCY AND PREVENT THEM FROM RESPONDING TO THEIR CLASS?

There are always trade-offs when curriculum decisions are made. Wherever learning content is specified, an opportunity is removed for a teacher to make a choice about what is to be learned. However, in the case of texts used in reading lessons, the advantages of specifying components of a curriculum outweigh the disadvantages. Only through conscious selection of texts can we guarantee that pupils' reading experiences are suitably varied and that teachers can make connections to pupils' prior knowledge. And making clear curriculum decisions allows schools to invest in class sets of texts, something that has a major impact on the ease with which reading can be taught to a high standard.

However, primary teachers often have books, poems or other texts they treasure and want to share with pupils. It is worth providing flexibility that allows for this, especially in the daily shared reading that teachers do (see Chapter 17). It might also be beneficial to leave flexibility in the curriculum to allow for some reading lessons that spend time exploring texts that matter deeply to individual teachers. This can be achieved through the addition of some optional texts in each year group's curriculum.

HOW CAN WE AFFORD THE WHOLE-CLASS SETS OF STORYBOOKS FOR A READING CURRICULUM?

There are several ways a school can reduce the cost of buying the whole-class sets of storybooks that facilitate high-quality teaching of reading. But first it should be pointed out that compared to many of the investments schools make – for example, tablet computers and online programs – books simply aren't *that* expensive. And the alternative – constant printing of sheets for pupils to read – is more expensive in the long run. Once a school has thought carefully about the selection of texts it wants in its reading curriculum, there is probably no single investment decision a school can make that is as cost-effective and impactful as buying class sets of books.

That said, how can a cash-strapped school minimise the cost of buying class sets of storybooks for their reading curriculum?

First, if a school contains more than one class in a year group, classes could engage with different books at different points in the academic year so that only enough books for one class would be required. Alternatively, different classes in the same year group could teach reading at different points in the school day so that a single class set of books could be shared.

Second, for most purposes, one book between two pupils will suffice, but this is less than ideal as it prevents pupils from studying their own copy and also prevents pupils from independently engaging with books during extended reading lessons, a valuable part of instruction with more fluent readers (see Chapter 9). However, sharing one book between two is far better than constantly reading printed extracts. Books can also often be purchased second-hand although finding them can be time-consuming and thus represent a false economy.

Third, the cheapest option is not to buy class sets at all and for the whole class to use the teacher's copy of the text, displayed on an interactive whiteboard via a document camera. Again, this prevents more fluent readers from independently engaging with books during extended reading lessons, and short texts would still need to be printed for fluency reading lessons, but it is still better than a curriculum diet composed mainly of printed extracts.

Regardless, over the longer term, every school should be aiming to acquire class sets of storybooks for every year group from years 2 to 6, alongside class sets of decodable books and other age-appropriate texts for scaffolded reading lessons in year 1.

Naturally, a reading curriculum develops over time. Your school might decide it wants to introduce a new storybook into the reading curriculum to replace one that isn't working as well as others. This sort of reflection and gradual adaptation is a good thing. Any curriculum should always be evolving, and this is especially true of a reading curriculum, given the wonderful array of new children's books that are published each year. In this circumstance, the class set of books that is to be replaced can be added to book corners and/or the school library.

WHAT ABOUT THE REST OF THE READING CURRICULUM – INFORMATION TEXTS, BIOGRAPHIES, LETTERS, DIARY ENTRIES, ETC.?

In some cases, textbooks are available that provide collections of non-fiction texts, and a class set of poetry anthologies with poetry for different age groups can be used across the school. But many texts we might want to include in our curriculum are not available in this format. What then? The short answer is that this aspect of the reading curriculum tends to require patience and a willingness to gradually accumulate texts. In some cases, this will mean writing brief information texts to match a subject you want pupils to read about (or cautiously using AI to do this). In others, it will mean saving examples of letters, biographies found online, myths from books in the school library, etc. (copyright permitting). Ideally, these texts can then be printed into a single booklet that can be used year after year, something that is far more convenient for teachers and more environmentally friendly. Table 16.1 is an example of a school's set of texts that were created, accumulated and printed into a reading booklet for year 5.

The set of texts in Table 16.1 constituted around half of the year group's reading content used in reading lessons, with the other half devoted to storybooks. The choices here are not random. These texts were chosen for a variety of reasons. For example, the information text about World War II and evacuation was chosen to prepare pupils for the storybook in the curriculum *Letters from the Lighthouse* by Emma Carroll. Naturally, pupils can learn a lot about these subjects from their reading of the story, but it was decided that their appreciation could be enhanced through some supportive prior reading on the subject. Likewise, information texts on the UK parliament, Millicent Garrett Fawcett and Emmeline Pankhurst complemented the study of developments in UK democracy in the history curriculum, including the story of the campaign for voting rights. And some texts were chosen to supplement aspects of the wider curriculum. For example, the school's geography curriculum ensures pupils study countries from around the world, considering every continent. And yet given the size and rapid population growth of Nigeria, it was felt to be a glaring omission that pupils did not learn about the country, so this was included in the reading curriculum as an information text.

Table 16.1 Example set of additional texts used across year 5

	Block 1	
Weeks 1 & 2	World War II and evacuation	*information text*
Weeks 3 & 4	Famous ships through history	*information text*
Weeks 5 & 6	The Black Death	*information text*
	Block 2	
Weeks 1 & 2	Jabberwocky	*poetry*
Weeks 3 & 4	Famous explorers	*information text*
Weeks 5 & 6	Rapunzel	*traditional tale*
	Block 3	
Weeks 1 & 2	Leonardo da Vinci	*biography*
Weeks 3 & 4	Greenpeace	*letter and newspaper article*
Weeks 5 & 6	Theseus and the Minotaur	*myth*
	Block 4	
Weeks 1 & 2	Mount Olympus and the ancient Greek gods	*information text*
Weeks 3 & 4	Pandora's Box	*myth*
Weeks 5 & 6	Recycling guide	*explanation*
	Block 5	
Weeks 1 & 2	Human brain and nervous system	*information text*
Weeks 3 & 4	Genghis Khan	*biography*
Weeks 5 & 6	Nigeria	*information text*
	Block 6	
Week 1 & 2	The UK parliament	*information text*
Week 3 & 4	Millicent Garrett Fawcett & Emmeline Pankhurst	*biography*
Week 5 & 6	The Highwayman	*poetry*

Of course, this is not where pupils' reading ends. The school's science curriculum includes basic information texts for each topic, alongside brief biographies of notable figures like Charles Darwin, Marie Curie and Katherine Johnson. And other school subjects include texts related to each topic, ready for teachers to use in their classroom teaching.

None of this was achieved overnight or just by one person in the school. It was a gradual creation and accumulation of texts that reflected the school's ethos about the value of ongoing curriculum development.

SHOULD THE STORYBOOKS IN OUR READING CURRICULUM CONNECT TO THE WIDER CURRICULUM?

The settings and plots of storybooks offer opportunities to make connections across the wider curriculum. For example, if a storybook chosen for the reading curriculum involves the evacuation of a protagonist during the Blitz, it might be advantageous for pupils to read that book at the same time – or shortly after – learning about World War II in history lessons. Equally, a story that includes an earthquake as a central plot point might be timed to align with pupils' learning about tectonic plates in geography. However, these sorts of connections are a mere bonus. They should not be a limiting factor when choosing the storybooks to include in a reading curriculum. While slight adjustments can be made to take advantage of potential connections with the wider curriculum, by far the most important considerations when choosing storybooks are the variety of language experiences they offer to pupils and the age-appropriateness of the texts.

DOES POETRY DESERVE SPECIAL TREATMENT IN OUR CURRICULUM?

One of the great joys of primary teaching can be found in learning poetry with children. In weeks where a poem is studied, teachers should be encouraged to explore the poem using reading lesson structures – fluency reading and close reading are particularly apposite – but also to take time to learn the poem by heart. This can continue in subsequent weeks through little-and-often practice. Where appropriate, pupils can devise and learn actions to support their performance of the poem. The learning of poetry by heart can become part of a school's culture, something that is supported by opportunities to perform in front of an audience, such as during assemblies.

--- This Chapter in a Nutshell ---

- The ability to read consists of constrained and unconstrained capabilities. The former benefit from being analysed into components that can then be listed in a curriculum; the latter cannot be productively specified in this way.
- An effective reading curriculum is likely to contain:
  - A general statement of end-of-school expectations.
  - A scope and sequence relating to the chosen systematic phonics programme.
  - A list of the comprehension strategies to be introduced and details of when these are likely to become more explicit in reading lessons.
  - A list of the texts that pupils will experience in different ways and their aspects: structure, themes, tense, perspective, familiarity of content and other language choices in these texts.

- Extracts can play a useful role in a reading curriculum, but most reading lessons should be spent reading complete texts.
- A good starting point for choice of texts is to aim for half of the texts in a reading curriculum to be storybooks and the other half to be everything else (e.g. information texts, short biographies, speeches, letters).
- Consider texts in terms of their structure, theme, tense, perspective, familiarity of content and other language choices. Aim for a suitable variety in these areas within age-appropriate texts. Specifying details related to aspects of texts helps with curriculum planning and classroom teaching.
- Consider the diversity of texts in your curriculum in terms of three interconnected dimensions: diversity of perspective, diversity of content and diversity of language.
- Allow opportunities for teachers to share texts that matter deeply to them. This can primarily be done through shared reading (i.e. story time), but also through some flexibility in the texts used in reading lessons.
- Over the long term, buying whole-class sets of storybooks is an important investment, but costs can be minimised in the short term through book sharing, use of document cameras and careful timetable organisation.
- The reading material beyond storybooks is harder to organise and can take time to accumulate. An elegant solution to build towards is a booklet of photocopied texts (copyright permitting) that can be used again and again.
- Use texts to complement and supplement the rest of your wider curriculum.
- Take time to give pupils opportunities to learn poetry by heart and then perform it as part of your reading curriculum.

Further Reading

- *Understanding and Teaching Primary English* (Clements & Tobin, 2021)
- *Reflecting Realities: Survey of Ethnic Representation within UK Children's Literature 2022* (Centre for Literacy in Primary Education, 2023)
- *Reading Reconsidered* (Lemov et al., 2016)

Retrieval Quiz

- What aspects of texts might be worth specifying in your reading curriculum for the purposes of curriculum development and classroom teaching?
- What is a reasonable balance between storybooks and other texts in a reading curriculum?
- How might the teaching of poetry differ from that of other texts?

————————— Questions for Professional Discussions —————————

- Information texts play an important role in a reading curriculum. What might be the advantages and disadvantages of schools writing some of these to precisely match their wider curricular goals?
- How much of a reading curriculum do you think should be adapted to suit the interests of a class or the preferences of a teacher? What trade-offs are involved in adapting the curriculum in this way?
- Once a reading curriculum is established, what might be a sensible rate of adaptation of that curriculum, bearing in mind the value of stability in supporting teachers' planning and the value of adaptation in allowing a place for recently published books and other texts?

REFERENCES

Bishop, R. S. (1990). Windows and mirrors: Children's books and parallel cultures. In M. Atwell & A. Klein (Eds), California State University San Bernadino Reading Conference 14th Annual Conference Proceedings (pp. 3–12).

Carroll, E. (2017). *Letters from the Lighthouse*. Faber & Faber.

Centre for Literacy in Primary Education (2024). *Reflecting Realities: Survey of Ethnic Representation within UK Children's Literature 2023*. CLPE.

Clements, J. & Tobin, M. (2021). *Understanding and Teaching Primary English: Theory into Practice*. Sage.

DiCamillo, K. (2009). *The Miraculous Journey of Edward Tulane*. Candlewick Press.

Dougherty Stahl, K. A. (2011). Applying new visions of reading development in today's classrooms. *The Reading Teacher*, 65(1), 52–56.

Filderman, M. J., Austin, C. R., Boucher, A. N., O'Donnell, K. & Swanson, E. A. (2022). A meta-analysis of the effects of reading comprehension interventions on the reading comprehension outcomes of struggling readers in third through 12th grades. *Exceptional Children*, 88(2), 163–184.

Lemov, D., Driggs, C. & Woolway, E. (2016). *Reading Reconsidered: A Practical Guide to Rigorous Literacy Instruction*. John Wiley & Sons.

Mar, R. A., Oatley, K. & Peterson, J. B. (2009). Exploring the link between reading fiction and empathy: Ruling out individual differences and examining outcomes. *Communications*, 34(2009), 407–428.

Oatley, K. (2011). *Such Stuff as Dreams: The Psychology of Fiction*. John Wiley & Sons.

Paris, S. G. (2005). Reinterpreting the development of reading skills. *Reading Research Quarterly*, 40(2), 184–202.

Snow, C. E. & Matthews, T. J. (2016). Reading and language in the early grades. *The Future of Children*, 26(2), 57–74.

Zephaniah, B. (2000). *Wicked World!* Penguin UK.

17

NURTURING A READING CULTURE

WHY DOES INDEPENDENT READING MATTER SO MUCH?

Every educator knows that the ultimate goal of teaching reading is for pupils to become capable, confident readers who choose to read independently on a regular basis. This may involve them reading for the sheer pleasure of it or reading to learn something valuable. Predictably, there is a strong correlation between the amount of independent reading pupils do and their reading capability (Stanovich, 2009). It is likely a virtuous cycle exists between reading capability and how much a child reads independently, in which greater capability encourages more independent reading, and independent reading enhances a pupil's capability. There is some evidence that reading also accelerates pupils' spoken language development (Seidenberg, 2017). This is unsurprising when we consider the contribution of reading to our understanding of language (Duff et al., 2015). All of this means that setting pupils on the path to independent reading is an essential responsibility of a school.

HOW CAN WE SUPPORT PUPILS TO BECOME INDEPENDENT READERS?

There are two things schools must do to increase the chances their pupils will choose to read independently:

1   Teach reading well.
2   Demonstrate that reading is valued and valuable.

Most of this book is devoted to the first of these criteria. There is essentially no way to tempt a pupil to read independently on a regular basis if they struggle to read. The pleasure and utility of independent reading is accessible only to those whose reading capabilities allow them to read without feelings of inadequacy. We must do our utmost to ensure every pupil becomes a capable, confident reader through the development of spoken language, the teaching of initial decoding, the development of fluency and the teaching of comprehension through meaningful experiences with plenty of thoughtfully chosen texts. However, even though pupils require a certain degree of capability before they can be lured into independent reading, this does not mean we cannot demonstrate that reading is valued and valuable long before pupils are fluent readers.

Almost every imaginable method of demonstrating that reading is valued and valuable is potentially effective in building a culture of independent reading in a school. The challenge is balancing this aim with the extra workload such methods often place on classroom teachers. For example, asking teachers to create and update elaborate displays that show what books they have read this year is a nice way to show pupils the value of reading, but the time teachers devote to such things might be better spent. Here are a few ways to build a culture of independent reading that do not place disproportionate demands on teachers' time:

- *Read aloud to children and have spare copies available of these books.* Nothing demonstrates the value of reading quite like shared experiences of books. And reluctant independent readers sometimes fall in love with reading in the comfort of re-reading a book they have already enjoyed, so it's helpful to have spare copies of these books in the classroom or school library.

- *Think carefully about how to make your classroom reading areas accessible.* It is easy for pupils to feel overwhelmed when there is a huge selection of books to choose from. Even if your school has a library, it can be worthwhile to curate a smaller selection in your classroom. Ask pupils to organise this and to display books their peers might enjoy. From this, pupils often begin recommending books to each other, creating a buzz about certain titles or authors.

- *Recommend books to children.* Occasionally, suggesting a book to a pupil can provide the impetus required for them to persevere beyond the first few pages. This doesn't mean you should always assume what a pupil will like based on what you already know about them. However, by initially recommending books to pupils based on their interests, you can gain the trust that allows you to subsequently broaden their horizons with less-expected recommendations.

- *Ensure there are plenty of quality non-fiction texts available.* While stories hold a special place in the interests of many children, for others it is factual books that spark their curiosity and give them a reason to read on their own. Check that every classroom (or the school library) is adequately stocked with a variety of non-fiction books.

- *Never discourage pupils from taking home a book they have chosen because you think it might be too easy or too difficult for them.* Many schools have systems that attempt to assign books into categories of difficulty (often called book bands). There is no exact science to this, but it isn't necessarily problematic for books to be labelled in a way that allows teachers and pupils to get an approximate sense of their difficulty. What *is* problematic is any system that restricts pupils' book choices based on these labels. On several occasions I have seen reluctant readers inspired to read independently by the challenge of books that were considered to be far above their current reading attainment. Pupils also sometimes enjoy books that might be considered too easy for them. While we should gently encourage pupils to broaden their horizons as readers and challenge themselves, not every book pupils read for pleasure needs to be at the limits of their capabilities. Equally, comics and graphic novels are a perfectly valid form of reading as well as a useful point of entry to independent reading for many pupils.

- *Ensure the diversity reflected in the reading curriculum is matched in the books that pupils can choose from.* Pupils deserve access to books that reflect their lives, their communities and wider society.

- *Think carefully about any use of extrinsic rewards for reading.* If we want pupils to see reading as a worthwhile use of time, we probably want to minimise signals such as extrinsic rewards that subtly tell them that reading is a chore (Willingham, 2017). Rewards can backfire in other ways too – for example, by incentivising pupils to race through the shortest books they can find to win a competition. Where pupils do benefit from extrinsic rewards to help them build up initial reading habits, these should be phased out as soon as possible.

- *Make connections with your local library.* If your local library is within walking distance, consider collaborating with them to ensure every pupil signs up as a member and understands what is available.

- *Offer break-time and lunch-time clubs that give pupils somewhere peaceful to enjoy books individually and with their peers.* Sometimes all a pupil needs to start reading independently and talking about books with their peers is somewhere to do it.

- *Understand the reading preferences of your class and respond accordingly.* A productive activity early in the academic year is to conduct a survey to find out what the pupils in your class think about reading. By finding out what kind of texts they like (e.g. types of books, comics, newspapers) and what reading they do at home, you can consider what reading material to promote in your classroom to align with pupils' interests and to fill gaps in their experiences.

- *Find reasons to talk about reading.* This might involve occasionally reading a blurb of a well-loved book from the book corner. It might involve sharing a poem you love. It might involve reminding your class of a well-crafted phrase from a story you are sharing. One of the joys of primary teaching is that teachers spend a lot of time with just one class. Use the opportunities this provides to talk about reading and make time for pupils to chat with each other about what they are reading. Talking about reading in this way won't come naturally to many pupils, but if you model this sort of talk, pupils will soon catch on.

HOW IMPORTANT IS IT FOR TEACHERS TO KNOW ABOUT CHILDREN'S LITERATURE?

Every teacher of reading needs to be familiar with children's literature, including that written for a contemporary audience. Teachers who understand the artistry involved in the creation of children's books are better equipped to share the language contained within them and to offer better recommendations to the pupils in their class.

However, there are countless expertly written children's books worth our attention, and we can't ignore the opportunity costs that would be involved in asking teachers to regularly read children's literature. Teachers have surprisingly little time to dedicate to professional development. Once training related to safeguarding, administration and assessment is accounted for, teachers probably have little more than 20 hours a year of in-school professional development relating to pedagogy and subject knowledge across the entire curriculum. Even if every minute of this time were dedicated to reading children's literature, a teacher in key stage 2 might only read ten extra children's books each year. The unfortunate truth is that the only teachers who will ever develop a broad and deep knowledge of children's literature are those who read it for leisure in their own time. And given the working hours of the average teacher, I don't think this is a demand that can be reasonably made of those who would prefer to spend their free time in other ways.

So how do we ensure teachers have at least an adequate knowledge of children's literature despite the constraints on their time?

First, we need to ensure that the process of teaching builds this knowledge. One of the advantages of teaching reading primarily using whole texts rather than relying on extracts is that the act of planning and teaching requires teachers to improve their knowledge of children's literature by analysing and appreciating it.

Second, we need to give teachers time at least to become familiar with some of the books that are in the reading corner of their classroom or school library. A sensible starting point is to give teachers an hour of professional development time at the start of each academic year to familiarise themselves with the books that their children will choose from and to discuss children's preferences with colleagues. This is likely to involve reading blurbs, searching on the internet for plot summaries and choosing a selection of books that will be regular recommendations.

Third, we need to nurture a culture in which talking about children's literature is an everyday part of what we do. For example, in one school where I was a classroom teacher, colleagues regularly asked each other about books they might recommend for pupils with certain preferences and experiences. Initiating a culture of shared support can begin with just one or two teachers demonstrating this inquisitiveness about children's literature choices. There is no reason for teachers to rely solely on their own knowledge of children's books when they are surrounded by like-minded colleagues.

Finally, we need to value the teachers in our schools who have built up a broad and deep knowledge of children's literature. If a school doesn't have at least one exceptionally knowledgeable children's literature enthusiast among their staff, then this is something to consider when next making recruitment decisions.

SHOULD WE INCLUDE TIME FOR INDEPENDENT READING IN OUR TIMETABLE?

There are good reasons to question the use of free-choice independent reading in our classroom timetable. Asking relatively dysfluent readers to read independently does little to improve their capabilities. As Seidenberg (2017, p. 139) suggests, 'Children who struggle when reading texts aloud do not become good readers if left to read silently; their dysfluency merely becomes inaudible.' And when struggling readers are asked to read in silence, they often simply pretend to read, leading them to develop negative feelings about reading and diminishing their belief in themselves as readers. It is hard for a pupil to feel comfortable in any learning environment that pushes them to hide their difficulties from their teacher. Shanahan (2019) also points out that devoting curriculum time to independent reading is almost certainly less productive than using that time to teach reading in a way that allows us to guide pupils' understanding.

So, does this mean we can dismiss this practice entirely? Not necessarily. There are a few reasons why we might continue to include some independent reading in our timetable:

First, there is some research that suggests that free-choice independent reading improves pupils' attitudes to reading (Bus et al., 2024).

Second, it is almost certainly true that encouraging pupils to read independently outside of school is beneficial. Admittedly, the available research only shows a relationship between time spent reading and reading ability (Stanovich, 2009); it doesn't show that one causes the other. But it would be a surprise to learn that reading was the only capability known to humankind that wasn't improved through practice and experience. One might argue that we have no evidence to suggest that independent reading in the classroom encourages pupils to read beyond the school gates. However, it seems reasonable to suggest that the independent reading habits we build in the classroom can transfer to pupils' reading outside of it.

Third, independent reading in the classroom can afford teachers opportunities to support struggling readers. While fluent readers in the classroom read silently, the teacher can undertake small-group instruction with those who need support with initial decoding or fluency. In this way, classroom time devoted to independent reading can close the gap between struggling readers and their peers, rather than widen it. (See Chapter 12 for more on this.)

Fourth, it's important to remember the limitations of research. To quote Rose and Eriksson-Lee (2017, p. 5): 'Evidence in education acts more like a compass: Once we know where we want to go, it can help point us in the right direction for getting there – but it cannot tell us where we're trying to go in the first place.' Ensuring we maximise the chances that pupils become capable readers is obviously a central goal of education, but it is not the *only* goal. It is perfectly reasonable for a school to decide they think every pupil is entitled to some time each day to choose from a wide selection of books, read in a peaceful setting and have a chat with their peers about their reading. Such a choice might be especially understandable in schools where some pupils do not have such opportunities at home. We must remember that we are not *only* setting pupils up for the rest of their lives. We have a responsibility to consider pupils' day-to-day experiences of childhood as well.

None of this is to suggest that independent reading should have a lot of time dedicated to it in every school. And independent reading should not displace reading instruction in which the teacher takes an active role in guiding pupils. If a choice must be made between reading instruction and independent reading, the former is always preferable. However, on the assumption that relatively dysfluent readers are not left to struggle on their own and the trade-offs have been considered, independent reading in the classroom might well deserve its place in a school's timetable.

HOW CAN WE MAXIMISE THE IMPACT OF SHARED READING WITH PUPILS?

As we saw in Chapters 9 and 10, reading aloud to pupils can be a beneficial component of reading lessons. But it is also essential we spend some part of each school day reading aloud to pupils in ways that prioritise enjoyment. Sharing wonderful books in this way is one of the great privileges of being a teacher and one of the great joys of being a pupil.

Every teacher brings their own personality to the classroom, and some find it quite natural to read aloud with enthusiasm and clarity. Others, however, find it more difficult. We need to recognise that reading aloud is a key competency for all teachers and, where required, devote time to practising it. This might mean practising alone or with a trusted colleague who can offer sensitive feedback.

As discussed in Chapter 16, teachers often have books that matter deeply to them that they wish to share with the pupils they teach. Likewise, a class might have interests or experiences that mean they are an ideal audience for a specific book. There should always be room for the sharing of such books even if a school curriculum might profitably determine some of the books for shared reading.

The type of discussion teachers engage pupils in when sharing books should change to reflect the reading that pupils undertake across the rest of the curriculum. For pupils at the start of their journey towards reading proficiency, shared reading is both an opportunity for a communal experience with a book and a chance to engage in discussions about the language used (though plenty of reading should still, of course, be undertaken for the sheer joy of it). However, once pupils engage in close reading as a regular part of their reading timetable, it is then best to minimise the discussion of language choices in shared reading time, saving this part of the school day purely for free-flowing, absorbing experiences with books.

HOW CAN WE MAKE THE MOST OF THE SUPPORT OFFERED BY PUPILS' FAMILIES?

All aspects of education benefit from collaboration between pupils' families and their school, and reading development is no exception. Part of a school's responsibility is to maximise the support offered by pupils' parents/carers and to react when this support is unavailable.

First, this means communicating clearly with parents/carers about how reading is taught in the school, especially at the earliest stages. They can be invited into school to observe the teaching of reading and engage in workshops that explore how reading at home might be managed effectively. (See Chapter 22 for more on one-to-one reading.) For those unable to attend in person, it can be helpful to create videos or simple written guides that show this, both of which can be made accessible on a school's website. None of this is to suggest that schools should attempt to restrict how parents/carers engage their children with books at home. However, advice about how to practise with decodable books and read together can be helpful.

Second, you should make clear recommendations around the frequency of reading at home. Encourage families to build daily routines around reading, with a focus on hearing their child reading aloud. Even relatively fluent readers benefit from reading aloud to someone at home. It is much harder for pupils to develop habits around reading when it only happens on some days of the week. Recommendations can be emphasised when parents/carers come into school to discuss their child's progress. These meetings can also give families an opportunity to inform the school if they are unlikely to be able to offer reading support at home. This, of course, needs to be done with due sensitivity. There is no value in passing judgement on families that, for whatever reason, are not able to support their children's reading development as much as others.

Third, we can prioritise reading at home as the central component of pupils' homework. While schools might set homework relating to other foundational academic capabilities (e.g. mental arithmetic), and they might also offer optional creative activities, reading aloud to a family member should be seen as the most important aspect of any school-related learning that takes place at home.

Fourth, we need to remove any administrative obstacles that might get in the way of pupils reading to their parents/carers. Asking parents/carers to write on a reading record to show they have heard their children read might seem like a way for a school to hold families accountable for the support they offer. However, this rarely works the way schools hope, and reading records often become an extra, unnecessary job for families who do hear their children read. Even worse, reading records are sometimes used to reward pupils who read at home, which disproportionately advantages those already more fortunate. Generally, all that is required for pupils to read at home are clear recommendations from the school and a book selected by the pupil based on their own preferences.

The final and most important thing to say about the support that is offered by pupils' families is that ultimate responsibility for pupils' reading development must lie with schools. There are myriad reasons why a family might not be able to support their child with their reading development. A school's approach to reading must offer everything pupils need to become capable, confident readers, and the support potentially offered by parents/carers should be considered as a welcome bonus. Any school that *relies* on family support to secure pupils' progress in reading is doing a disservice to those pupils who do not benefit from such support.

HOW CAN WE ENSURE BILINGUAL AND MULTILINGUAL PUPILS ARE SUPPORTED AND THEIR LANGUAGE CAPABILITIES ARE NURTURED AND CELEBRATED?

When pupils first arrive at primary school, their prior experiences with spoken English vary greatly. Some pupils have spent their entire childhood until this point surrounded only by spoken English. Other pupils arrive with relatively little or almost no experience of spoken English and with an ability to speak one or multiple other languages.

Teaching pupils who are new to English provides a mixture of challenges and opportunities. While initial communication with pupils who are new to the English language can make it more difficult for teachers to communicate new concepts, research suggests there are potential advantages to pupils acquiring more than one language, beyond the obvious and profound advantage of proficiency in multiple languages (Sharples, 2021). For example, bilingual and multilingual pupils have been found to be more likely to meet key stage 1 academic targets than their monolingual peers with equivalent proficiency in English (Whiteside et al., 2017).

By far the most important way we can support the spoken language and reading development of pupils who are new to English is to engage them in spoken English while encouraging them to also continue to express themselves in other languages they know (e.g. thinking aloud in these languages). However, it is important to note that pupils who are new to English often go through a 'silent period' as they become accustomed to English (The Bell Foundation, 2024a). This is where a pupil communicates rarely or not at all in speech as their initial grasp of spoken English develops. Pupils experiencing this should not be pressured to talk in English, but they should be given the same experiences of spoken language as the rest of the class and be supported to develop friendships. It can be intimidating for any pupil to enter a school where they cannot immediately communicate with their peers or adults. Technology can be employed to facilitate communication between a pupil who is new to English and their teacher, but it is also valuable for adults to learn some basic words and phrases in the pupil's home language that will help the pupil to express their most important needs (e.g. use of the toilet). The best support that can be offered to pupils new to English is to ensure they feel entirely safe and included in the school.

In English schools, pupils who are thought to speak a language at home other than English are often described as speaking English as an additional language (EAL) (Department for Education, 2020). It is essential to recognise that the category of EAL describes a heterogenous group (Hutchinson, 2018): nothing can or should be assumed about a pupil's proficiency in English, current attainment or cultural experiences based on this category. However, where pupils who speak English as an additional language appear to have difficulties with spoken English, it can be useful to use assessments that investigate pupils' spoken language in the language they use at home. The Bell Foundation (2024b) is a charity that provides excellent advice and resources to help schools better support pupils who speak English as an additional language.

Building a reading culture depends on helping every pupil to become a capable, confident reader. Bilingual and multilingual pupils benefit from evidence-informed approaches to reading in the same way as their peers who speak only English. However, building a reading culture also depends on pupils feeling included in the school community. A central part of this involves celebrating the array of languages and dialects used by pupils and teachers, and recognising the valuable contribution to school life that comes from the diversity of pupils' cultures.

--------------------------- This Chapter in a Nutshell ---------------------------

- Pupils' reading development is accelerated if they read independently outside of school. Schools should nurture a culture that encourages this.
- The most important things schools can do to encourage pupils to read independently are to teach reading well and demonstrate that reading is valued and valuable.

(Continued)

- It is crucial to read aloud to pupils and enable them to find books they will enjoy.
- Independent reading time can be a valuable part of a school's timetable as long as relatively dysfluent readers are given appropriate support..
- Reading aloud to pupils is not something that comes naturally to all educators. It is a pedagogical capability that warrants professional development time.
- Schools are ultimately responsible for pupils' reading development, but pupils' families can be encouraged to offer support through clear communication and recommendations about reading at home.
- The best support for pupils new to English is a welcoming environment that includes them in spoken interactions while encouraging them to also use the other languages they speak.
- Pupils defined as speaking EAL are a heterogenous group. As with all pupils, the support they need should match their individual learning needs and not be based on assumptions related to a particular category or label.

Further Reading

- *Approaches to Reading and Writing for Pleasure: An Executive Summary of the Research* (Cremin et al., 2023)
- *Tell Me: Children, Reading and Talk* (Chambers, 1993)
- *Teaching EAL: Evidence-Based Strategies for the Classroom and School* (Sharples, 2021)
- The Bell Foundation website (2024) www.bell-foundation.org.uk/
- Reading for pleasure (Biddle, n.d.) https://padlet.com/Jon_Biddle/reading-for-pleasure-woam2an149vg
- CLiPPA – the CLPE poetry award (Centre for Literacy in Primary Education, n.d.) https://clpe.org.uk/poetry/CLiPPA
- Empathy Lab (n.d.) www.empathylab.uk/

Retrieval Quiz

- In brief, what are the two most important things a school can do to encourage pupils' independent reading?
- Describe two ways schools can show that reading is valued and valuable.
- Why is it important for schools to take ultimate responsibility for pupils' reading development?

——————————— Questions for Professional Discussions ———————————

- To what extent is independent, free-choice reading part of the timetable in your school? And how are relatively dysfluent readers supported during this part of the school day?
- How confident are you and your colleagues in reading aloud to pupils? And has this area of teaching ever been the focus of professional development during your career?
- How does your school help the families in your community to support their children with their reading development?

REFERENCES

Biddle, J. (n.d.). *Reading for pleasure.* https://padlet.com/Jon_Biddle/reading-for-pleasure-woam2an149vg

Bus, A. G., Shang, Y., & Roskos, K. (2024). Building a stronger case for independent reading at school. *AERA Open, 10*(1), 1–17.

Centre for Literacy in Primary Education (n.d.). *CLiPPA – the CLPE poetry award.* https://clpe.org.uk/poetry/CLiPPA

Chambers, A. (1993). *Tell Me: Children, Reading and Talk.* Thimble Press.

Cremin, T., Hendry, H., Chamberlain, L. & Hulston, S. (2023). *Approaches to Reading and Writing for Pleasure: An Executive Summary of the Research.* The Mercers' Company.

Department for Education (2020). *English Proficiency of Pupils with English as an Additional Language.* www.gov.uk/government/publications/english-proficiency-pupils-with-english-as-additional-language

Duff, D., Tomblin, J. B. & Catts, H. (2015). The influence of reading on vocabulary growth: A case for a Matthew effect. *Journal of Speech, Language, and Hearing Research, 58*(3), 853–864.

Empathy Lab (n.d.). *Empathy Lab.* www.empathylab.uk/

Hutchinson, J. (2018). Educational outcomes of children with English as an additional language. Education Policy Institute and The Bell Foundation. https://dera.ioe.ac.uk/31500/1/EAL_Educational-Outcomes_EPI-1.pdf

Rose, N. & Eriksson-Lee, S. (2017). *Putting Evidence to Work: How Can We Help New Teachers to Use Research Evidence to Inform Their Teaching?* Teach First. www.teachfirst.org.uk/sites/default/files/2017-10/Putting_Evidence_to_work_2017.pdf

Seidenberg, M. (2017). *Language at the Speed of Sight: How We Read, Why So Many Can't, and What Can Be Done About It.* Basic Books.

Shanahan, T. (2019) Isn't independent reading a research-based practice. Blog. www.shanahanonliteracy.com/blog/isnt-independent-reading-a-research-based-practice

Sharples, R. (2021). *Teaching EAL: Evidence-Based Strategies for the Classroom and School.* Multilingual Matters.

Stanovich, K. E. (2009). Matthew effects in reading: Some consequences of individual differences in the acquisition of literacy. *Journal of Education, 189*(1–2), 23–55.

The Bell Foundation (2024a). *EAL and SEND: A Framework for Integrated Provision in Schools*. www.bell-foundation.org.uk/app/uploads/2024/02/The-Bell-Foundation_EAL-SEND.pdf

The Bell Foundation (2024b). Changing lives and overcoming exclusion through language education. www.bell-foundation.org.uk

Whiteside, K. E., Gooch, D. & Norbury, C. F. (2017). English language proficiency and early school attainment among children learning English as an additional language. *Child Development, 88*(3), 812–827.

Willingham, D. T. (2017). *The Reading Mind: A Cognitive Approach to Understanding How the Mind Reads*. John Wiley & Sons.

PART VI

READING DEVELOPMENT ACROSS THE CURRICULUM

18

DEVELOPING VOCABULARY

WHY IS VOCABULARY DEVELOPMENT SO IMPORTANT?

There is a well-established association between the extent of a pupil's vocabulary and their language comprehension capabilities (National Reading Panel, 2000; Ouellette, 2006; Quinn et al., 2015). Naturally, a pupil's understanding of word meanings is fundamental to their understanding of language in both spoken and written forms. It is estimated that more than 90% of words in a text need to be understood by a reader for comprehension to take place (Cunningham, 2005; Nagy & Scott, 2000). Willingham (2017, p. 90) goes further, suggesting that 98% of words need to be grasped for what he terms 'comfortable comprehension' although this is dependent on the specific text being read and the specific unknown words.

An illuminating way to think about vocabulary development is through the concepts of **vocabulary breadth** and **vocabulary depth**: vocabulary breadth is a measure of how many words someone knows; vocabulary depth is a measure of how much someone knows about those words. For example, a four-year-old child and a literate adult are likely to both recognise the word 'tree' and use it accurately in some contexts. But the adult is likely to know various species of trees, what it means for a tree to be evergreen or deciduous and metaphorical uses of the word 'tree' such as a 'family tree'. Put another way, the adult has greater vocabulary depth, which comprises the multitude of connections between the concept of 'tree' and other concepts in their mind. Our responsibility as teachers is to ensure we increase both the breadth and depth of our pupils' vocabularies.

WHAT IS THE MOST IMPORTANT CONTRIBUTION WE CAN MAKE TO PUPILS' VOCABULARY DEVELOPMENT?

Most vocabulary is learned implicitly through experiences of spoken and written language in varied contexts, an example of what Seidenberg (2017) calls 'statistical learning'.

Given that pupils add approximately 3,000 words per year to their vocabulary (McGuinness, 2006), we should be grateful this is the case. It would be an overwhelming task to explicitly teach all the vocabulary required for our pupils to become literate adults.

All of this means that, regardless of the benefits of explicit instruction, the most important way we build pupils' understanding of words is by providing a diverse array of meaningful experiences with the English language. This is where literature excels. While opportunities for pupil talk are obviously important, even adult speech cannot compete with the sophistication of language found in many children's books, both in terms of the frequency of rarer words and the complexity of sentence structure (Cunningham & Stanovich, 1998; Korochkina et al., 2024; Nation et al., 2022). Increasing the amount and quality of reading we undertake with pupils is likely the most effective contribution we can make to their vocabulary development.

While pupils will learn plenty of vocabulary through these experiences alone, we may choose to briefly describe some words as we are reading, especially those crucial to the text's meaning. This teaching of what Biemiller (2010) calls 'drop-in words' is most effective for words that relate to real objects or experiences of the world (e.g. 'twilight', 'archipelago', 'translucent') and words that have familiar synonyms (e.g. 'exhilarated', 'desire', 'quandary').

HOW CAN WE EXPLICITLY TEACH VOCABULARY?

As described above, many words can be introduced by sharing a quick description that is supported by the context in which the word is experienced. Many words may not need any description at all. But occasionally it can be beneficial to go into more detail or even teach some words before a text is read, especially if we think a word is crucial to a text's meaning and too unfamiliar or complicated for pupils to grasp through 'drop-in' teaching. To do this well, we should consider characteristics of effective vocabulary instruction (Beck et al., 2013; Such, 2021; Zimmerman & Reed, 2017):

1   A pupil-friendly definition is given, and connections are made to what pupils already know.
2   The word is contextualised in sentences, including non-examples (i.e. ways the word would *not* be used) where necessary.
3   Pupils are exposed to the word multiple times.
4   Pupils actively use the word.

Let's look at an example of what this might look like in a classroom explanation:

'The word "declare" means "to say something forcefully". It is usually reserved for when we say something important. I probably wouldn't declare to my friends that I was feeling a little hungry. However, a headteacher might declare in assembly that the school had won an important competition.'

Here we see the first two characteristics of effective vocabulary instruction. Whether or not we would continue with the final two depends on the classroom situation. If we were pausing during reading to provide an in-the-moment description of an unfamiliar word, then we might just move on or perhaps note down the word for active use and retrieval at a subsequent time. However, if we were teaching this word on its own before reading, as part of a spelling lesson or perhaps even as part of a discrete vocabulary lesson, we would be likely to demonstrate the final two characteristics of effective vocabulary instruction – for example:

> 'Let's have a go at using this word in a sentence. Say this sentence starter to your partner and then complete the sentence: "The police officer declared..."'

Alternatively, pupils could be asked to write a sentence including the target word. The word could then be revisited in later lessons, perhaps as part of an ever-growing list of new words noted down by the classroom teacher for this purpose.

WHAT WORDS MIGHT WE PRIORITISE?

When reading or teaching pupils about new concepts, it makes sense to prioritise words we deem to be most crucial to pupils' understanding. However, often there are opportunities to think more strategically about the words we teach. To have a better chance of learning the curriculum provided by a school, pupils obviously benefit from being taught words that are useful across the breadth of that curriculum. And they benefit from being taught words they are less likely to learn from their day-to-day experiences outside of the classroom (Beck et al., 2013). By combining these ideas, we can see that words that would fit in the overlap in Figure 18.1 are exceptionally useful to teach.

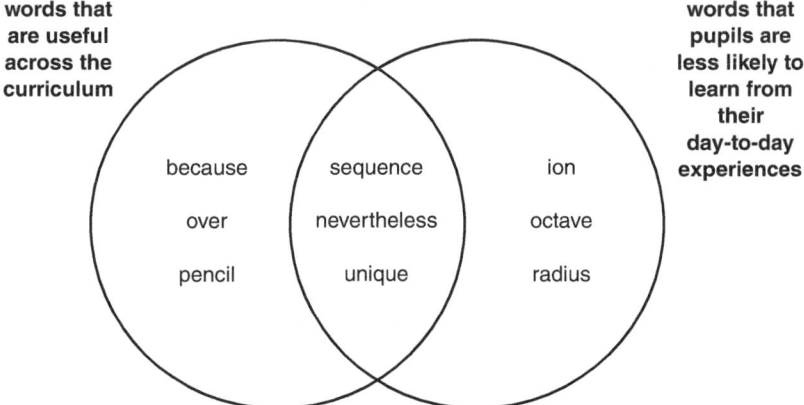

Figure 18.1 Prioritised words for explicit teaching

A list of such words that are appropriate for primary schools can be found on my blog (Such, 2019a) and in my previous book (Such, 2021).

HOW CAN WE HELP PUPILS REMEMBER THE WORDS WE TEACH THEM?

Learning involves the integration of new ideas with prior knowledge that is activated in working memory (Simonsmeier et al., 2022). In effect, this means teachers need to try to make connections between new ideas and what pupils already know (Cottingham, 2023). When teaching vocabulary, we can make links between words by using synonyms, antonyms, examples and non-examples. Another way to build connections between words is to discuss morphology (i.e. the chunks of meaning within words). By drawing attention to this, we can help pupils to see patterns that are likely to support learning. This has the added benefit of providing them with knowledge that can give them a head-start with unfamiliar words containing familiar morphemes. Let's look at an example.

Take the word 'deformed'. Within this word, we can identify morphemes using a word equation:

deformed → de + form + ed

de: suggests 'the opposite' or 'undo'

form: suggests 'shape' or 'fashion'

ed: suggests the past tense

We might even consider the way other morphemes modify 'form' using a word matrix such as Figure 18.2:

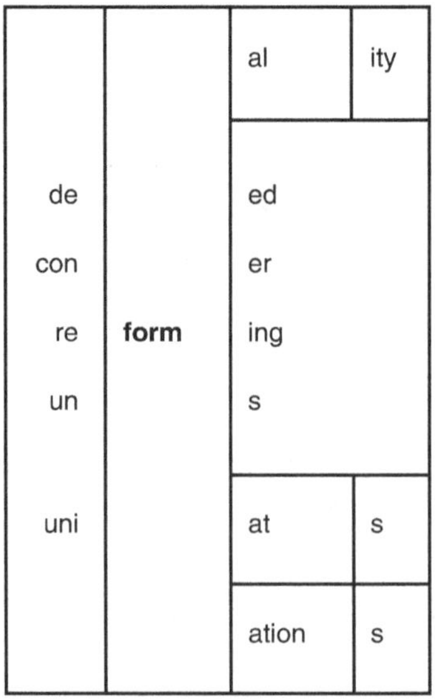

		al	ity
de con re un	**form**	ed er ing s	
uni		at	s
		ation	s

Figure 18.2 Example of a word matrix

Exactly how we discuss morphemes with children is less important than the fact that this discussion happens. It doesn't mean we have to recognise and point out every morpheme within every word. However, where we do recognise a chunk of meaning we know has consistent meaning across multiple words, then we can help pupils to become word detectives by sharing this understanding with them.

We can also point out the patterns in language by referring to etymological elements within words that are familiar to us, such as Latin and Greek roots. These are particularly useful because more than half of all words in English contain a Latin or Greek root (Green, 2020). For example, we might point out that the Latin root 'cred' in the word 'incredible' relates to belief or faith and then spell out the connection to words such as 'credulous', 'credit', 'credentials'. This doesn't mean teachers need to spend hours studying the most common Latin and Greek roots, although this is a surprisingly productive way to increase your understanding of English words. But it does mean that where we *do* recognise patterns within words, we should make these explicit to pupils. As teachers, it is our responsibility to nurture pupils' curiosity about the fascinating tapestry of written English, and an introduction to morphology is a key part of this.

HOW MIGHT WE EMBED VOCABULARY ACROSS THE WIDER CURRICULUM?

A central part of developing a curriculum in any academic subject is choosing the most important concepts we want pupils to understand. This is supported by clear thinking about the words and phrases that pupils need to grasp. Teachers should know in advance the essential words and phrases that need to be introduced in a unit of study and the essential words and phrases that have already been introduced earlier in the curriculum. Curriculum documents should make this explicit so that teachers are free to consider how to plan effective lessons. Examples of what this might look like in primary science, history and geography can be found on my blog (Such, 2019b).

HOW MIGHT WE EMBED READING ACROSS THE WIDER CURRICULUM?

Reading can be included in many other aspects of the academic curriculum. The lesson structures described in Part III of this book can be used as a jumping-off point for how different texts will be read. Texts, or parts of texts, that are relevant to an aspect of the academic curriculum can be used in lessons. Shorter texts might even be included in a booklet of additional texts that are used year after year (as we saw in Chapter 16). Beyond this, your school might consider using curriculum products for some subjects that include integrated texts. Alternatively, as part of your curriculum development, your subject leaders might write basic information texts to match the key content of each topic within an academic subject. Again, examples of what this might look like in primary science, history and geography can be found on my blog (Such, 2019b).

---------------------------------- This Chapter in a Nutshell ----------------------------------

- Pupils learn most of their vocabulary through words in context in spoken interactions and reading.
- The words in books tend to be considerably more varied and sophisticated than those found in speech. This means that arguably the most important contribution teachers make to pupils' vocabulary development is through ensuring the quality and quantity of pupils' reading experiences.
- Words that are particularly crucial to meaning in texts can be briefly described without overly interrupting the flow of reading. However, some words require greater focus and can be taught through careful explanation, active practice and retrieval.
- It might be worth prioritising words that are useful across the curriculum and less likely to be learned through pupils' everyday experiences.
- Sensitising pupils to the chunks of meaning within words can help pupils to remember words through the connections made to the rest of their vocabulary.
- The vocabulary to be introduced and retrieved in topics across the academic curriculum should be identified to support teachers in their planning.

---------------------------------- Further Reading ----------------------------------

- *Bringing Words to Life: Robust Vocabulary Instruction* (Beck et al., 2013)
- *Words in the Mind: An Introduction to the Mental Lexicon* (Aitchison, 2012)
- The Latin–Greek connection: Building vocabulary through morphological study (Rasinski et al., 2011)
- *The Art and Science of Teaching Primary Reading* (Such, 2021)

---------------------------------- Retrieval Quiz ----------------------------------

- What is meant by the terms 'vocabulary breadth' and 'vocabulary depth'?
- What are 'drop-in words'? And what words might particularly lend themselves to this sort of teaching?
- Identify the morphemes in the word 'untested'.

---------------------------------- Questions for Professional Discussions ----------------------------------

- When reading challenging texts with pupils, it is inevitable that some unfamiliar words will be left undiscussed by the teacher. What difficulties might be associated with this in terms of pupils' motivation? And how might these be minimised?

- What might be the advantages and disadvantages of including a discrete timetable slot for the teaching of vocabulary?
- To what extent is the vocabulary to be learned spelled out in your wider curriculum?

REFERENCES

Aitchison, J. (2012). *Words in the Mind: An Introduction to the Mental Lexicon*. John Wiley & Sons.

Beck, I. L., McKeown, M. G. & Kucan, L. (2013). *Bringing Words to Life: Robust Vocabulary Instruction*. Guilford Press.

Biemiller, A. (2010). *Words Worth Teaching: Closing the Vocabulary Gap*. McGraw-Hill SRA.

Cottingham, S. (2023). *Ausubel's Meaningful Learning in Action*. John Catt.

Cunningham, A. E. (2005). Vocabulary growth through independent reading and reading aloud to children. In E. H. Hiebert & M. L. Kamhi (Eds), *Teaching and Learning Vocabulary: Bringing Research to Practice* (pp. 45–68). Lawrence Erlbaum Associates.

Cunningham, A. E. & Stanovich, K. E. (1998). What reading does for the mind. *American Educator, 22*(1/2), 8–17.

Green, T. M. (2020). *The Greek & Latin Roots of English*. Rowman & Littlefield Publishers.

Korochkina, M., Marelli, M., Brysbaert, M. & Rastle, K. (2024). The Children and Young People's Books Lexicon (CYP-LEX): A large-scale lexical database of books read by children and young people in the United Kingdom. *Quarterly Journal of Experimental Psychology*. https://doi.org/10.1177/17470218241229694

McGuinness, D. (2006). *Early Reading Instruction: What Science Really Tells Us about How to Teach Reading*. MIT Press.

Nagy, W. E. & Scott, J. (2000). Vocabulary processes. In M. Kamil, P. Mosenthal, P. D. Pearson & R. Barr, R. (Eds), *Handbook of Reading Research* (Vol. 3), (pp. 269–284). Lawrence Erlbaum Associates.

Nation, K., Dawson, N. J. & Hsiao, Y. (2022). Book language and its implications for children's language, literacy, and development. *Current Directions in Psychological Science, 31*(4), 375–380.

National Reading Panel (2000). *Teaching Children to Read: An Evidence-Based Assessment of the Scientific Research Literature on Reading and Its Implications for Reading Instruction: Reports of the Subgroups*. National Institute of Child Health and Human Development, National Institutes of Health [in the US Department of Health and Human Services].

Ouellette, G. P. (2006). What's meaning got to do with it: The role of vocabulary in word reading and reading comprehension. *Journal of Educational Psychology, 98*(3), 554.

Quinn, J. M., Wagner, R. K., Petscher, Y. & Lopez, D. (2015). Developmental relations between vocabulary knowledge and reading comprehension: A latent change score modeling study. *Child development, 86*(1), 159–175.

Rasinski, T. V., Padak, N., Newton, J. & Newton, E. (2011). The Latin–Greek connection: Building vocabulary through morphological study. *The Reading Teacher, 65*(2), 133–141.

Seidenberg, M. (2017). *Language at the Speed of Sight: How We Read, Why So Many Can't, and What Can Be Done about It. Basic Books.*

Simonsmeier, B. A., Flaig, M., Deiglmayr, A., Schalk, L. & Schneider, M. (2022). Domain-specific prior knowledge and learning: A meta-analysis. *Educational Psychologist, 57*(1), 31–54.

Such, C. (2019a). Tier two vocabulary for primary teachers – the 3-4-5 list https://primarycolour.home.blog/2019/06/14/tier-two-vocabulary-for-primary-teachers-the-3-4-5-list

Such, C. (2019b). One-stop shop for @Suchmo83 resources https://primarycolour.home.blog/2019/11/02/one-stop-shop-for-suchmo83-resources

Such, C. (2021). *The Art and Science of Teaching Primary Reading.* Sage Corwin.

Willingham, D. T. (2017). *The Reading Mind: A Cognitive Approach to Understanding How the Mind Reads.* John Wiley & Sons.

Zimmerman, L. & Reed, D. K. (2017). Attributes of effective explicit vocabulary instruction. Blog. Iowa Reading Research Center. https://iowareadingresearch.org/blog/vocabulary-instruction-part-2

19
SUPPORTING READING THROUGH WRITING

HOW ARE READING AND WRITING LINKED?

Reading and writing are intimately connected and mutually supportive (Graham & Harris, 2017). Reading and related discussion, especially that which involves an author's choices, provides pupils with a better understanding of the craft of writing. And learning to write helps pupils to recognise how authors achieve their aims, enhancing their ability to analyse and appreciate texts.

In theory, it would be possible to integrate the teaching of reading and writing entirely rather than allocating each aspect of literacy its own discrete slot in the timetable. Or, in theory, reading and writing could both be integrated into the wider curriculum entirely so that all teaching of literacy took place in the context of science, history, geography, etc. However, attempts at such integration in practice often lead to the downplaying of key aspects of reading instruction, alongside less variety in the texts chosen for reading and fewer opportunities for pupils to become truly engrossed in books. In contrast, discrete reading and writing lessons tend to ensure all crucial aspects of instruction are addressed. The challenge then is to consider how to embed writing into reading lessons and vice versa, the subject of this chapter.

HOW MUCH WRITING SHOULD BE INCLUDED IN READING LESSONS (AND VICE VERSA)?

In most English schools, much more time is devoted to the teaching of writing than the teaching of reading, especially in year 3 and beyond. As we discussed in Chapter 10, this status quo means that in most schools it is wiser to embed more reading into writing lessons than the reverse.

Assuming a timetable includes approximately 30 minutes per day of reading lessons, there is no good reason for pupils in years 5 and 6 to spend more than 15 minutes *per week* writing multiple-sentence responses to questions in reading lessons. And such written responses are preferably avoided almost entirely for younger pupils whose precious reading lesson time is better spent developing fluency and building their experience with written texts. This is not to say pupils should not regularly write in response to text. They absolutely should. However, in the typical English primary school, this is mostly better achieved in writing lessons.

WHAT WAYS OF WRITING IN RESPONSE TO TEXT ARE MOST BENEFICIAL?

Some forms of writing in response to text appear to deepen comprehension. Graham & Hebert (2011) categorise these as the following:

- *Extended writing*: Lengthy responses based on pupils' own opinions and interpretations of a text, fostering reflection and personal involvement with a text.
- *Summary writing*: Shorter responses that encourage pupils to integrate ideas from a text and put them into their own words.
- *Note-taking*: Brief responses that encourage pupils to continually check their ongoing understanding of a text.
- *Answering and generating questions*: Responses that encourage pupils to make their thoughts explicit.

In short, we can support pupils to deepen their understanding of a text by asking them to express their own opinions, write about aspects of the text in their own words, take notes as a text progresses, answer questions and generate questions of their own.

WHAT PRINCIPLES UNDERPIN EFFECTIVE TEACHING OF SPELLING?

Beyond the obvious benefits for pupils' writing, teaching spelling supports pupils' ability to recognise words (Graham & Santangelo, 2014). Teaching spelling through application of knowledge of grapheme–phoneme correspondences (GPCs) is a fundamental part of initial reading instruction via systematic phonics (Department for Education, 2023). However, the nature of the English writing system means teaching spelling requires much more than this (Treiman, 2018).

Four principles underpin effective spelling instruction:

1   Build on pupils' knowledge of GPCs, understanding the complexities of these *and* parts of words where assigning phonemes to every letter is not productive (e.g. cupboard, Wednesday, Gloucester).

2   Teach pupils about the chunks of meaning within words (morphemes) and how these contribute to spelling (e.g. the reason why there are two 'ns' in 'unnatural'

and one 'n' in 'unfair' can be made salient by discussing how 'un' is a prefix in both words). This might include consideration of a word's history (i.e. etymology)

3   Teach pupils common spelling patterns (e.g. affixing patterns that explain the difference in the vowel sound represented by 'o' in 'hoped' and 'hopped'). This is not the same thing as asking pupils to use rules like 'i before e, except after c'.

4   Ensure pupils are regularly writing words as part of their spelling instruction (Cunningham & Stanovich, 1990).

Alongside these principles, it can be helpful to use a spelling voice for certain words (e.g. 'Wednesday' said as 'Wed-nez-day') and to ask pupils to focus on whichever part of a word they find most challenging (e.g. the spelling of the /ee/ sound in 'fiend'). It can also be beneficial to embed particularly useful vocabulary into spelling lessons. (See Chapter 18 for more on this.)

Moreover, there are common practices that are ineffective or even detrimental that should be avoided:

*   Avoid exposing pupils to inaccurate spellings (McGuinness, 2006). In the early stages of spelling development, pupils are likely sometimes to use their initial knowledge of GPCs to make plausible but inaccurate guesses at words. This does *not* mean teachers should ever model spelling words in this way. Activities that provide pupils with a mixture of accurate and inaccurate spellings to select from are also best avoided.

*   Avoid spelling activities that waste time by not getting pupils to think carefully about how words are spelled (e.g. wordsearches, bubble writing).

HOW CAN WE TEACH GRAMMAR AND PUNCTUATION IN A WAY THAT SUPPORTS READING?

Common conventions of grammar and punctuation are often taught merely as a set of technical rules pupils must follow, not least because of the existence of standardised tests that propagate this perspective. However, language is not defined by a list of unchanging rules. Instead, it is a tool for communication with conventions that exist because of agreement within a language community or at least significant parts of it. While this is a subtle idea, a crucial responsibility of teachers is to introduce pupils to this reality, rather than relying on the fiction of universal, unchanging rules.

One way to build this understanding is to discuss grammar and punctuation in terms of the meaning that can be conveyed through their use. After all, this is primarily why conventions come to exist in the first place. And the technical language that exists relating to language is useful because of how it helps us to discuss these conventions and the way grammar and punctuation impact meaning.

For example, teaching pupils about the concepts of 'subject' and 'verb' can seem arcane and pointless. But if we keep our focus on meaning, we see just how valuable these concepts are. We can discuss with pupils the fundamentals of how ideas are communicated in clauses such as 'the cat purred' or 'it disappeared'. Crucially, this sort of discussion of how grammar and punctuation impact meaning aligns with attempts to support pupils' comprehension of texts.

--------------------- This Chapter in a Nutshell ---------------------

- Reading and writing are connected and mutually supportive. Teaching one supports the development of the other.
- It is possible to integrate reading and writing into the same lesson entirely or even integrate both into every other curriculum subject. However, discrete reading and writing lessons tend to provide greater assurance that all crucial aspects of reading instruction are addressed.
- Reading should take place in writing lessons and writing should take place in reading lessons. The amount of each depends on how much time is dedicated to reading and writing in a school's timetable. In most English schools, less time is allocated to reading lessons, so it makes sense to keep lengthy written responses to texts in reading lessons to a maximum of 15 minutes per week for older pupils. Younger pupils may benefit from not writing lengthy responses to text in reading lessons at all.
- When pupils write in response to text, it is particularly worthwhile for them to express their own opinions, summarise aspects of text, take notes, answer questions and generate questions of their own.
- Teaching spelling should build on pupils' understanding from phonics and build pupils' knowledge of morphology, etymology and common spelling patterns.
- Punctuation and grammar should be taught to pupils primarily in terms of the meaning that different choices can convey.

--------------------- Further Reading ---------------------

- *Understanding and Teaching Primary English* (Clements & Tobin, 2021)
- *The Reading Framework* (Department for Education, 2023)
- *Teaching Elementary School Students to Be Effective Writers* (Graham et al., 2012)
- *The Writing Revolution* (Hochman & Wexler, 2017)

--------------------- Retrieval Quiz ---------------------

- What ways of responding to text in writing appear to be beneficial in deepening comprehension?
- What practices should be avoided in the teaching of spelling?
- How might we best frame the teaching of grammar and punctuation?

—————————— Questions for Professional Discussions ——————————

- In terms of the amount of time dedicated to it in your weekly timetable, what is the balance between reading and writing in your school? To what extent does this reflect a conscious decision based on the way these aspects of literacy support each other?
- Pupils are often asked to do a lot of writing while their spelling of many common words is still inaccurate. What might be the advantages and disadvantages of doing this?
- To what extent is the teaching of grammatical terminology (e.g. subject, verb, clause) embedded into the teaching of writing in your school? And is it commonly used to discuss how language can be manipulated to convey meaning?

REFERENCES

Clements, J. & Tobin, M. (2021). *Understanding and Teaching Primary English: Theory into Practice*. Sage.

Cunningham, A. E. & Stanovich, K. E. (1990). Early spelling acquisition: Writing beats the computer. *Journal of Educational Psychology, 82*, 159–162.

Department for Education (2023). *The Reading Framework*. https://assets.publishing.service.gov.uk/media/65830c10ed3c34000d3bfcad/The_reading_framework.pdf

Graham, S. & Harris, K. R. (2017). Reading and writing connections: How writing can build better readers (and vice versa). In C. Ng and B. Bartlett (Eds), *Improving Reading and Reading Engagement in the 21st Century. International Research and Innovation* (pp. 333–350). Springer.

Graham, S. & Hebert, M. (2011). Writing to read: A meta-analysis of the impact of writing and writing instruction on reading. *Harvard Educational Review, 81*(4), 710–744.

Graham, S. & Santangelo, T. (2014). Does spelling instruction make students better spellers, readers, and writers? A meta-analytic review. *Reading and Writing, 27*, 1703–1743.

Graham, S., Bollinger, A., Olson, C. B., D'Aoust, C., MacArthur, C., McCutchen, D. & Olinghouse, N. (2012). *Teaching Elementary School Students to Be Effective Writers*. National Center for Education Evaluation and Regional Assistance, Institute of Education Sciences.

Hochman, J. C. & Wexler, N. (2017). *The Writing Revolution: A Guide to Advancing Thinking through Writing in All Subjects and Grades*. John Wiley & Sons.

McGuinness, D. (2006). *Early Reading Instruction: What Science Really Tells Us about How to Teach Reading*. MIT Press.

Treiman, R. (2018). Teaching and learning spelling. *Child Development Perspectives, 12*(4), 235–239.

20

PREPARING PUPILS FOR EXTERNAL ASSESSMENTS

WHAT PROBLEMS HAVE BEEN CAUSED BY EXTERNAL ASSESSMENTS AND ACCOUNTABILITY PRESSURES?

As discussed in Chapter 2, it is a sad reality across many English schools that the existence of external assessments – such as the National Curriculum assessments, usually called SATs – has indirectly undermined the teaching of reading. If such assessments didn't exist, it is hard to imagine any teacher would think it a good idea to conceptualise reading comprehension almost entirely as the ability to answer a limited set of question types. However, beneath the looming presence of these accountability measures, many primary schools – guided by companies selling specious solutions – reverse-engineered their reading lessons to follow the surface structure of National Curriculum assessments. This resulted in reading lessons that didn't involve much reading, with predictable consequences for pupils' attainment and motivation. I suspect this is why national improvements in initial decoding have not yet translated into a significant increase in subsequent reading capabilities: learning the basics of decoding is of little use if you do not then read enough in lessons to become fluent and develop your knowledge of written English.

None of the above necessarily means external assessments are a bad thing under all circumstances although we should perhaps be unsurprised that an accountability metric distorted the very thing it sought to measure (Muller, 2018). As educators, we need to be wary of assuming that the structure of any assessment is an accurate reflection of the underlying capability being measured by that assessment. In other words, we shouldn't decide how to teach pupils based on how assessments are organised. This is especially true of complex, unconstrained capabilities like reading comprehension.

HOW SHOULD WE PREPARE PUPILS FOR EXTERNAL COMPREHENSION ASSESSMENTS?

External comprehension assessments exist, and almost all of our pupils will be required to take them at some point. Part of our responsibility as teachers is to ensure our pupils can feel confident in such situations. This means we need to dedicate a proportionate amount of time to this goal. In the case of the National Curriculum assessments taken towards the end of year 6 in English schools, there are a few things that you can do to support pupils:

- In the weeks before the National Curriculum assessments, help pupils to understand the different question formats that are likely to appear (e.g. multiple-choice, ordering events, questions that require justification using details from the text). A little bit of modelling, guided practice and independent practice goes a long way.
- In close reading lessons across years 5 and 6, very occasionally introduce pupils to the sorts of questions they will encounter in the National Curriculum assessments. This should *not* become a central focus of teaching, but it can be a way to gently prepare pupils for the assessment without taking their attention away from the text they are studying.
- Intentionally build pupils' reading 'stamina' through the incrementally increasing expectations for independent reading in extended reading lessons (see Chapter 9). The value of this goes far beyond supporting pupils to feel confident in assessments, but it does also help with this goal.
- Build test strategy habits. This means teaching pupils to:
  - Read the question carefully
  - Underline components of the question they might forget to follow (e.g. how many answers need to be selected)
  - Take a sensible guess where possible
  - Circle question numbers for tricky questions to come back to later, rather than getting stuck and spending too much time on them.
- Familiarise pupils with the way the assessment is presented and the expectations of the assessment in terms of pace by doing a few past papers.

From my experience as a year 6 teacher, I would estimate that around 5% of a pupil's score comes down to the extent to which they have been prepared for the structure of the reading comprehension assessment. The other 95% of their score comes down to their reading fluency and their knowledge of written English and the world it describes, which we develop through the meaningful teaching of reading. It would be both counterproductive and ethically dubious to spend countless hours explicitly preparing primary pupils for external assessments.

HOW SHOULD WE PREPARE PUPILS FOR THE PHONICS SCREENING CHECK IN YEAR 1?

Pupils should undertake almost no preparation for the phonics screening check. In the week before the check, it might be helpful to briefly introduce pupils to the idea of 'alien' words (i.e. pseudo-words like 'vip' and 'flom'). However, undertaking extensive teaching using pseudo-words is a poor use of instructional time that should be used instead to learn about real words (Shanahan, 2016).

This Chapter in a Nutshell

- Pupils should feel confident and prepared when taking external reading assessments. This means schools should spend a proportionate amount of time preparing pupils for them.
- Pupils can be introduced to the structure and question formats of assessments alongside test strategy habits.
- The most important support pupils can be given to succeed in external reading assessments is meaningful reading instruction that develops reading fluency and builds their knowledge of written English and the world to which it relates.
- Do not spend a lot of time preparing pupils for the phonics screening check. Pupils' learning in phonics should be focused on real words.

Further Reading

- *The Reading Framework* (Department for Education, 2023)

Retrieval Quiz

- Which reading lesson structure might best allow for occasional use of question formats that match the National Curriculum assessment?
- How might we support a pupil not to overlook important aspects of a question in an assessment?
- How might we support a pupil not to lose a lot of time on a single tricky question in an assessment?

———————— Questions for Professional Discussions ————————

- To what extent has the teaching of comprehension in your school been warped by the perceived need to prepare pupils for external assessments?
- How much time is spent in your school on familiarising pupils with the structure of external reading assessments? To what extent is this done for the direct benefit of the pupils in question?
- Imagine external assessments were phased out. Do you think this would change the teaching of reading in your school? If so, in what ways?

REFERENCES

Department for Education (2023). *The Reading Framework*. https://assets.publishing. service.gov.uk/media/65830c10ed3c34000d3bfcad/The_reading_framework.pdf

Muller, J. (2018). *The Tyranny of Metrics*. Princeton University Press.

Shanahan, T. (2016). What doesn't belong here? On teaching nonsense words. www. shanahanonliteracy.com/blog/what-doesnt-belong-here-on-teaching-nonsense-words

PART VII

ASSESSING AND SUPPORTING PUPILS

21

IDENTIFYING AND ADDRESSING BARRIERS TO READING DEVELOPMENT

WHY DO SOME PUPILS FIND IT MORE DIFFICULT TO LEARN TO READ THAN THEIR PEERS?

It is an undeniable reality of education that learning to read is more difficult for some pupils than others. The reasons behind this are complex. While our genes do not determine our learning outcomes, our unique neurobiology can increase or decrease the challenge we experience in learning to read (Little & Hart, 2022; Yeatman, 2022). This does not mean reading difficulties have a simple explanation. Pupils can struggle more than others to learn to read due to persistent absence, undiagnosed medical issues and issues beyond the classroom that impact their ability to learn. Crucially, inadequate instruction is another reason why pupils may struggle. We must ensure classroom teaching is effective, not least because this reduces the number of pupils needing support through intervention, allowing us to focus more attention on those who need it most.

HOW CAN WE BEST SUPPORT PUPILS EXPERIENCING DIFFICULTIES IN LEARNING TO READ?

Support for struggling readers begins with identification of their barriers to reading development. Primarily, this involves teachers informally assessing pupils as an ongoing part of phonics and fluency teaching and providing timely help. This might mean in-the-moment scaffolding, extra time in the school week to help pupils 'keep up' with the class or interventions designed to help pupils 'catch up'.

It is worth reiterating that the pace of learning for a class is an arbitrary standard that may not align well with the present capabilities of some pupils. While the unavoidable constraint of teaching pupils in large groups means we should support as many pupils as possible to 'keep up' or 'catch up', we should bear in mind that some pupils will learn at rates that are considerably different to most of their peers. It is right to offer greater support to those who find learning to read more difficult, but we should not prevent any pupils from accessing large swathes of the rest of the curriculum in our understandable haste to 'catch them up' to their peers. This is especially true in the earliest stages of education where pupils' spoken language, physical development and personal, social and emotional development are the priority. A reasonable guideline is that interventions might be used to double the amount of time struggling pupils focus on reading, but more time than that is likely to have diminishing returns and potentially even negative consequences for pupils' experiences of school.

At any one time, a pupil might have barriers that relate to multiple aspects of reading. For example, a pupil might appear to have little prior knowledge relevant to the texts read in class. They might have apparent difficulty with reading fluency or difficulty decoding individual words. In this situation, it can be hard to know what support to prioritise. The short answer to this question is that we should target the most foundational aspect of a struggling pupil's reading development, something that will be described in more detail below.

HOW CAN WE IDENTIFY WHICH PUPILS REQUIRE SUPPORT AND WHICH READING BARRIERS TO TARGET?

There is a bewildering array of assessments that might be used to identify pupils' reading barriers. In the hands of a special educational needs and disabilities coordinator (SENDCo), these assessments can be employed to identify bespoke support for the minority of pupils who require it. However, beyond this, what is required is a systematic approach to assessment that can be employed with all pupils. One way to achieve this is to use a combination of a phonics assessment (i.e. a decoding assessment), an oral reading fluency assessment and a comprehension assessment.

In reception and year 1, assessment and intervention focus on pupils' decoding development – something undertaken as a consistent part of classroom instruction – and their spoken language development – something informally observed by teachers with additional help from the school's SENDCo where required.

In year 2 and beyond, the systematic approach to assessment I advocate involves termly oral reading fluency assessments and standardised comprehension assessments used as a starting point, alongside a decoding assessment for those identified as relatively dysfluent by the oral reading fluency assessment (see Figure 21.1).

HOW DOES A DECODING ASSESSMENT WORK?

Decoding assessments work by giving pupils isolated words to decode. Ideally, they should include pseudo-words (i.e. words that don't exist) so that a pupil's ability to use grapheme–phoneme correspondences (GPCs) in unfamiliar words can be assessed. A decoding assessment is likely to be included in your school's phonics programme. If not, previous phonics screening checks (Department for Education, 2023) can be used to get a sense of the following:

1   A pupil's knowledge of GPCs
2   A pupil's ability to blend
3   A pupil's ability to decode polysyllabic words.

To differentiate between (1) and (2), the pupil can be asked to 'sound out' words they are unable to decode (i.e. say the individual phonemes represented by the graphemes before attempting to blend them together). This will show whether the pupil recognises common GPCs or not. To confirm whether a pupil has a specific difficulty with blending, the relevant phonemes of words that cannot be decoded can be said aloud by the teacher for the pupil to try to blend. From this information, pupils can be provided with the most appropriate support (see Figure 21.1).

HOW DOES AN ORAL READING FLUENCY ASSESSMENT WORK?

An oral reading fluency assessment usually involves a teacher hearing a pupil read aloud for a short period from an age-appropriate text and from that calculating their accuracy and reading rate (words correct per minute). Where pupils get stuck on a word, they should be told the word after a couple of seconds. A subjective assessment of whether the pupil is able to read with prosody can also be made. As a general rule, once pupils are reading at more than 100 words correct per minute with prosody (i.e. their reading sounds close to their natural spoken voice), they can be considered fluent enough for their fluency to no longer require assessing. Assessment materials, including oral reading fluency assessments, can be found on the University of Oregon's website (University of Oregon, n.d.). The texts used in these oral reading fluency assessments contain American English spellings, so – although I have never encountered issues while using the texts in their original form – it might be worth translating them into British English. Alternatively, any age-appropriate text can be used.

Oral reading fluency assessments provide helpful information when used alongside approximations of pupils' oral reading fluency at different ages (see Table 21.1). However, the information is only ever a rough guide to support decision-making. As with any assessment, teachers should not place too much emphasis on any single result, not least because pupils tend to score a bit higher or lower depending on the text being used. Also, because the difficulty of texts increases as pupils age, a relatively stable score across two assessments isn't necessarily an indicator that no progress has been made. What matters is that such assessments give a quick overview of which pupils' reading fluency is approximately on track and which pupils might benefit from further support. In the process, any pupils who struggle to accurately decode words can then be assessed using a decoding assessment.

There is no reason why a pupil undertaking an oral reading fluency assessment should be made aware that their reading fluency is being assessed. Teachers should ensure that any annotating of incorrect words is done out of the pupil's sight. Otherwise, the pupil can become distracted, undermining the assessment. An oral reading fluency assessment should be experienced by a pupil as nothing more than a brief spell of reading aloud to a teacher.

Oral reading fluency assessments provide useful information on the reading capabilities of most pupils. However, there are pupils for whom such assessments are ill-suited. For example, oral reading fluency assessments will not provide useful information about pupils with significant speech dysfluency (sometimes known as stuttering or stammering) or pupils who communicate in speech less readily or not at all. As with any use of assessment, oral reading fluency assessments should only be used when they are likely to provide useful information or when they will not cause distress to the pupil in question.

Table 21.1, which shows approximations for pupils' oral reading fluency for different ages, is created from aggregated data from English schools provided by Fischer Family Trust from its Reading Assessment Programme (Fischer Family Trust, 2024). There are no guarantees this data is exactly representative of oral reading fluency across all English schools, but it is a data set based on hundreds of thousands of oral reading fluency assessments. Pupils scoring below the score for the 25th percentile for their year group for oral reading fluency are prime candidates for a fluency intervention or, if decoding is an issue, a decoding intervention.

Table 21.1   Oral reading fluency data collected by Fischer Family Trust (2024)

	Percentile	Autumn term WCPM	Spring term WCPM	Summer term WCPM
Year 2	75	77	88	98
	50	**45**	**60**	**73**
	25	18	30	45
Year 3	75	101	113	116
	50	**68**	**84**	**91**
	25	39	50	62

	Percentile	Autumn term WCPM	Spring term WCPM	Summer term WCPM
Year 4	75	118	123	127
	50	**88**	**97**	**101**
	25	60	65	73
Year 5	75	124	129	133
	50	**102**	**108**	**111**
	25	71	80	83
Year 6	75	139	140	144
	50	**108**	**111**	**114**
	25	79	83	87

WPCM – words correct per minute

For those working in an American context, similar approximations for pupils' oral reading fluency for different ages can be found via Hasbrouck & Tindal's (2017) freely available paper on the subject.

HOW DOES A STANDARDISED COMPREHENSION ASSESSMENT WORK?

Standardised comprehension assessments work by providing pupils with texts to read and questions to answer based on their understanding of these texts. Because such assessments are standardised using data from many pupils, the achieved score can be associated with a particular reading capability relative to the age of the pupil who has taken the assessment. This score can be shown as a number between 50 and 150, with 100 indicating that a pupil achieved an average score. The score can also be shown as a 'reading age', where the pupil's current reading ability is estimated using the average scores of different ages as a benchmark.

It is important to bear in mind that comprehension assessments are an imprecise measure of a pupil's current reading ability, not least because a pupil's background knowledge relating to the content in the texts can affect their score. However, multiple assessments over a longer period can provide some useful information to a pupil's teacher and their parents/carers. On its own, a comprehension assessment is of very little diagnostic value for an individual pupil, offering as it does only a vague overview of their reading capability. However, when coupled with other assessments, a comprehension assessment can occasionally reveal the rare instances of pupils whose comprehension is surprisingly weak despite relatively strong reading fluency. These pupils often benefit from support that guides them towards the active 'detective work' they need to undertake to deal with tricky texts (see Figure 21.1). As ever, classroom teachers should seek advice from their school's SENDCo when a pupil displays unusual difficulties with an aspect of learning.

HOW CAN WE IDENTIFY THE INTERVENTIONS THAT ARE LIKELY TO BE MOST BENEFICIAL FOR PUPILS USING THESE ASSESSMENTS?

Figure 21.1 shows how a combination of an oral fluency assessment, a standardised comprehension assessment and a decoding assessment can be used to identify the most appropriate reading interventions for pupils.

Let's consider some example pupils to see how this flow diagram might be used in practice.

Pupil A is a boy in the spring term of year 3. His most recent comprehension score is somewhat below average, giving him a reading age about a year less than his actual age. His oral reading rate is 38 words correct per minute, significantly below the 25th percentile according to the table of oral reading fluency approximations. A follow-up decoding assessment suggests that his knowledge of GPCs is adequate, but he struggles to blend adjacent consonants in words. A quick check of his score in the phonics screening check, undertaken at his previous school, suggests he scraped a 'pass' mark of 32 out of 40 and was not considered in need of further support on this basis. As a result of this assessment, Pupil A is added to an intervention group that focuses on blending and segmenting across the range of GPCs taught in the school's phonics programme. As with the other pupils in this intervention, his progress in blending words will be monitored. He is also added to the list of 'vulnerable readers' who are heard reading aloud at least once a week.

Pupil B is a girl in the autumn term of year 5. Her most recent reading comprehension score is about average despite her significantly above-average speaking and listening capabilities (according to her class teacher). The oral reading fluency assessment seems to suggest few if any issues with decoding individual words accurately, which is unsurprising as three years ago she scored 38 out of 40 on the phonics screening check. However, her oral reading rate is 67 words correct per minute, just slightly below the 25th percentile according to the table of oral reading fluency approximations. A follow-up decoding check confirms that Pupil B has no obvious issues with decoding, but her reading fluency is likely holding back her comprehension. She is added to an intervention group that undertakes extra fluency reading twice a week, and her progress is monitored.

Pupil C is a boy in the summer term of year 6. Like most of this class, he hasn't undertaken an oral reading fluency assessment in the last two terms as the strength of this aspect of his reading is immediately evident. However, his most recent comprehension assessments both showed scores significantly below average. He was assessed for developmental language disorder by the SENDCo when he was in year 2, but his spoken language capabilities have developed considerably since then. There is no reason to suspect that his linguistic knowledge or knowledge of the world are impediments to his ability to comprehend texts. Based on this information, Pupil C is given extra support in the classroom to encourage him to undertake the 'detective work' required to resolve

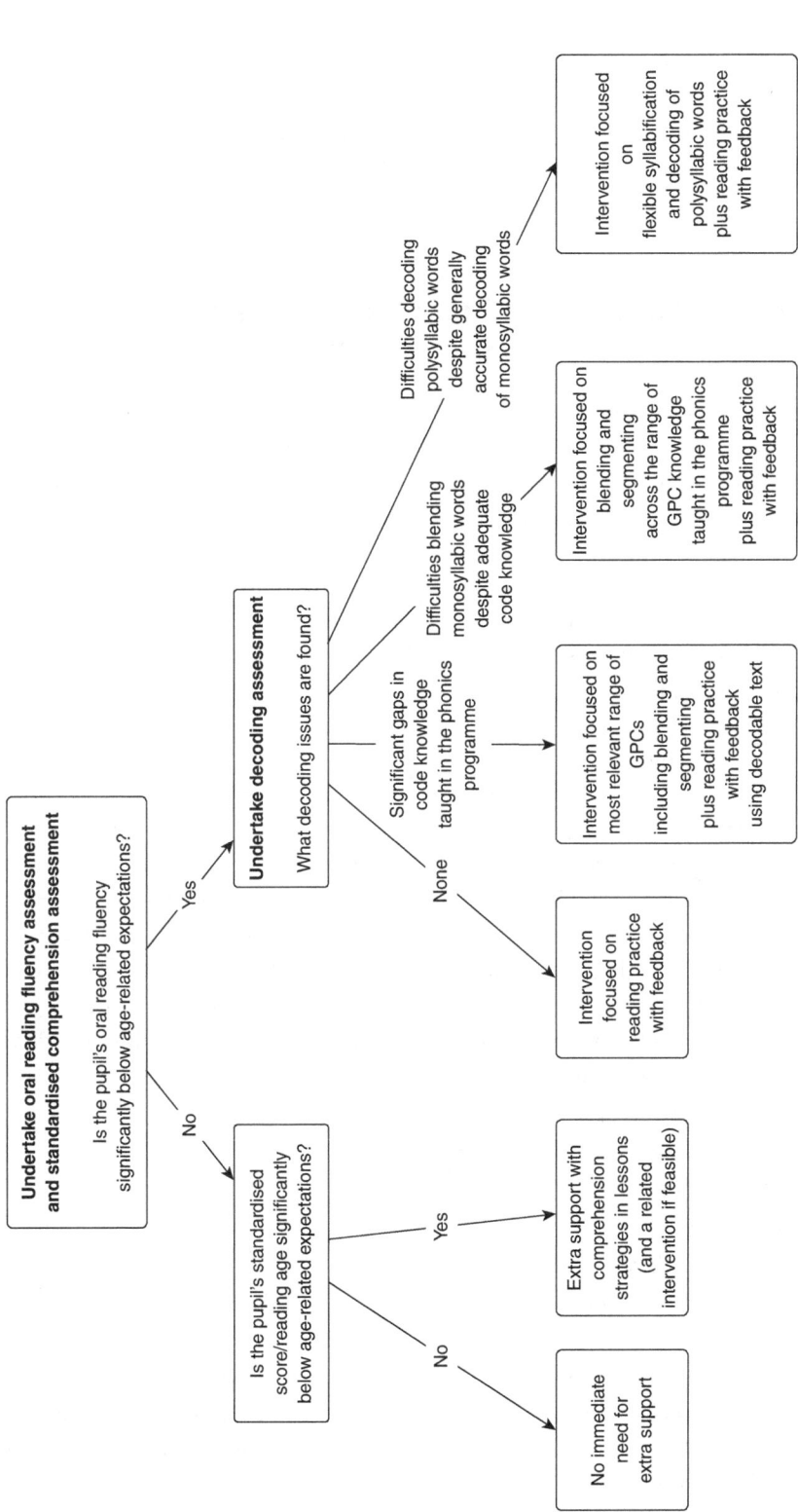

Figure 21.1 Assessment and intervention flow diagram

ambiguities in challenging texts. His parents, who are keen to support, are asked to encourage him to summarise bits of texts after he has read them aloud and to identify passages that are worth re-reading because of the challenge they provide. He finds this increasingly easy as his teacher has taken extra time to model this in the classroom and gives pupils occasional opportunities to practise these comprehension strategies.

WHAT MIGHT DECODING INTERVENTIONS LOOK LIKE?

The range of decoding interventions your school offers will depend on what is logistically feasible. At a bare minimum, pupils with significant decoding difficulties should be taught using the routines and structures of your school's phonics programme. Ideally, however, pupils should receive more targeted support:

- Pupils with significant gaps in the GPC knowledge taught in the school's phonics programme should be taught this alongside blending and segmenting. Where possible, different groups will target different GPC knowledge (e.g. one group might focus on the most basic GPCs of the first year of the phonics programme while another group moves more quickly through the GPCs of the second year of the phonics programme).
- Pupils with adequate GPC knowledge but significant difficulties with blending should practise blending and segmenting words across the range of GPC knowledge in the school's phonics programme. In particular, adjacent consonants (consonant clusters) should be targeted. This might involve one-to-one practice in reading a range of decodable texts with modelling and practice of blending where the pupil struggles and subsequent spelling of these words. Alternatively, if working with a group, words with adjacent consonant clusters can be systematically targeted. For example, pupils might practise decoding words with specific consonant clusters:
  - crack, crush, crisp
  - tusk, flask, whisk
  - ramp, stump, limp
  - plan, plucky, plot

  After decoding these in sets (blocked practice) to build confidence with explicit modelling and guided practice, the pupils can then decode and spell these words in a jumbled order (interleaved practice).
- Extra scaffolding for blending can be provided through progressive blending of words by elongating sounds that allow this (e.g. 'mmmiiilllk' → 'milk') (Gonzalez-Frey & Ehri, 2021). Where pupils have extreme struggles with blending, it can be useful to begin practice with simple words where all the sounds can be elongated (e.g. 'slam' → 'sssllllaaammm'). It can also be helpful to incrementally reveal

graphemes, blending each time, making sure to reveal letters together if they are part of the same grapheme (e.g. chomp: 'ch' → 'cho' → 'chom'→'chomp'). This is best thought of as a scaffold to the usual step-by-step decoding used in your school's phonics programme.

- Pupils who struggle specifically with decoding polysyllabic words can be taught to flexibly syllabify words (i.e. break words into syllables), starting with compound words where syllabification is relatively straightforward (e.g. football, toothbrush, cupcake) and moving onto words where syllabification is less clear cut (e.g. market, praising, overdue). Once a word is seen as a set of syllables, pupils should be taught to decode each syllable and then reconstitute the word. Pupils should be encouraged to do this flexibly, rather than following a rigid set of rules (Bhattacharya & Ehri, 2004; Shanahan, 2021). For example, if a pupil divides 'overdue' into 'over-due' (i.e. not fully syllabified) because they can decode 'over' easily, then that is fine. The aim is to give pupils tools to deal with polysyllabic words that they can use with increasing automaticity and flexibility, not to enforce a strict procedure that they must follow. Helping pupils to recognise the boundaries between morphemes, as is the case with 'overdue' being divided into 'over-due', can be useful too.

All teaching of decoding should emphasise the meaning of the words being decoded. It is also a good idea to finish any decoding intervention with some shared reading and discussion of text. Even when pupils are working on a particular aspect of reading, it is worth reminding them that the end goal is making meaning from texts.

WHAT MIGHT FLUENCY INTERVENTIONS LOOK LIKE?

The ideal fluency intervention is one-to-one reading of the sort described in Chapter 22 (i.e. with modelling and feedback). However, it is usually more efficient to undertake fluency interventions with small groups of pupils (between two and six pupils is a sensible group size). In this case, the intervention can run in the same manner as a whole-class fluency reading lesson. In the transition between modelling and paired reading, it can be beneficial to build confidence through sentence-by-sentence echo reading (i.e. the teacher reads a sentence followed by the pupils).

WHAT MIGHT COMPREHENSION STRATEGY INTERVENTIONS LOOK LIKE?

In most cases, pupils can be supported to use comprehension strategies through extended reading and close reading in whole-class reading lessons. Occasionally, however, a pupil or a small group of pupils might benefit from brief support with comprehension strategies in an intervention. This involves engaging pupils in either an extended reading or close reading lesson but with much greater focus on asking pupils to re-read, summarise and create pertinent questions relating to challenging bits of text.

Pupils who are relatively fluent readers can regularly struggle with reading comprehension if they lack background knowledge, vocabulary, knowledge of sentence structure and knowledge of text structure relevant to the texts they are reading. It is tempting, thus, to think that this should be addressed in an intervention. However, these aspects of comprehension can and should be addressed in everyday teaching. The resources required to run such interventions are almost certainly better dedicated to supporting pupils who struggle to decode or read fluently.

ARE THESE THE ONLY WAYS TO UNDERTAKE DECODING, FLUENCY OR COMPREHENSION STRATEGY INTERVENTIONS?

The forms of intervention described above are merely examples of reasonable ways to tackle pupils' potential barriers to reading development. As long as an intervention is designed to target one of these barriers and is delivered in a way that provides modelling and practice, it is likely to be equally effective as the examples given above.

HOW CAN WE ADAPT INTERVENTIONS TO MEET THE NEEDS OF ALL PUPILS?

Naturally, not all pupils will be able to easily 'keep up' or 'catch up' with their peers through extra support (i.e. interventions). These pupils will benefit most from sensitive, persistent support that takes account of extra challenges to their motivation and self-efficacy. There is no single 'correct' way to achieve this because it will be specific to the needs of the pupil in question. However, here are some adaptations that can be used to support the learning of struggling pupils:

- *Alter the teacher–pupil ratio.* Small-group interventions are generally a more efficient use of time and should be the default, but some pupils will require one-to-one support.
- *Alter the length and frequency of intervention sessions.*
- *Alter the amount of modelling by adults.* Struggling pupils often require significantly more modelling of decoding than is seen in most phonics lessons, for example.

It is essential that the impact of interventions is evaluated to allow for the sort of adaptations described above and, potentially, for more appropriate interventions to be chosen. Such evaluation should involve assessment of the component of reading addressed in the intervention. It makes sense to use the same sort of assessment that was used to recognise the barrier to reading development in the first place. For example, if a pupil were assigned to a phonics intervention because a decoding assessment suggested they lacked basic alphabetic code knowledge, then a similar decoding assessment should be used to see if progress has been made in acquiring this knowledge. Equally, the impact of a reading fluency intervention is likely to be best evaluated using an oral reading fluency assessment. However, be cautious in assuming that slow progress means a pupil needs something completely different. If you have used assessment to identify the pupil's barrier to reading, be confident that attempting to directly address this barrier is the best way forward. Instead of automatically changing tack, consider how the intervention might be adapted in the three ways described above.

Providing small-group or one-to-one interventions for pupils requires the use of scarce resources and a timetable that allows for such support, something that inevitably reduces pupils' access to other aspects of the curriculum. This is a decision that should never be taken lightly. However, there are few priorities quite as pressing as ensuring pupils secure the foundations of literacy, so this is an area where compromises are necessary.

HOW CAN WE BEST SUPPORT PUPILS WITH DYSLEXIA AND OTHER READING-RELATED SPECIAL EDUCATIONAL NEEDS AND/OR DISABILITIES (SEND)?

There is no universally accepted definition of dyslexia. However, it is widely accepted by those who study dyslexia that it is characterised by difficulties with word recognition and spelling that are neurobiological in origin (Wagner et al., 2022). To be precise, dyslexia relating to initial reading development is **developmental dyslexia**. Dyslexia that results from damage to the brain is **acquired dyslexia**. When educators discuss dyslexia, it is almost always developmental dyslexia to which they are referring, so I will use 'dyslexia' as shorthand for 'developmental dyslexia' for the remainder of this chapter. Difficulties with word recognition and spelling that can be accounted for by environmental causes such as inadequate instruction, absence from school, etc. are not considered to be indicative of dyslexia.

There is no single cause of dyslexia. As Wolf (2007, p. 324) states, there is 'no one form of dyslexia; instead there is a continuum of developmental reading disabilities'. In other words, many interconnected capabilities are coordinated in learning to read, and weaknesses in any one of these can be considered as a risk factor for dyslexia. Phonological difficulties (i.e. difficulties in recognising and manipulating speech sounds) are commonly associated with dyslexia (Kilpatrick & O'Brien, 2019).

Despite common perceptions, decades of research investigating links between visual processing and dyslexia have found nothing conclusive (Fletcher et al., 2018; Vellutino et al., 2004). Those with dyslexia are more likely to have spoken language disorders

(Seidenberg, 2017), attention-deficit hyperactivity disorder, maths impairments and relative weaknesses in aspects of executive function such as working memory (Farah et al., 2021; Wagner et al., 2022). However, it is important not to make assumptions about individual pupils based on such correlations. For example, advice is sometimes offered to teachers that *all* dyslexic pupils should sit at the front of the class because these pupils will inevitably have issues with attention. Such advice is bogus, as is any attempt to suggest that a pupil will inevitably align with the generalisations of a specific label. A fundamental principle of supporting pupils with difficulties in any area of learning is to identify and support them based on their individual barriers to progress (Education Endowment Foundation, 2021).

Weaknesses in any area of reading can cause pupils to struggle with the ultimate goal of reading, comprehension of texts. The following principle should be adhered to for all pupils with any form of reading difficulty, regardless of whether this difficulty forms part of a defined special educational need or disability: through robust assessment, identify the pupil's individual barriers to reading development, and then provide teaching that targets the highest-priority barrier(s). In other words, there is no *qualitative* difference between the methods of instruction required for those with recognisable reading difficulties and their peers. There is, however, a *quantitative* difference: some pupils are likely to need significantly more time and practice than others, often to an extent that requires small-group support or even one-to-one support. As with any area of learning where a pupil struggles more than their peers, teachers should also be sensitive to the potential impact this can have on the pupil's motivation and self-efficacy.

HOW MIGHT WE SUPPORT PUPILS WITH SPECIAL EDUCATIONAL NEEDS AND/OR DISABILITIES RELATING TO SPOKEN LANGUAGE?

Speech, language and communication needs (SLCN) is the umbrella term for areas of special educational needs and disabilities directly related to literacy (I CAN, 2021). SLCN include speech dysfluency, hearing impairments, selective mutism and language disorders.

Language disorders are one category of SLCN that are especially relevant to reading development (I CAN, 2021). They are defined as lifelong difficulties related to comprehending and/or producing spoken language. Where these difficulties are not linked to a specific biomedical condition (such as autism), genetic condition (such as Down's syndrome) or intellectual disability, this is called developmental language disorder (DLD).

Spoken language difficulties such as DLD show themselves in a wide variety of ways (I CAN, 2021). Most obviously, such difficulties can be observed in pupils' own speech. They might struggle to formulate their thoughts into words or use immature language for their age. They might struggle to retrieve sounds from memory or pronounce specific sounds. Or they might use words in an unpredictable order. Equally, spoken language difficulties can manifest in pupils' understanding of spoken language, in other aspects of literacy and in their social behaviour more generally.

Not every instance in which a pupil struggles with an aspect of spoken language is a result of significant, ongoing difficulties with spoken language development. Some pupils will overcome such issues through brief, targeted support in the classroom. However, other pupils might need support beyond the classroom. Evidence suggests that early interventions relating to spoken language can be effective in supporting pupils' spoken language skills and decoding (Sibieta et al., 2016). And frameworks such as those from the Communication Trust (2007) can help teachers and leaders to identify which difficulties might be addressed within the classroom and which difficulties require further support. (While the Communication Trust no longer exists, useful resources it created can still be found online.) Classroom teachers and school leaders should always seek the expert advice of the school's SENDCo who can, where appropriate, seek further support from external agencies.

HOW MIGHT WE SUPPORT PUPILS WITH HEARING IMPAIRMENTS?

Although reading outcomes vary widely among children with significant long-term hearing impairments, on average these pupils are at higher risk of reading difficulties (and other literacy difficulties) than their peers with unimpaired hearing (Adlof et al., 2022). This is unsurprising given the centrality of the representation of sound in the English writing system. The most crucial protective factors for pupils with a hearing impairment are exposure to language (e.g. through management of hearing loss or access to sign language), evidence-informed reading instruction and interventions relating to spoken language and aspects of reading where necessary, based on observed barriers to reading development.

Temporary hearing loss can also make learning to read more difficult and can affect a pupil's spoken language development. Teachers and school leaders should be aware of signs of otitis media with effusions (commonly called 'glue ear') in their pupils, especially during the early stages of learning to decode (National Health Service, 2023). This condition can result in pupils experiencing hearing loss in one or both ears, earache, tinnitus and/or problems with balance. Otitis media with effusions is usually temporary, lasting around three months, but pupils' parents/carers should still be advised to contact their doctor immediately if their child displays any of these symptoms. While a pupil has this condition, classroom adaptations should be considered, such as sitting the affected pupil closer to the teacher.

As with all other forms of special education needs and disabilities, where hearing impairments provide barriers to learning, collaboration with the school's SENDCo is essential to ensure the pupil's needs are met and, where necessary, support from external specialists can be sought.

WHAT DATA SHOULD BE TRACKED BY TEACHERS AND LEADERS RESPONSIBLE FOR READING ACROSS A SCHOOL?

All data collection and analysis should have a clearly defined purpose and should be minimised wherever possible. The reasons to gather data relating to pupils' reading are as follows:

- *To inform classroom teaching or interventions.* Information about the needs of a class can be garnered from assessment data. For example, a year 5 class might need considerably more support with fluency development than previous cohorts, something shown by analysing their fluency assessment data. Equally, an individual pupil's barriers to reading development can be assessed, as described above. Tracking this data allows teachers to recognise what progress has been made, what support appeared to work and what further support might be needed.
- *To assess the impact of teaching approaches.* Changes made to teaching approaches rarely show immediate results. In the short term, there is too much 'noise' in the data to reliably see the impact of changes. Over the long term, however, patterns within data can provide some insight. For example, over several years, tracked data might hint at the impact of a change of phonics programme.
- *To inform parents/carers of their child's progress.* Parents/carers are usually keen to understand their child's reading development. Information gathered from assessments over time can be sensitively used to help pupils' families understand the progress being made and the support they might offer.

An example of the data that might be usefully tracked is shown in Table 21.2.

Table 21.2 Example of tracked reading assessment data

Name	Year group	Knowledge of GPCs taught in the phonics programme	Phonics screening check score (most recent)	Fluency (words correct per minute)	Fluency (prosody)	Reading age
Pupil A	Reception	On track	N/A	N/A	x	N/A
Pupil B	1	Receiving support	N/A	N/A	x	N/A
Pupil C	2	✓	38/40	68	x	8y 1m
Pupil D	3	Receiving support	24/40	15	x	N/A
Pupil E	4	✓	35/40	75	x	7y 4m
Pupil F	5	✓	36/40	114	✓	9y 5m

In reception and year 1, more detailed results from ongoing phonics assessments might also be tracked by classroom teachers to inform 'keep up' or 'catch up' interventions.

Beyond data relating to decoding, fluency and comprehension, the only other information that might be worth gathering relates to a pupil's relationship to reading, specifically useful information about their reading preferences, motivation and contributions to classroom discussions about texts. However, it is not essential that this information is tracked, as long as it is available to teachers when they begin teaching an unfamiliar class of pupils.

This Chapter in a Nutshell

- Some pupils find it significantly more difficult to learn to read than their peers.
- Every school should implement a systematic approach to assessment and interventions that addresses barriers to reading development. One way to do this involves the use of oral reading fluency assessments and standardised comprehension assessments alongside a decoding assessment.
- In terms of interventions that directly address aspects of reading, supporting pupils with decoding and reading fluency issues should be the priority.
- Interventions can be adapted to pupils' needs by:
  - Altering the teacher–pupil ratio
  - Altering the length and frequency of the sessions
  - Altering the amount of modelling by the adult running the intervention.
- Pupils with special educational needs and/or disabilities – such as dyslexia, spoken language difficulties or hearing impairments – should be supported on the basis of their individual barriers to learning. Collaboration with the school's SENDCo is essential.
- Minimise the collection and analysis of data. Only track data that is useful for informing classroom teaching/interventions, assessing the impact of teaching approaches or informing parents/carers about their child's progress. As a general rule, data relating to decoding, fluency and comprehension fulfil this remit.

Further Reading

- *Special Educational Needs in Mainstream Schools: Guidance Report* (Education Endowment Foundation, 2021).
- *Teacher Handbook: SEND* (NASEN, 2024)
- *Universally Speaking* (Communication Trust, 2007)
- National Deaf Children's Society website: www.ndcs.org.uk/ (n.d.)

---------------------------------- Retrieval Quiz ----------------------------------

- What does a systematic approach to assessment and intervention relating to reading focus on in reception and year 1?
- How does an oral reading fluency assessment work?
- What might a comprehension strategy intervention look like? And why might this not be a high priority compared to other aspects of reading?

---------------------------- Questions for Professional Discussions ----------------------------

- To what extent is there already a systematic approach to assessment and intervention relating to reading difficulties in your school? How does it compare to the one described in this chapter?
- What are the logistical impediments to providing small-group interventions and, where required, one-to-one interventions in your school?
- In your teaching experience so far, how have you addressed the issues relating to motivation and self-efficacy that can occur when pupils struggle with persistent reading difficulties?

REFERENCES

Adlof, S. M., Chan, J., Werfel, K. & Catts, H. W. (2022). The neurobiology of literacy. In M. J. Snowling, C. Hulme & K. Nation (Eds), *The Science of Reading: A Handbook* (pp. 533–555). John Wiley & Sons.

Bhattacharya, A. & Ehri, L. C. (2004). Graphosyllabic analysis helps adolescent struggling readers read and spell words. *Journal of Learning Disabilities*, *37*(4), 331–348.

Communication Trust (2007). *Universally Speaking*. ICAN. www.fis.cityoflondon.gov.uk/asset-library/tct-univspeak-5-11.pdf

Department for Education (2023). Phonics screening check: 2023 materials. www.gov.uk/government/publications/phonics-screening-check-2023-materials

Education Endowment Foundation (2021). *Special Educational Needs in Mainstream Schools: Guidance Report*. https://d2tic4wvo1iusb.cloudfront.net/production/eef-guidance-reports/send/EEF_Special_Educational_Needs_in_Mainstream_Schools_Guidance_Report.pdf?v=1711454708

Farah, R., Ionta, S. & Horowitz-Kraus, T. (2021). Neuro-behavioral correlates of executive dysfunctions in dyslexia over development from childhood to adulthood. *Frontiers in Psychology*, *12*, 708863.

Fischer Family Trust (2024). Reading Assessment Programme. https://fft.org.uk/literacy/reading-assessment-programme

Fletcher, J. M., Lyon, G. R., Fuchs, L. S. & Barnes, M. A. (2018). *Learning Disabilities: From Identification to Intervention*. Guilford Press.

Gonzalez-Frey, S. M. & Ehri, L. C. (2021). Connected phonation is more effective than segmented phonation for teaching beginning readers to decode unfamiliar words. *Scientific Studies of Reading*, *25*(3), 272–285.

Hasbrouck, J. & Tindal, G. (2017). *An Update to Compiled ORF Norms*. Technical report # 1702. Behavioral Research and Teaching, University of Oregon.

I CAN (2021) *Developmental Language Disorder: A Guide for Every Teacher on Supporting Children and Young People with Developmental Language Disorder (DLD) in Mainstream Schools*. www.wholeschoolsend.org.uk/search?search_api_fulltext=developmental+language+disorder

Kilpatrick, D. & O'Brien, S. (2019). Effective prevention and intervention for word-level reading difficulties. In D. A. Kilpatrick, R. M. Joshi & R. K. Wagner (Eds), *Reading Development and Difficulties* (pp. 179–212). Springer International Publishing.

Little, C. W. & Hart, S. A. (2022). Genetic and environmental influences on learning to read. In M. J. Snowling, C. Hulme & K. Nation (Eds), *The Science of Reading: A Handbook* (pp. 515–532). John Wiley & Sons.

NASEN (National Association for Special Educational Needs) (2024). *Teacher Handbook: SEND*. www.wholeschoolsend.org.uk/resources/teacher-handbook-send

National Deaf Children's Society (n.d.). www.ndcs.org.uk

National Health Service (2023). Glue ear. www.nhs.uk/conditions/glue-ear

Seidenberg, M. (2017). *Language at the Speed of Sight: How We Read, Why So Many Can't, and What Can Be Done About It*. Basic Books.

Shanahan, T. (2021). On eating elephants and teaching syllabication. Blog. www.shanahanonliteracy.com/blog/on-eating-elephants-and-teaching-syllabication

Sibieta, L., Kotecha, M. & Skipp, A. (2016). *Nuffield Early Language Intervention: Evaluation Report and Executive Summary*. Education Endowment Foundation.

University of Oregon (n.d.). DIBELS (Dynamic Indicators of Basic Early Literacy Skills), 8th edition. University of Oregon. https://dibels.uoregon.edu

Vellutino, F. R., Fletcher, J. M., Snowling, M. J. & Scanlon, D. M. (2004). Specific reading disability (dyslexia): What have we learned in the past four decades? *Journal of Child Psychology and Psychiatry*, *45*(1), 2–40.

Wagner, R. K., Zirps, F. A. & Wood, S. G. (2022). Developmental dyslexia. In M. J. Snowling, C. Hulme & K. Nation (Eds), *The Science of Reading: A Handbook* (pp. 533–555). John Wiley & Sons.

Wolf, M. (2007). *Proust and the Squid: The Story and Science of the Reading Brain*. Harper.

Yeatman, J. D. (2022) The neurobiology of literacy. In M. J. Snowling, C. Hulme & K. Nation (Eds), *The Science of Reading: A Handbook* (pp. 533–555). John Wiley & Sons.

22

MAXIMISING THE IMPACT OF ONE-TO-ONE READING

WHICH PUPILS SHOULD WE TARGET FOR ONE-TO-ONE READING?

Every experienced teacher of reading recognises the power of one-to-one reading support. In an ideal world, every pupil would be heard reading aloud daily on a one-to-one basis in school. However, this is simply not possible, so it makes most sense to prioritise pupils who are at the early stages of reading proficiency (i.e. those in reception and year 1). Extra attention should also be directed towards nascent readers who are unlikely to receive support at home in their reading development and struggling readers in older year groups. However, small-group interventions with older readers are often just as effective as one-to-one support (Miles et al., 2022), so the latter should be reserved for when it appears to be essential.

HOW CAN WE MAXIMISE THE IMPACT OF ONE-TO-ONE READING?

Opportunities for one-to-one reading are difficult to organise across a school, and asking a teacher or teaching assistant to focus their attention on just one pupil has an obvious opportunity cost. As such, where we commit to one-to-one reading, we need to know we are doing it well. Here is a list of things to consider to ensure you make the most of one-to-one reading opportunities:

- From their reading experience, almost all pupils will immediately and automatically recognise at least a few of the words they encounter. The key to effective one-to-one reading is the support you offer to pupils with words that are *not* immediately and automatically recognised. With each one of these unfamiliar words, support pupils to decode throughout the word by paying attention to all the letters and the sounds that are represented. Specifically, we want pupils to apply their knowledge of grapheme–phoneme correspondences (GPCs). Model this decoding whenever pupils get stuck on a word, and then ask the pupil to repeat what you did (e.g. 'ch-a-m-p' 'champ').

- Keep an eye out for pupils who take a guess at the whole word after decoding only the first sound or two that is represented within it. This 'partial-decode-then-guess' strategy can appear successful for some pupils, but it is counterproductive over the long term, often drastically so. Again, a key aim is to support pupils to use decoding through the entire word as their go-to strategy for recognising any unfamiliar word.

- When a pupil decodes a word using GPCs they know but then comes unstuck (e.g. they decode 'cafe' as 'caif' or 'caffee'), help them use mispronunciation correction. To do this, ask them if they know a word that sounds similar and fits with the word's context. If not, tell them what the word is, what it means and point out the GPCs in this word (e.g. pointing to the 'e' in this word, say, 'This letter spells "ay" in this word: "c-a-f-e" "cafe".') In this way, you are priming the pupil to learn new GPCs by applying the ones they already know (Colenbrander et al., 2022; Shanahan, 2022). This orthographic learning is essential to reading development. The teaching of mispronunciation correction is one reason why it is essential that *all* nascent readers receive some one-to-one reading time, especially as they make the transition from decodable books to 'normal' books in their independent reading practice.

- Where a pupil struggles to decode polysyllabic words (i.e. words with more than one syllable), model breaking the words into syllables and decoding these piece by piece (e.g. 'unhelpful': 'u-n' 'un'; 'h-e-l-p' 'help'; 'f-u-l' 'ful'; 'un-help-ful'). Again, get the pupil to practise this immediately after modelling. Some argue that there are rules we should follow when breaking words into syllables. However, teaching pupils to syllabify words flexibly appears to be more beneficial (Bhattacharya & Ehri, 2004; Shanahan, 2021).

- As discussed in Chapter 21, nascent readers frequently find blending to be a persistent barrier to progress. This is often because of the load placed on their working memory: by the time a pupil gets to the end of the word, they have forgotten the first sound they recognised. Scaffolds can help with this. Consider progressively blending challenging words by elongating sounds that allow this (e.g. 'mmmiiilllk' 'milk'). It can also be helpful to incrementally reveal graphemes, blending each time, making sure to reveal letters together if they are part of the same grapheme (e.g. chomp: 'ch' 'cho' 'chom' 'chomp'). This is best thought of as a scaffold to the usual step-by-step decoding used in your school's phonics programme.

- Until a pupil has developed the habit of paying attention to all the GPCs within an unfamiliar word, it makes sense for their decoding practice to be undertaken with decodable text. As discussed in Chapter 3, the transition to 'normal' books depends on the pupil, and it should be carefully managed to ensure pupils do not revert to a counterproductive 'partial-decode-then-guess' strategy described above.

- Where pupils are capable of decoding individual words without much help but are still particularly dysfluent, give them occasional opportunities to re-read sentences, aiming for a little more fluency the second or third time around. Again, this can be modelled for the pupil.

- Where pupils struggle so much that motivation or attention become a factor, consider taking turns with the pupil. This might be on a sentence-by-sentence or page-by-page basis. You should try to read to them at a pace that is fluent but steady. You should also point at the words as you read them, modelling how to decode particularly challenging words.

- Where a pupil's reading is relatively dysfluent and/or decoding is still laborious, they will need help to make sense of the text as they read. Support meaning-making by briefly discussing and summarising what the text has said. If you want a relatively dysfluent reader to make sense of a chunk of text independently, they will probably need to re-read it to the point where it does begin to flow. Some degree of prosody (i.e. natural-sounding stress and intonation) in the pupil's reading is often a sign that comprehension is more likely. This prosody can be modelled and supported.

- As described above, it makes sense to target one-to-one reading at pupils who are struggling most with foundational aspects of reading. However, in the rare circumstances that a pupil is relatively fluent yet has significant issues with comprehension relative to their peers, one-to-one reading can emphasise the active role pupils need to play in making meaning. This can be achieved by supporting the pupil to summarise what they have read, by showing where to re-read tricky bits and by emphasising the 'detective work' that is often required to make sense of a text, such as when a word or phrase refers to something that has come before.

- Where it becomes apparent from one-to-one reading that a pupil struggles with a particular aspect of decoding, allow this to inform the interventions you might use beyond one-to-one reading (see Chapter 21). If someone other than a teacher is undertaking one-to-one reading with pupils, it is helpful for them to give feedback to the teacher on pupils' individual progress with decoding and fluency.

- In some schools, volunteers – usually parents/carers or governors – come into school to support pupils with their reading. This support can be beneficial for those who are well on their way to decoding proficiency but who lack fluency. However, pupils who are struggling most with the foundations of reading are best served by support from teachers and teaching assistants who have had the training required to understand reading development in theory and practice.

- Above all, make clear to every pupil exactly what a pleasure it is to witness their improvement, and tell them how worthwhile their efforts are. Helping pupils to develop as readers is one of the joys of being a teacher. Let pupils know this through your words and actions.

─────────────── This Chapter in a Nutshell ───────────────

- Pupils at the start of their journey to reading fluency, including older pupils still struggling with foundational aspects of reading, should be prioritised for one-to-one reading.
- The teaching of mispronunciation correction is one reason why it is essential that *all* nascent readers receive some one-to-one reading time, especially as they make the transition from decodable books to 'normal' books in their independent reading practice.
- Ensure that whoever is reading with pupils on a one-to-one basis understands the routines and techniques of the school's phonics programme and applies these where appropriate.
- Where pupils struggle to decode a word, model the decoding before giving the pupil the chance to have another attempt.
- Use one-to-one reading to keep an eye out for pupils reverting to a 'partial-decode-then-guess' word recognition strategy.
- Consider pupils' attention and motivation. Take turns reading if this helps maintain their effort.
- While volunteers might help with hearing the reading of pupils who are well on their way to becoming fluent readers, pupils who are struggling with the foundations of reading should be supported by teachers and teaching assistants.

─────────────── Further Reading ───────────────

- Maximising access to reading intervention: comparing small group and one-to-one protocols of Reading Rescue (Miles et al., 2022)
- Teaching children to read irregular words: A comparison of three instructional methods (Colenbrander et al., 2022)
- Graphosyllabic analysis helps adolescent struggling readers read and spell words (Bhattacharya & Ehri, 2004)

—————————————— Retrieval Quiz ——————————————

- Which pupils are best targeted with one-to-one reading?
- What is meant by a 'partial-decode-then-guess' strategy?
- How might we support pupils who decode monosyllabic words adequately but who struggle to decode polysyllabic words?

—————————— Questions for Professional Discussions ——————————

- Which pupils are supported through one-to-one reading in your school? And who undertakes this reading support?
- What training have those undertaking one-to-one reading support been given in your school?
- Under what circumstances might older struggling readers be better supported by one-to-one reading rather than a small-group intervention? And vice versa?

REFERENCES

Bhattacharya, A. & Ehri, L. C. (2004). Graphosyllabic analysis helps adolescent struggling readers read and spell words. *Journal of Learning Disabilities*, *37*(4), 331–348.

Colenbrander, D., Kohnen, S., Beyersmann, E., Robidoux, S., Wegener, S., Arrow, T., Nation, K. & Castles, A. (2022). Teaching children to read irregular words: A comparison of three instructional methods. *Scientific Studies of Reading*, *26*(6), 545–564.

Miles, K. P., McFadden, K. E., Colenbrander, D. & Ehri, L. C. (2022). Maximising access to reading intervention: Comparing small group and one-to-one protocols of Reading Rescue. *Journal of Research in Reading*, *45*(3), 299–323.

Shanahan, T. (2021). On eating elephants and teaching syllabication. Blog. www.shanahanonliteracy.com/blog/on-eating-elephants-and-teaching-syllabication

Shanahan, T. (2022). Phonics and flexibility. Blog. www.shanahanonliteracy.com/blog/phonics-and-flexibility

PART VIII

SETTING

PRIORITIES

23

SELECTING AND ACTING ON PRIORITIES

WHAT SHOULD I PRIORITISE AS A SCHOOL LEADER RESPONSIBLE FOR READING?

Arguably the hardest part of being responsible for reading across a school is knowing where to begin. Before making any decisions about what to prioritise, it is important first to ensure you have a sound grasp of the various aspects of reading across the school. There is no one correct way to categorise this, but I tend to approach it by checking the extent to which the following five priorities are being met:

1   Pupils who are struggling to learn to read receive timely support to address their individual barriers to reading development through a systematic approach to assessment and intervention.
2   Initial reading is taught to a high standard through responsive teaching of phonics, opportunities to develop spoken language capabilities and shared reading.
3   Fluency is explicitly developed through whole-class structures that allow for decoding practice (e.g. scaffolded reading and fluency reading).
4   Comprehension is taught meaningfully (e.g. through extended reading and close reading).
5   The wider curriculum and school culture encourages independent reading, appreciation of books and curiosity about language.

Investigating these aspects of reading requires you to consult curriculum documents (including the school's phonics programme), observe teaching, take feedback from colleagues and gauge the views of pupils. Once this understanding of a school's reading provision has been established, the aspect that is least developed should be tackled first. If in doubt – for example, because all aspects appear equally to require attention – start at the top of the list. All five aspects are crucial, but each aspect relies on the ones above it.

In some circumstances, it might be possible for more than one aspect of reading to be addressed at once, especially if this does not require teachers to focus on different priorities at the same time. For example, professional development for teachers in reception and year 1 might focus on the teaching of phonics while teachers in years

2 to 6 focus on how to support fluency development. In general, however, it makes sense for a school leader to target one aspect at a time, using the 'explore-prepare-deliver-sustain' cycle discussed in Chapter 14.

WHAT SHOULD I PRIORITISE AS A CLASSROOM TEACHER?

Ideally, as a classroom teacher you will be supported by senior colleagues to focus on aspects of your teaching of reading that are the highest priority for your pupils. In some circumstances, however, you might need to decide for yourself what aspect to focus on.

For classroom teachers in reception and year 1, considering the following four priorities is a good place to start:

1   Phonics teaching is effective.
2   Shared reading and discussion supports pupils' understanding and appreciation of written language and provides opportunities for them to develop their spoken language capabilities.
3   Pupils who are struggling in phonics lessons receive timely 'keep-up' or 'catch-up' support.
4   Alongside frequent opportunities for meaningful discussion for all pupils, those struggling with spoken language receive extra support through conversations with adults and peers.

Consider which of these aspects is furthest from where you would like it to be and target the area of greatest immediate need.

An important caveat here is that the above assumes a specific focus on improving reading. It is worth bearing in mind that in reception – and beyond, where required – the prime areas of the EYFS framework (communication and language; physical development; personal, social and emotional development) should be prioritised.

For classroom teachers in year 2 or above, considering the following four priorities is a good place to start:

1   Pupils who are struggling to learn to read receive timely support to address their individual barriers to reading.
2   Relatively dysfluent readers are given plenty of successful decoding practice (e.g. in fluency reading lessons).
3   Pupils are building experience with a wide variety of texts (e.g. in extended reading lessons).
4   Classroom reading discussions explore authors' language choices and themes effectively and build pupils' understanding of themselves as readers (e.g. in close reading lessons).

Consider which of these aspects is furthest from where you would like it to be and target the area of greatest immediate need.

AFTERWORD

In the introduction, I stated that my aim was to share in detail my approach to teaching reading, from classroom instruction to whole-school implementation. However, it will have become apparent that following my approach to the letter is not the only way to make use of this book. Even if you decide to plot a completely different course through the terrain of evidence-informed reading instruction, I like to think that this account of my preferred route will have provided a valuable perspective. With this in mind, forgive me for returning to the guiding principle behind everything you have read:

Any approach to teaching reading should be judged both on the scope it provides for expert teachers to excel and on the support it provides for novice teachers to achieve adequacy.

Crafting an approach to teaching reading that stands up to such judgement is a complicated task, but we mustn't make a virtue of unnecessary complication. If you want to create something that will actually work in the wonderful, unrelenting swirl of a primary school, my advice is to get a clear vision of what you want to achieve, and then simplify it as much as possible. Classroom instruction naturally evolves towards increasing elaboration. Teachers are irrepressibly innovative, adding glorious complexity to the most elemental of ideas. By beginning this evolution from the sort of simple structures advocated in this book, schools can derive an approach to reading instruction that is sophisticated yet coherent, liberating yet supportive, meaningful yet efficient. Our pupils deserve no less.

GLOSSARY

accuracy an aspect of oral reading fluency relating to whether words are correctly identified

acquired dyslexia significant difficulties in learning to recognise and spell words that are the result of a brain injury

affix a morpheme other than a root that can be added to a word to change its meaning

automaticity an aspect of oral reading fluency relating to the rate and effortlessness of word recognition

blending reconstituting words by combining the phonemes identified within a word

close reading a core reading lesson structure that prioritises deeper exploration of texts

constrained capability a component of a person's reading ability that is limited in scope and can be usefully identified in a list within a curriculum

decodable text/book a text/book that primarily contains grapheme–phoneme correspondences and words that are already familiar to the reader

decoding using knowledge of grapheme–phoneme correspondences and blending to identify a word

developmental dyslexia significant difficulties in learning to recognise and spell words that manifest as a person naturally develops

etymology the history of a word, potentially including its origin and changes in meaning

extended reading a core reading lesson structure that prioritises breadth of reading experience

fluency reading a core reading lesson structure that prioritises fluency development through accurate decoding practice

grapheme the smallest functional unit of a writing system; in English, a grapheme is a letter or small group of letters that usually represents a phoneme

grapheme – phoneme correspondence (GPC) a relationship within a word between an individual letter or a small group of letters and the represented phoneme

mispronunciation correction a strategy for recognising unfamiliar words that involves imperfect decoding followed by identifying a similar-sounding word already in the reader's vocabulary; also known as set for variability.

morpheme the smallest chunk that has consistent, identifiable meaning across different words

morphology the study of morphemes

orthography the conventional writing system of a given language

phoneme the smallest unit of sound that can distinguish one word from another; phonemes can be productively thought of as basic chunks of spoken sound identified within words for the purposes of reading and spelling

phonemic awareness the ability to identify and manipulate phonemes

phonics the teaching of relationships between letters and sounds and how to use them to identify words

prefix an affix that precedes a root to modify the meaning of a word

prosody an aspect of oral reading fluency relating to the extent to which it sounds like natural speech (i.e. natural-sounding stress and intonation)

reading fluency the extent to which words flow as a person reads; reading fluency can be identified most easily when pupils read aloud through observation of accuracy, automaticity and prosody, but these are imperfect proxies for the underlying construct of reading fluency

responsive teaching teaching that uses ongoing assessment to identify and address pupils' misconceptions and other learning needs

root a morpheme within a word that provides the central meaning of the word and to which affixes can be added

scaffolded reading an introductory reading lesson structure that is designed to give year 1 pupils decoding practice through repeated reading while introducing them to whole-class reading

segmenting identifying the individual phonemes within a word

suffix an affix that follows a root to modify the meaning of a word

synthetic phonics the teaching of phonics in which pupils are introduced to GPCs individually and shown how to blend these into words

systematic phonics the attempt to teach phonics with a defined scope and sequence (i.e. an organised curriculum of what will be taught and in what order, starting with the simplest and most common GPCs and incrementally introducing greater complexity)

unconstrained capability a component of a person's reading ability that is effectively unlimited in scope and cannot be usefully identified in a list within a curriculum

vocabulary breadth a measure of how many words a person knows

vocabulary depth a measure of how much someone knows about the words in their vocabulary (i.e. the connections between the words they know and others)

INDEX

Page numbers in *italics* relate to Tables and Figures and those in **bold** relate to Glossary definitions.